ALEXIS KORNER

ALEXIS KORNER

THE BIOGRAPHY

HARRY SHAPIRO

*Discography and additional research
by Mark Troster*

BLOOMSBURY

First published in Great Britain 1996

Bloomsbury Publishing Plc, 2 Soho Square, London W1V 6HB

Copyright © 1996 by Harry Shapiro

Discography © 1996 by Mark Troster

The moral right of the author has been asserted

A CIP catalogue record for this book
is available from the British Library

ISBN 0 7475 2725 3

10 9 8 7 6 5 4 3 2 1

Typeset by Hewer Text Composition Services, Edinburgh
Printed in Great Britain by Clays Ltd, St Ives plc

To my dad, who by example has taught me to 'roll with it'

CONTENTS

PREFACE

When Alexis Korner died, in January 1984, he was on the brink of a new career in the music business as a film and radio programme maker, documenting all the diverse traditions of the music he loved – the blues. What has happened since makes his early death seem all the more tragic. He was unable to be a part of the CD revolution and missed the chance to be involved in compiling and writing the notes for anthologies of classic or obscure blues, gospel and jazz, or to bring fresh artists to the fore through his production company. He missed out on the latest blues boom – although it is unlikely his enthusiasm for this would have been total – and he died in advance of the rapid expansion of 'world music', the increasing opportunities for broadcasting through the proliferation of stations and the exciting possibilities of the new electronic media. The fragmentation of the music scene would have suited Alexis down to the ground, creating as it has new audiences for a broad church of music.

Whether he would have ever escaped the tag 'Father of the British Blues' or 'the man who gave the Stones their big break' is doubtful, but perhaps all this modern-day diversity might have enabled him to broaden his reach and increase his chances of escaping the straitjacket. Because Alexis hated narrowing the options of music, neatly parcelling it up for the marketing department. For him, there were only two kinds of music – good and bad – and for bad read 'dishonest' – music played by musicians who were not true to their own spirit, but simply in it for the money. If this book is anything, it's the journey of a musician holding on to his soul.

I picked up the challenge of writing the book first from my old friend John Platt and then from singer and journalist Ellie Buchanan, who came to know Alexis well in the latter years of his life. I am grateful to both for the gracious way in which they passed on the baton. A biography was first proposed back in 1985, just a year after Alexis died, but for the family the pain of bereavement was too acute. The project was left fallow until I stuck my nose in during the winter of 1993. Alexis was too strong a spirit for the raw ends of grief to be fully cauterized even then, so I have to extend my deepest thanks to his wife Bobbie, his son Damian and daughter Sappho for not only giving their blessing to the book, but also sharing with me some highly personal memories of somebody whose star still burns bright in their lives.

I would like to thank Del Taylor, formerly Alexis' manager and now boss of Indigo Records, and radio producer Jeff Griffin for their unstinting co-operation throughout the book.

Thanks are due to all of the following for their time and assistance: Mick Abrahams, Jochen Albrecht, John Alcock, Rupert Allason MP, Themi Aperguis, Ginger Baker, Long John Baldry, Chris Barber, Norman Beaker, Chris Bell, Val Berry, Colin Bowden, Vernon Bown, Geoff Bradford, Pete Brown, Victor Brox, Beryl Bryden, Graham Burbidge, Raphael Callaghan, John Cameron, Steve Clyne, Karl Dallas, Tomaz Domicelj, Lonnie Donegan, Ronnie Dunn, Pete Dyer, Madalena Fagandini, Hughie Flint, Pete Frame, Andy Fraser, Marek Garztecki, Herbie Goins, Alan Grace, Davy Graham, Stan Grieg, Alexis Grower, Bob Hall, Bob Harris, Richard Hattrell, Brenda Havenhead, Dick Hawdon, Dick Heckstall-Smith, Trevor Hill, Colin Hodgkinson, Kevin Howlett, Mick Jagger, Karsten Jahnke, Paul Jones, Ronnie Jones, Anthea Joseph, Pete King, Brian and Marie Knight, George Körner, Bill Leader, Harry Lee, Dave Lunt, John Marshall, John Mayall, Tom McGuinness, George Melly, Cliff Michelmore, Zoot Money, Bryan Morrison, Mickie Most, James Moyes, Paul Oliver, Johnny Parker, Ottilie Patterson, Harold Pendleton, Viv Perry, Duffy Power, Chris Pyne, Mick Pyne, Phil Roberge, Tom Robinson, Willi Schlosser, Keith Scott, Gordon Snell, Nick South, Dave Stevens, Trixie Stevens, Art Themen, Danny Thompson, John Timperly, John Tobler, Guido Toffoletti, Tony Vines, Ian Wallace, Ray Warleigh, Teddy Warwick, Charlie Watts, Klaus Welleshaus, Wally Whyton, Val Wilmer, Jack Winsley, Art Wood and Pam Wynne.

I would like to acknowledge the assistance of the following: Ken Jones

PREFACE

of the National Jazz Foundation Archive, Graham Langley of the British Institute of Jazz Studies, Uli Twelker, John Cowley, Axel Reisenhofer, Stuart Booth, Joachim Kirstein, Jackie Krendel, Don Strange, Brian Rance and Areta Hautman of the King Alfred School, Christopher Dean of St Paul's School; Chris Barber's archivist, Julian Purser, Mark Troster and Sherry Daley and Liz Watley from the Rolling Stones' office.

Special thanks to Guido Toffoletti for permission to use his unpublished interviews with Keith Richard, Eric Burdon and B. B. King. I am also very grateful to John Lyward for permission to examine and use material from the archives of Finchden Manor.

A doff of the cap to David Reynolds at Bloomsbury for saying yes when others said no.

No book of mine will ever be complete without planet-busting gratitude to Kay, my partner, my very best friend and my sternest editor. What makes her slash-and-burn approach to my finely wrought prose so inexplicably acceptable is that we are both in hysterics while she's doing it.

Harry Shapiro
March 1996

All quotes attributed to Alexis Korner for which a source is not specified come from a variety of published sources, radio interviews with Alexis, comments he made on his own shows and from the interview I conducted with Alexis for my biography of Graham Bond.

1

BLUES BEFORE SUNRISE

Being Jewish in Austria has never been one of life's easier options. However, by the late nineteenth century there was a thriving Jewish community in Vienna composed largely of financiers, merchants and traders. It was into this society that Emil Körner was born on 11 November 1872.

Emil was the middle boy of five children born to Herman and Sophie Körner: he had two elder brothers and two younger sisters. Herman worked for an insurance company and the family were reasonably comfortable, living close to the centre of Vienna: Emil went to school in Gymnasiastrasse. Until 1857 the well-to-do had been virtually walled in within the city centre, with all the other districts laid out in concentric circles around it. Then the city walls came down, inaugurating a new period of civic building and the development of middle-class suburbs. Nevertheless, the prime housing stock was still in the centre, where families like the Körners lived.

The strong foothold enjoyed by the Jewish community of Vienna by the time Emil was born had been tenuous for the previous generation and before that downright dangerous. At the time of Maria Theresa's accession to the throne in 1740, there were only about 300 Jewish people left in the whole of Austria and they were 'tolerated Jews', accorded this status under special permit because of the financial services they provided. Even when conditions eased, Jewish families living in Vienna had to renounce their faith in favour of Roman Catholicism or be forced to leave. In the more liberal climate of the nineteenth century, families still converted, but for reasons of social expediency and business advantage rather than legal dictate. It was probably under these latter conditions that the Körner family became Catholics. George Körner, Emil's son and Alexis' half-brother, now eighty-seven years old, remembers that 'his [Emil's] original Jewish background was acknowledged, but played no further part in our lives'.

All went well for the Körners until 1886, when Emil's father died. The family had to move out of the city centre to Dobling, an ordinary residential suburb, and they were in deep financial difficulties until some wealthy relatives intervened and ensured that Sophie and her children could enjoy a life restored to something of its former comfort.

Emil passed his grammar school exams, which allowed him to serve only one year's military service in the Austro–Hungarian Imperial Army instead of the otherwise statutory three. By 1892 he had left the Army with the rank of lieutenant, although he was permanently on the list of reservists for potential call-up in time of war. What was he to do now? One of his two elder brothers had emigrated to Argentina to be a teacher in the German College in Buenos Aires while the other, something of a maverick, had fallen out with the family and disappeared to America.

According to George, Emil was a well-balanced person, not particularly adventurous, but intelligent and certainly enterprising. The problem was that since the end of the Napoleonic Wars, Vienna, and indeed the whole of Austria, had been stifled by a smug complacency. Vienna, linked to the music of Liszt, Brahms and Beethoven, saw itself bathed in an aura of romanticism, but to Europe at large, in an era before modern trans-European travel, Austria was regarded as a remote and isolated country and dubbed 'Europe's China'.

Austria was in the hands of an autocratic ruler commanding a secret service which required a heavily censored press and put spies on every street corner. Emil could have followed in his father's footsteps, pursuing in Vienna a career in insurance or some other commercial field, a life played out against the background of the quiet conservatism and studied aloofness of the city's middle classes. But Emil had other ideas. He may not have been recklessly adventurous, but he was an opportunist, and in 1894 he accepted a job with an Austrian trading company in Moscow and left home.

If Austria was considered remote in the late nineteenth century, Russia was virtually unknown. It was still, by and large, a medieval country run on feudal lines by the Tsars. But in the Caucasus, in southern Russia, there was the beginning of an industrial revolution funded almost entirely by foreign capital and controlled by foreign managers. This was frontier land with plenty of opportunity for speculators and entrepreneurs to make a financial killing in the oilfields and by exploiting the region's vast untapped wealth of minerals. Emil was sent to Grozny, a grim, dirty frontier town of some 30,000 people on the River Sunzha, eight miles south of the oil derricks.

Before long Emil found himself a partner and set up his own import business to bring in oil pipes and other machinery for the industry, as well as the agricultural implements needed to improve farming techniques to feed the growing local population of industrial workers. He settled into the life of a *Mestchinstvo*, joining the bourgeois estate of capitalist entrepreneurs which also included doctors, lawyers, teachers and academics. Established in this station in life, he found himself a wife.

Nina Popich was the daughter of a circuit judge and, according to George Körner, a cultured, attractive woman and an accomplished pianist who, by the standards of the day, had received a good education. Her family came from Georgia and it was there that Emil and Nina's first son, Herman, was born on 12 June 1903. George (known as Youra in Russian) arrived on 30 December 1909. In between the two births, Nina contracted TB and was sent away to the mountains, altitude then being the only known way to deal with the disease.

A few years passed and Emil and his business partner began looking for a base that would give them easier access to the trade routes to and from Western Europe. By this time railways were reasonably well developed and they made the 230-mile train journey from Grozny via the garrison town of Vladikavkaz, through the Caucasus mountains, across the Steppes and over the River Don to Rostov. Perched on the river's lofty right bank, Rostov was, after Odessa, the best-built city in southern Russia.

Before long they had found both offices and town houses in respectable areas. Business flourished; Emil and his partner built up trading links across southern Russia, importing and distributing their goods throughout the region. Emil's circle of friends were mainly from the ranks of businessmen and professionals, many of them German, Austrian and English expatriates. Herman and George went to a private school and there were family holidays in Austria, Switzerland and other parts of Europe.

Then, in June 1914, came the assassination of Archduke Franz Ferdinand in Sarajevo. The complex time bomb of alliances and treaties which had been ticking away for decades was triggered, and Europe collapsed into war. All over Europe expatriates suddenly found themselves in enemy territory. Police and secret service agents in a dozen countries began checking the papers and backgrounds of 'alien' populations. The Tsarist police discovered that Emil was a reservist in the Austrian Army and, as in the most banal spy thriller, came knocking at four o'clock in the morning. Emil, along with several others, was interned in a house in Soligavich, about halfway between Moscow and the northern port of Archangel. George recalls his father telling him: 'It was in the woods deep in the country with no transport to anywhere else. If you did try to get a horse everybody would know about it and if you had found one — where would you go?'

Back home, Emil's partner managed to keep the business going, paying Nina an income to feed and clothe the family. But in 1917 it went bust and the family fell on very hard times. During the years leading up to the First World War, the Körners had maintained a veneer of respectability, with Nina the dutiful wife; but the marriage had long been in trouble and Emil's internment finished it off. Nina left Emil and married a man described by George as 'an engineer and an intellectual'. George, just nine years old, stayed with Nina and his stepfather, 'who treated me perfectly well and I had no complaint except that he was not my father, who was somewhere else and who I hardly remembered'. But Nina's mother (also called Nina) was absolutely furious with her daughter's desertion.

While in exile, Emil managed to keep up a correspondence with his mother-in-law and between them it was decided that Herman should live with her and her husband, Herman's grandparents. The war between Russia and Germany ended about six months before that involving the Western Allies and as soon as it was over, Emil and his fellow prisoners were liberated by the Bolsheviks.

In 1918 Herman and George's grandfather died. The following year Emil, now sick at heart with his misfortunes in Russia and divorced from his wife, left the country for good, taking Herman with him back to Austria. Herman stayed for a while with Emil's mother in Vienna. George meanwhile had left his mother's new home and went to live with Grandma Nina. Eventually, in 1922, Grandma Nina Popich took George to Vienna to be reunited with his brother and father and she stayed too.

Given the disruptive, peripatetic existence of the war years, and all its emotional turmoil, Emil might have been expected to settle down as quickly as possible to an quiet, ordered existence. But his was clearly a restless spirit, a trait no doubt exacerbated by his four years' incarceration, and he began looking for business opportunities elsewhere.

On his return to Vienna he had started up his business again, but transferred it to Berlin in 1923. At the same time he set up in London a company called Continental Contractors with two partners, Karl Berlin (who changed his name to Bentley to make himself appear more English) and a man named Nakhimoff. Emil knew both men from his time in Russia: Bentley had worked for him in Rostov, and Nakhimoff he had known in Grozny. Emil's business connections spread out across Europe and even back into Russia, where, although he had no desire to return, there were increasingly excellent financial returns for a enterprising businessman eager to trade with a Bolshevik regime obsessed with industrialization.

One of Emil's properties was an apartment in Paris and it was to here that the whole family moved, George being sent to the Russian school. Meanwhile Emil was spending most of his time in London, building up the business. There he met a young Greek, Themi Aperguis, who was a pupil at the Lycée Français in South Kensington with the sons of Bentley and Nakhimoff. One of Themi's elder sisters was named Sappho.

In interviews, Alexis relished saying that his mother was from a Greek–Turkish background, knowing full well the deep hostility which existed between the two nations. When Alexis died, Themi Aperguis took the trouble to write to journalist Bill Harry, who had written an obituary in the *Daily Express*, to put him straight on the point. There is a Turkish connection in that Sappho was one of seven brothers and sisters born to Nicholas Aperguis and Cleoniki Mesiki in the midst of the Greek community resident in Constantinople (now Istanbul). Sappho, born in 1898, was the eldest, followed by Marie, George, Mildiages, Helene, Calliopi and finally Themi on 3 July 1908. The family business was shipping.

Themi came to London in 1916, when he was eight years old. 'My father had always been a friend of this country, absolutely loved it. At the time of the First World War, Greece had King Constantine on the throne; Queen Sophia's brother was the Kaiser, so the Allies and Greece didn't get on. He used to travel extensively and had to have special permission to travel to Britain.'

Relations between Greece and Turkey were very bad; Nicholas Aperguis in London had sent word to his wife in Constantinople to pack up and leave, which they did just before the Turks expelled the Greek community altogether. The Aperguis family escaped just in time through Bulgaria and got back to Greece. However, Greek 'refugees' returning from Turkey were not well received. Life was made very uncomfortable for them and after a year Nicholas, Cleoniki and the children, plus relatives on Cleoniki's side, all left Greece together. Nicholas took his family to London, while the francophone Mesiki family opted for Paris.

Emil met Sappho in 1926. With his businesses going well, his thoughts turned to family life; he was anxious to be a married man again. Sappho was twenty-nine years old at a time when unmarried women 'of a certain age' were heading for the label 'spinster'. Theirs was not a passionate romance and it is doubtful if Sappho could have said she was truly 'in love' with Emil. But he offered security, affection and respect; it was a relationship of 'social understanding', as George puts it. On 17 March 1927 they married at Kensington Register Office. Sappho quickly became pregnant. 'They expected a girl,' says George, 'but it wasn't.' On 19 April 1928, four months after Emil's fifty-fifth birthday, Sappho gave birth to Alexis Andrew Nicholas.

2

JUVENILE DELINQUENT

Convinced she would receive better medical care in France than England, Sappho insisted that Alexis be born in Paris, although at the time of the birth the Körners were firmly established in London. When they first married they had a flat in Hampstead Garden Suburb; Emil then bought a detached house not far away at 11 Armitage Road, Golders Green. The rest of the family came over from France, George by then aged seventeen and Grandma Popich, but Herman stayed in Paris to become a prominent violinist. Sappho's father, Nicholas, died in 1926, so her mother, Cleoniki, was also living at the new house.

Settled into business and family life once more, Emil aspired to a life of high culture. He enjoyed listening to Sappho play the piano for him and there were dinner parties for his business associates, European musicians and singers who were performing in London and other stars of the London literary world – including the notorious Brian Howard.

Howard visited them at a house in Bandol in the south of France owned by a friend of Sappho's sister Calliopi (known as Cali) where the Körners often spent their summer holidays. Howard was part of the 'Brideshead' generation who went to Eton and then Oxford in the company of Harold Acton, Cyril Connolly, John Betjeman and Evelyn Waugh. His milieu was that of the wealthy Old Etonians whose lifestyle was underpinned by money and homosexuality and who ate, drank and screwed (mainly each other) to excess and did very little work. A published (although not very accomplished) poet, he befriended the spy Guy Burgess and was active in Nancy Cunard's fund-raising activities on behalf of the Republicans during the Spanish Civil War.

However, Howard was not well liked; Waugh described him as 'mad, bad and dangerous to know' and in *Put Out More Flags* modelled the character of Ambrose Silk on him. Harold Acton told Waugh's biographer Martin Stannard that Howard would 'let anyone down . . . and if he could get a man or woman away from the person they were fond of, he would do so. He was completely amoral.' During the Second World War Howard secured a minor post with British Intelligence and was later described by Andrew Boyle in his *Climate of Treason* as 'a reject freelance of the old, unreconstructed MI5'. His drunkenness and general unreliability rendered him useless for the work and he was quickly dismissed. What the Körners saw in him is difficult to fathom unless they gained a vicarious thrill from his company. But the link between them and Howard may have given rise to a curious story about Emil told by Alexis but almost certainly invented or misunderstood from fragments of truth.

The story went that Emil first came to London in 1939 with a Russian trade delegation and that, on the eve of the war, he was granted British citizenship while the rest of his colleagues were deported back to Russia as spies. There are no records of such a delegation visiting Britain at the time although Emil's company did deal with Acos in London, part of the permanent Russian trade delegation based in the UK. The company also had a partner in Russia who was shot as a spy and there was a family friendship with a husband-and-wife 'second division' spy team, one of whom was called Bunny. George says that Emil was naturalized around 1936 or 1937, although Alexis said that rather than being 'given' British citizenship in 1939 he was advised to apply for it by a friend of the family who was 'a member of what . . . people jokingly referred to as MI5' (almost certainly Brian Howard) on the grounds that otherwise, as an Austrian national, he could be interned. Given Emil's experience in Russia, this would have made eminent sense.

So while the nub of the 'spy' story appears incorrect, nevertheless there are some tantalizing hints of infamous connections and half-truths. A pastel portrait of Alexis as a young boy, commissioned from Alexis' nanny by Brian Howard, with a dedication to Emil and Sappho, still hangs in the London flat now owned by Alexis' wife, Bobbie.

Life for Alexis was less romantic. Everyone loved him, but the house was unsuited to the needs and demands of a young child. Emil was frequently away, but even when at home he wasn't much involved in his son's day-to-day life. He was not tolerant of the natural rampages of a boisterous little boy; his was the era of the child who was seen but not heard, cared for instead by nurses and nannies. But in the period after the First World War this lifestyle was only for the well-to-do. While they were not exactly poor, the Körners' business was nowhere near good enough to employ servants. Besides, Emil was in poor health and so, as Alexis wrote regretfully some years later, 'was not able to go cycling with me'.

The child care fell upon Sappho, but she was often caught between the differing opinions about childbearing expressed by her mother and Emil's mother-in-law from which there was no escape, living as they were all under the same roof. Nina Popich and Cleoniki Aperguis spent much of their time tut-tutting in the wings and disagreeing with each other. Emil was detached, but nevertheless had high expectations of a boy clearly developing an above-average intelligence; Alexis could speak French, German and Russian, plus smatterings of Greek, Italian and Spanish.

Sappho tended to smother her only child – and since she was already in her thirties, the only child she was likely to have, given the ethos of the day – trying to compensate for Emil's much sterner approach with what she later admitted was overindulgence. Alexis was thus caught between all these conflicting views and emotions and in his search for unconditional love, he became overeager to please. He was also quite a lonely boy; the house was unwelcoming for an influx of playmates and it seems he had few boyhood friends apart from one who grew into the famous Russian economic historian Alex Nove, who died in 1994.

In his isolation Alexis began to weave fantasies in his head about his life and his family which in adolescence became more evident and which later passed into his publicity biographies unchallenged. The espionage story cited above was one example. Another which was subsequently widely quoted depicted Emil as the dashing cavalry officer, unhappy with the politics of the Habsburg monarchy, surrendering a whole platoon of Austrian soldiers to the Communists. This was probably a bit of mischief-making by Alexis, similar to the claims of Turkish ancestry. Although Emil was liberated from internment by the Bolsheviks and traded with them after the First World War, their politics would have been complete anathema to him.

Although he claimed he was constantly on the move as a child, Alexis did have a relatively stable schooling between 1931 and 1938 at King Alfred School in Hampstead. Founded in 1897, this was known as a 'Rational School', what might nowadays be called 'progressive', although the school would deny the label, if for no other reason than that its classes have never been optional either for staff or students.

Even so, the school's current prospectus presents an ethos of child development that would have chimed with Alexis both as man and boy. 'We make no apologies for giving our children as much freedom as is reasonably compatible with sound education and for putting the individual child before dogma.' Certainly the atmosphere would have been in sharp contrast to a home background confusingly alternating between impatience and indulgence.

Alexis' schooling was interrupted when he was eight and nine years old, after he contracted TB and was sent away on his own to Switzerland without being told the nature of his illness. This would not have been his first time away from home. While he may have slightly exaggerated his gypsy existence, it does seem that during the summer holidays, for example, he did not necessarily spend the time with his parents, often being sent to France to stay with a relative. He once summed this up by saying that 'I was where my father wasn't' and it could have done little for his self-esteem or sense of belonging to be (as he would have seen it) 'dumped' in this fashion.

In the special circumstances that are the subject of the next chapter, Alexis wrote down what happened to him during his extended stays in Europe between 1938 and 1940. He recalled going to German-speaking Switzerland and staying for 'some months' at the 'Helios' in a well-known ski resort called Adelboden. He describes it as a 'pension', but it appears to have been some kind of nursing home. Alexis was not happy there. 'I did not like it very much, but was not allowed to say so as our letters I think were censored, but I'm not sure about this. I remember very clearly that we were given castor oil every Sunday after lunch. The lunch always consisted of chicken and rice. The first time they gave me castor oil, I immediately vomited. They always had a bowl of sugared black coffee ready for me after that first time . . . Then mother and father came to take me away.'

Rather than returning to England to continue his schooling, Alexis then turns up in another part of Switzerland, at Villars-sur-Ollon, where he was placed in a boarding school. 'We were awarded marks for our work; if it was very bad we got black marks, if it was just bad we got a green mark, fair was blue, good was yellow and if very good, red.

Those who had more than a certain number of black or green marks at the end of the week were forbidden entry to the big hall where the cinema show which we had every Sunday was on. I was often banned from the shows.' He was probably away from home for about a year because he commented that he 'enjoyed the skiing and the skating in the winter most of all and also the swimming in the summer'.

By now the fortunes of the Körner family were in decline. Emil had been involved in business speculations, including a proposal to build oil tanks on Canvey Island, in the Thames estuary, in partnership with a former manager of the Thames Haven Oil Wharfs. This and other ventures didn't quite work out and Emil was forced to sell the house in Golders Green for a flat in a residential complex known as Ealing Village, in west London. Space now for the household was at less of a premium: George had his own small place and, sadly, Grandma Popich had been killed outright when she stepped in front of a lorry in Kensington High Street. Now in his late sixties, Emil was in failing health and increasingly in need of Sappho's constant attention, which almost certainly accounts for Alexis' being kept out of the way.

Alexis was off again, this time to Paris, where he spent a night at Herman's apartment (probably the last time he ever saw him) *en route* to La Ciotat, near Marseilles, in the company of a woman called Blanchette. She worked for a Dr Chaumont. Emil was very ill with bladder trouble and was at Dr Chaumont's sanatorium for treatment. It had been decided that this time Alexis should accompany his parents rather than be left in England with Sappho's mother, Cleoniki. But Sappho had to be with Emil; Alexis was sent to a children's home a few miles away.

The home was run by a Dr Met and his wife, 'who I called Auntie Machi'. A Rumanian kid called Lionel tried to bugger Alexis, 'but I wasn't having any of it . . . Auntie Machi called us both into her office the following morning and told us this was the way that you caught TB.' Which would have somewhat confusing for Alexis had he been told about his TB at the time.

Many years later Alexis presented his own version of *Desert Island Discs* on Radio 1, with himself as the castaway. Recalling his time at the home, he said: 'The kids gave concerts every now and then and I was forced one day to my absolute horror . . . they dressed me up in a miniature American sailor's suit and stuck a fake ukulele in my hand, stuck me on the stage and said, "Sing this." I hated every second of it – it was my first appearance on stage and it was loathsome. I was so embarrassed and so full of hate for these people who were making me do this. And the song I had to sing was (God help me) "San Francisco Open Your Golden Gates". I was also very good at winning fancy-dress contests dressed as a hula girl. It was a disgusting childhood, it really was. Never mind, I got over it.' He probably did recover from superficial humiliations of this kind, but the deeper hurts remained.

'I was in the sea when war was declared. Somebody came to the edge of the beach and said, "They've declared war." It didn't mean anything – I was eleven years old. War doesn't mean anything, death doesn't mean anything.

'My parents left it a bit late getting out of France. It was 1940, France had collapsed and it wasn't so easy to get out. We had to go via Toulon and got a refugee ship. The Italians came over and bombed us as we were leaving, but they didn't hit anything.

'It was a great adventure. A lot of us got on this very small ship, a French merchant cruiser with very light armament. I think it had a twelve-pounder in the bow and that was all.'

It took five days to get from Toulon to Oran, and they were attacked on the way by Italian submarines, the attacks seeming, to Alexis, 'futile but exciting'. They changed ship in Oran, to an 800-ton coastal collier with hundreds of people draped everywhere. A day later they reached Gibraltar, where they transferred to the *Empress of India*. Emil was very ill and had his own cabin, where Sappho took care of him. This left Alexis to run riot all over the ship. Alexis the castaway described the war at sea as 'like a strip cartoon come to life' as enemy planes swooped down on to the Allied shipping lanes and the escort ships returned fire. They met the British fleet going in the opposite direction *en route* to take on the Italian Navy in the Mediterranean.

Two days out of Gibraltar, Alexis was 'sick as a dog', though this doesn't appear to have dampened his enthusiasm for what was in truth a hazardous journey. 'The first dead bodies I ever saw were on that trip back because the ships in the convoy from Gibraltar to Plymouth were torpedoed.' Right into Portsmouth harbour, five days after leaving Gibraltar, they still weren't safe as a Junkers 88 bomber made one last attempt to sink the boat with its thousands of passengers. The Körners got home unscathed, away from one kind of trouble and right into another.

★　　★　　★

When George Körner settled in London in 1927, he went to the London School of Economics; like his father, he was destined for life as a businessman and his relationship with Emil was very close. Herman had become slightly distant – 'he was more demanding of my father than I was' – but George remembers his father with great affection. The house language was French, but 'my language with my father was either Russian or German if he wanted to tell me something that wasn't to be heard by Sappho'. But George had much respect for Sappho; 'she was very patient, bearing in mind she had a teenage stepson, a new baby and her husband's mother-in-law by his first marriage all living in the house'.

Alexis, on the other hand, presented his family with all kinds of problems. When the family finally got back to England, Alexis went to Colet Court Preparatory School and then to the associated main school, St Paul's. The schools were on adjacent sites in Hammersmith, west London, but because of the war, had been evacuated to Berkshire. So barely back from France, Alexis was sent away from home again.

Life was hard for Alexis at St Paul's; his swarthy looks marked him out as a foreigner, which during wartime meant a spy or, failing that, a Jewish refugee – equally demonized and despised by cruel peers lacking knowledge of what was happening in Germany and Poland. He began calling himself Andrew (one of his middle names) and in an attempt to appear more English dropped the umlaut from his surname, so changing its pronunciation from 'Kerner' to 'Korner'. (For a brief period his friends chose to call him Sandy rather than Andrew, which annoyed him intensely.) To ingratiate himself with whatever gang was 'in' at the time, he would distribute cigarettes bought with money stolen from other boys. He began smoking himself, outraging his parents by his use of the word 'fags'. One housemaster, apparently very kind to Alexis, supplemented the pocket money that he said he wasn't receiving from home. Alexis also had a friend, who introduced him to jazz records, named, appropriately enough, Benny Goodman.

Emil and Sappho were called to the school on a number of occasions and were deeply shocked by what they heard. For Emil, Alexis was a huge disappointment and he made little attempt to hide his anger. Alexis later claimed that his father wanted him to be a diplomat. 'My father had very specific plans for all his sons. My older brother was meant to be a bishop (Herman), the middle brother was meant to be the sharp businessman (George) and I was due to be the diplomat, a sort of gay, elegant boy about town. The problem was that he forgot that being an Austrian national, naturalized British, born in France, it would be terribly difficult to decide what sort of diplomat I was.' But whatever career Emil had wished for his son, petty criminal was not one them.

In the summer of 1942 Alexis passed all the elements of the School Certificate with the exception of maths, but the discipline problems had got so bad that the headmaster, Mr Oakenshott, had no option but to expel Alexis at the end of the summer term. However, he realized that this highly intelligent boy was not simply a yob run wild, but a sensitive teenager with problems. In August that year he sent Alexis to see a psychiatrist, H. Crichton-Miller, who founded the Tavistock Clinic in London. At one time he was also medical director of the Bowdon House Clinic in Harrow, a residential bolt-hole for a number of the rich and famous trying to come off drugs and alcohol, including, in their time, Keith Richard and Marianne Faithfull.

Crichton-Miller saw Alexis eight times during the remainder of 1942, after which he persuaded Oakenshott to take him back. However, this didn't work out and Alexis was expelled again for the last time in December 1943. He was now sent to a cramming school in London's Notting Hill Gate to acquire sufficient maths to complete the School Certificate.

At home, Alexis started hanging round the Ealing Village residents' club and fell in with the ubiquitous 'bad lot'. In their midst, he found a golden opportunity to rebel against his background and upbringing, to bolster his failing sense of self-worth and to find an identity for himself outside the expectations of his family. The rite of passage into this particular gang was to change his life for ever.

'On Saturday afternoons we used to go down the Shepherd's Bush Market and nick 78s from the stalls. You had to have a bicycle saddle bag at least twelve inches big before you could join the club because you had to be able to slip the records in fast and vanish. And one of the first records to vanish into my saddle bag was Jimmy Yancey's "Slow And Easy Blues".'

Alexis had been forced to learn piano from a very early age and had had a reasonable classical grounding, but really no interest in playing piano until he heard Jimmy Yancey pounding out boogie-woogie. Inside his mother's piano stool, beneath all the Bach concertos, he had come across some sheet music of popular songs of the day which Sappho might play when her husband was not around. So Alexis had a soul mate in wanting to subvert the cause of high culture, but Emil would have none of it. With boogie, as opposed to Bach, 'I found a music that I was totally involved with straight away. One day my father came back to find me playing boogie-woogie and he blew his top, totally and absolutely. He slammed down the lid of the piano and locked it, saying, "You don't play stuff like that on my piano." '

The music had an immediate emotional impact on Alexis. He possessed nothing of the vast knowledge he was to acquire of blues and jazz; this was an instinctive reaction that went straight to the heart. Alexis spontaneously tuned in to the visceral intensity of the music, with its notes chopped, bent, halved, twisted, augmented and stretched – a far cry from the sequential nature of European harmony. That it represented the complete antithesis of his father's cultural background and preferences, a herald for the 'shiny barbarism' of Americana, as Richard Hoggart put it, made it all the more attractive.

Boogie-woogie was the pop music of its day; it spawned great individualists like Yancey, Albert Ammons and Pete Johnson, and in Britain Winifred Atwell, but reached the mass audience rather through its inclusion in swing-band repertoires. Alexis grabbed everything he could find, 'anything with boogie-woogie in the title I bought. I didn't even want to hear what it was . . . "The Boogie Woogie Bugle Boy of Company B–"; "Beat Me Daddy Eight to The Bar"; "Scrub Me Mama With A Boogie Beat".' Note the word 'bought': not all Alexis' records were acquired illicitly. George Körner offered Alexis his stamp collection, which Alexis took eagerly, only to sell it shortly afterwards to buy records. In his clipped, understated tone, George admits to being 'disappointed' at the fate of his stamp collection.

Crichton-Miller was still seeing Alexis, but was at a loss as to how to proceed. Alexis was truanting regularly from the school in Notting Hill Gate and his parents were at their wits' end. The boy's last remaining hope of avoiding a life of crime, Crichton-Miller decided, was to stay at a very special establishment called Finchden Manor.

3

HONOUR THE YOUNG MAN

George Lyward was a remarkable man. Born into a humble and rather unstable family background in London, he suffered bouts of ill health, but was blessed with a great intellect and survived to become at eighteen a teacher at a private school and later a history graduate of St John's College, Cambridge.

Various teaching jobs followed graduation and by his late twenties he was head of the sixth form at Glenalmond, a public school in Scotland, where he was also in charge of English and History and acted as both school librarian and rugby team coach.

But it is not for his academic, teaching, organizational or sporting achievements that George Lyward has been remembered over the years with so much love and respect by many hundreds of men (some now in highly eminent positions) and their parents. While at Glenalmond he revealed a deep empathy for those boys who, for a variety of reasons, could not cope with the demands and expectations of their parents and the rigours of the public school system.

These boys were the damaged, the unloved, the misfits, the non-conformists. Many had parents who were divorced, or who lived abroad, or who exercised rigid discipline through the father and overindulgence through the mother. They often came from homes that were not exactly broken, because they had never been made. These were boys made to lead lives not their own, subject to family pressures to 'succeed'. As a consequence they were hurried through childhood to 'be a man' and 'stand on your own two feet'. The rich variety of life's options was denied these boys at a very early age; their views and opinions counted for very little, if they were heard at all, and many simply retreated into themselves or became 'delinquent' and were tagged 'maladjusted'. As Philip Larkin so famously put it: 'They fuck you up, your mum and dad.'

After many strenuous years at Glenalmond, George Lyward had a breakdown. But he had come into contact with doctors who had become acquainted with his skills and asked him to see boys who were having problems at school. He went to live in Coulsdon, Surrey on a farm called Guildables, owned by a friend. Some of these troubled boys came to work on the farm. His reputation spread, space on the farm was limited and so new premises were sought. In 1935 Lyward and his wife discovered Finchden Manor on the road between Tenterden and Appledore in Kent. The black-and-white timbered house, part Jacobean, part Victorian, was hidden behind a wilderness of briars which, over the next few years, the Lywards reclaimed for the grounds.

When they moved into Finchden Manor, they had around twenty boys in their care, rising to forty by the outbreak of war. Then many of the staff were called up, the Army requisitioned the house for soldiers evacuated after the fall of France and most of the boys had to be sent home for two weeks while new premises were found. The Lywards moved to a rectory at Pipe Aston near Ludlow, Shropshire, and then, for the rest of the war, not far north to Marrington Hall, Chirbury, almost on the border with Wales. However, because 'Finchden Manor' became as much a way of life as a place, the rest of this chapter set in wartime will nevertheless refer to Finchden.

What was Finchden? It would be easier to say what it wasn't: not a school, although lessons were available if Lyward thought them appropriate; not a hospital, rehabilitation unit or clinic, although Lyward would use the term 'patient' if he thought somebody from outside, for example a parent, needed a particular point emphasized. It wasn't a children's home. 'Therapeutic community' might be a slightly better definition, although Lyward's methods in no way depended on a particular therapeutic model. The best description might be 'community' or 'halfway house', though that suggests an establishment run on social-work lines with rules and regulations, codes of practice and the like which simply did not apply at Finchden.

And yet in a sense it was all of these, because what happened to any individual was entirely focused on his own needs at any given time and so it might be appropriate for a boy to be treated or to regard himself as a patient or a member of a community or even on holiday. This is why the word 'Finchden' describes not only the location, but a unique undertaking in the restoration of submerged identities.

How was this achieved? Lyward demurred on the notion that he had a gift. 'I rule myself out as having any experience at all and become one of them.' In fact he had a number of gifts for helping the boys, one of the most important being timing and thus, by definition, the willingness to wait. The process of reinvention, restoration or growth for a boy might take six months or six years, and along the way there would be calculated times for acts of great generosity or toughness by Lyward and the staff. But Lyward had an instinct for exactly what should be delivered and when. Those few parents who took their sons away against his advice came to regret their decision.

In this short chapter it is impossible to convey the precise nature of Finchden and how it worked. A journalist, Michael Burn, wrote a partly successful account of Finchden in 1956, a book entitled *Mr Lyward's Answer*, after much rewriting (and anguish) by Lyward himself. Lyward always said it would take a poet to write about Finchden, an indication of the depth of sensitivity required to avoid pat theorizing about the mental health of the boys who went there and to discern the true nature of the nurturing devices by which he 'repaired' individual psyches on an individual basis. Lyward's own account remains unpublished, although fragments of his thoughts and methods reside in correspondence, articles and the magazine he edited for many years, *Home and School*.

In grossly simplified form, what Finchden offered was firstly respite and liberation from expectations, demands and pressures; secondly, a means by which a life which had been usurped or hijacked by parents trying to live their lives through their children could be restored to its rightful owner; and thirdly, a process of weaning. In Lyward's opinion, many of these boys had had their childhood taken from them; they had reached their mid or late teens without becoming seven years old. Part of the job of helping them to move forwards, therefore, was to give them 'permission' to slip backwards without having to deal with the weight of outside opprobrium.

It is doubtful whether, in its arrogance, the psychiatric profession ever really understood Finchden. Crichton-Miller was an exception. He had first met George Lyward when he helped Lyward through his own mental illness and it was to the pioneer of Finchden that he now turned for help with the insoluble problem of a juvenile delinquent known as Alexis Korner.

In his letter to Lyward of 4 February 1944, Crichton-Miller displays the ingrained British attitudes to foreigners which slip the leash during wartime; he says that Emil is Jewish 'claiming to be Roman Catholic' and that Sappho's allegiance to the Orthodox Greek Church was 'in name only'. He generally marks them down as Jewish refugees from the war in Europe, when in fact they had simply been caught out when war was declared. He found Alexis 'perfectly charming, very intelligent but facile and I never really got down to any significant repressed material'.

Further on he comments rather crudely on his perception of Alexis' unctuousness: 'I think that were he in Greece where he really belongs, he would be doing excellent work in the underground movement and at the same time making himself persona grata with the occupying forces. I think he would do well with a good long spell at Chirbury.' These and similar comments below about Alexis and his family were clearly of their time, but appear outrageous from the perspective of multicultural society in the late-twentieth century.

Crichton-Miller broached the idea of Finchden with Emil and Sappho, who then wrote to Lyward on 25 February 1944: 'Since he came home from school, he has been unable to settle down to any serious work and feels very unhappy about it.' In the same letter Emil raised the issue of the fees, which were eight guineas a week, stating that 'this is beyond any financial possibilities in present circumstances' and taking up Lyward's offer of a 'reasonable reduction'. Money was never an issue with Lyward; nobody was refused entry for lack of funds, which left Finchden lurching from one financial crisis to another. Emil concludes by saying that he was too ill to travel so that Sappho would be bringing 'the boy' and would, at the same time, 'have a frank talk with you regarding my present financial situation'.

At the time when Crichton-Miller wanted to get Alexis into Finchden, the secretary, Mr Davies, was reluctant both because Lyward hadn't returned from holiday and because a boy had just died, blown to bits by a mortar shell he had taken to his room, where it exploded, killing him and causing extensive damage. But Crichton-Miller was insistent; he wrote again in March reiterating his previous report and adding: 'I don't see what chance he has except with you.' And because of the difficulties of travelling during wartime and because 'the friction between himself [Alexis] and his parents is becoming intolerable for all parties', he urged that they should take Alexis in straight away, waiving the normal pre-entry interview and 'vetting' of parents which were part of Lyward's standard practice. The urgency of the situation is underlined by the fact that, apart from persistent truanting from his crammer school, Alexis' most recent escapade had cost his family a ten-shilling fine at Chelsea Juvenile Court when he was caught fare dodging on the London Underground.

Eventually Davies agreed to take Alexis on Crichton-Miller's recommendation, although he couldn't guarantee that Alexis would be able to stay indefinitely as Lyward had not been involved in the decision to admit him. Perhaps inevitably, Alexis did not arrive at Finchden with either of his parents, but travelled alone on Friday 23 March 1944 from Paddington to Welshpool via Shrewsbury.

Lyward returned and had no hesitation in allowing Alexis to stay until the time was right for him to leave. There would have been about forty other boys there at the time; they had all come with their own unique set of problems, their own stories to tell, their own weighty baggage to unload. Some had been severely mentally or even physically abused by parents or schoolmasters, some would have such severe mental illness as to be beyond Lyward's help and would have to be sent on to mental hospitals. Some would end up writing to Lyward, or 'Chief' as he was known to staff and boys alike, from prison; others would become the judges who put boys like them there. At that point in Finchden's history they would probably have all been from public schools; it was only after the war that local education authorities began to refer boys from state schools to Finchden. But wherever they came from, all the boys would have been highly intelligent. Lyward required of all would-be entrants an IQ of 125 or above, on the grounds that they needed to be involved in the process of working through their problems and understanding how they came to have them in the first place.

Alexis settled in quickly; the 'Finchden day' was built around the routines of 'four square meals and bedtime', as Lyward once said. Breakfast was from nine to ten a.m.; elevenses were taken in the kitchen; lunch one to two p.m.; tea four to five p.m.; supper seven to eight p.m.; and lights out at ten-fifteen. The boys were expected to cook, clean, work in the garden and generally take on the housekeeping. But beyond that an answer to the question 'What did boys at Finchden do?' would be similar to the one Lyward gave to Michael Burn when the journalist was writing his book. 'I have a rough idea. I can tell you that three are in London. Two, as you see, are playing croquet. One has just been given twenty pounds to start breeding budgerigars. Another is thinking about making a telescope, but won't get a penny till he shows that he means it. And one has run away.'

The whole point was to relieve the pressure of expectations from the boys' shoulders, to allow a natural growth. But Finchden was very far from anarchic; Lyward had little truck with so-called 'progressive schools' such as Beacon Hill, run by Bertrand Russell's wife, Dora, where 'children run around with no clothes on'. As Lyward's answer indicates, however disturbed a boy might be (and some came with a dreadful record of disruption and violence) he was invariably coaxed from his shell to take on something he wanted to do. Boys might spend their time reading, making models, fishing, looking after the animals and taking lessons in various subjects in which they had shown an interest (rather than being educationally force-fed for examinations).

The other members of staff (many of whom had been to Finchden as boys) all had various teaching skills and experiences to help the boys along whatever paths they chose. A firm favourite was Syd Hopkins, a large, strong man, later crippled by an injury to his spine, who helped the boys make wireless sets and who encouraged Alexis to make his first guitar. Burn wrote of Syd: 'The loss of his physical vigour may have deepened the resources of a spiritual and speculative nature already deep . . . He took things quietly, humorously and without hurry; and to many of the boys, especially the young and more excitable, his mere appearance had the effect of a caress.'

By 4 April 1944, two weeks into his stay at Finchden, Alexis' parents hadn't even heard that he'd got there safely. But rather than contact the school direct, they wrote to Crichton-Miller, who confirmed their son's arrival and told them that he had insisted on being called 'Andrew', although he continued to sign his letters home as 'Alexis' or 'Alexy'.

On 5 April Lyward wrote to Sappho and Emil saying that he would be sending monthly reports on Alexis, but that it was his policy never to write to parents until the boy had written home first. He felt it important that the boy should be given the chance to describe what was going on without the parents' view being coloured by what Lyward might have said first. But Lyward was scrupulous in keeping up contact with parents, not only sending the detailed reports as promised, but replying at length to any worries or problems. Concerning one boy, Burn found over 2000 pages in the files, spanning five years of correspondence.

Alexis had actually written home in a letter dated 3 April which described his journey, the physical environs of his new home and going to the 'flicks' in Shrewsbury. 'I'm sorry I didn't write earlier,' he continued, 'but this place is so full of life and all its various interests that it is honestly difficult at first to find time in which to sit down and write a letter.' And as a postscript, 'in my tuck parcel you might like to put a pound note and 50 to 100 odd fags (cigarettes). Both would be very welcome as a couple of my pals and I intend to make whoopee on my birthday by going into Shrewsbury to have some fun.'

His parents immediately wrote back to Lyward querying the request for money and cigarettes. Emil was particularly incensed at the use of words like 'flicks' and 'fags' even if Alexis had helpfully put 'cigarettes' in brackets. He was clearly against Alexis smoking, but not on health grounds (he himself was a very heavy smoker and, according to George Körner, had been told to give up by his doctor). 'Andrew should understand that he cannot have all that the other boys have and that he will still be among the privileged ones,' Emil explained. He goes on to say that he is 'very embittered by the great deception he has given me', but says that he 'must leave the decision on the steps to be taken entirely to your experience'.

In his reply, even though Alexis had only been at Finchden for two weeks, Lyward had come to an understanding of where the problems lay. 'There is nothing in what Andrew has done to be worried about still less to get embittered about. His actions are symptoms of the state of mind he is in and this relates back to the earlier years and what happened to him then. Far from wishing to deceive you, he is almost obsessed by a desire not to let people down – a much more serious matter as I hope you'll gradually see as our reports unfold the truth about him. Put briefly, if one part of him hadn't been made too good to be true, the other part wouldn't appear too bad to be loved. By the way is anybody too bad to be loved?'

Lyward's first 'official' report on Alexis was written on 15 April, just four days before his sixteenth birthday. 'It is most significant that his two most urgent regrets are that he never had an elder sister and that his father didn't get involved with his activities. Obviously there were reasons for both of the above . . . but the business of everybody interested in Andrew's welfare is to realize that this is the net result of what he was given when he would have been better without it (spoiling shall we call it?) and what he was denied which would have helped him to nourish his spirit and helped him outgrow the emotional condition of a small child. He did not outgrow that and is therefore inside, as it were, still a small child, in spite of such intellectual advances as he has made. He therefore feels small and has to cover that up by acting "big".

'We should do well to look upon this acting as nature's way of saving him from still more serious breakdown. We must certainly not have that up against him and waste energy by being sorry about that instead of sorry about the way he was undernourished emotionally as a small child and subjected prematurely to grown up standards.

'If he was introduced early to such notions as "not letting people down" then it is only to be expected that in taking these notions over ready-made, he would also have to balance them by taking over the habit and the sophistication (in his case false) of adults. Smoking is merely one of his ways of trying to keep up the "grownupness" which was induced too early while he was not allowed grow through the proper stages with normal companionship. It is probably the least harmful of all the bluffs he might be indulging in and I am only too glad that he can use that instead of more subtle methods. Not that he hasn't already started subtler methods of bluffing himself, but he is still young and I think the atmosphere will ease him up and satisfy the small child in him in ways which will make bluff unnecessary.'

Alexis had got it into his head that he wanted to join the Navy. Exactly where this came from is unclear, but it may have derived from his experiences of warships on the way back to England from France in 1940. In one of Sappho's first letters to Lyward, she comments that 'he is very keen on entering the French or British Navy'.

For 'Chief' this was not good news. 'The most serious problem from our point of view is his determination to get into the Navy by a fixed time. This may hold up his progress in the more important things that make for real life. Fixed goals are much to be deplored in cases like Andrew's. I haven't said anything about this last matter to him, for at present he is easily capable of talking morally about it. He is far too much impregnated with moral maxims, I fear at the moment. They do not help his development and hold him up because they are unrelated to his growth and his capacity of experiencing the truths they crystallize.

'I hope the above will serve as a preliminary introduction to our way of releasing people like Andrew from their lifelong trip of 1) hiding their real fears and disappointments under a casual air 2) estimating everything in terms of their own immediate satisfaction perfectly natural to small children – and he has remained one 3) trying to live up to pictures of themselves which have developed in their minds owing to unexamined repetitions to them of a moralizing order before they were ready for them. Above all, I hope that you will be able to see Andrew's recent behaviour as the logical outcome of earlier experiences and certainly not as reasons for ceasing to love him which is what being "embittered" strictly implies. Andrew at the moment is one of the huge number of children who feel that the love of other people depends on how they behave. Until he realises that love is a free gift, he cannot start his rebirth and his re-education.

'I feel sure you will co-operate with us in our work with him.

'PS I noticed in the letter he sent you that the signature is "Alexis". He told me he was known as Andrew at home . . . I hope incidentally that you realise how much you have to be thankful for in him asking for "fags" (whatever you and I may think about smoking). It is something that is done either openly or in secret and Andrew is being open about it. Boys generally smoke a good deal less after being here for a time. They tend to bite the hand that feeds them at first. We expect that.'

On 17 April, Alexis wrote a letter headed 'Dear parents' in which he said: 'Mr Lyward thinks my mental readjustment is more important than my studies . . . incidentally you probably know more about my mental stage than I do because you probably get weekly [sic] reports on it. Anyway, I have more or less been given to understand by Mr Lyward, that I am mentally too far advanced for my age. I have spoken to Mr Lyward about matric[ulation] and Naval Special Entry and he says all will come in good time. But I was not satisfied, so I pressed him again by asking him if he thought that I would be ready for the NSE exam next year and he said that he saw no reason why I should not be.'

In a PS he requested ten shillings plus envelopes and writing paper, adding, 'I hope you have not forgotten the fags as Mr Lyward does not mind you sending them. He says that if a boy wants to smoke there is no reason why he should not do so. Anyway, 100 cigarettes should last me a heck of a long time as I'm already smoking less than when I came down here . . .'

Written at about the same time is an internal report on Alexis' capabilities in maths written by one of the staff. While it belied the fact that Alexis failed the maths component of his school certificate, it said reams about what Alexis could achieve when the pressure was off. 'In test he appears to have the ability of a very high order indeed very much greater than that of anybody else who I have discussed the subject with here.'

Emil had washed his hands of Alexis and was content to let Lyward do what he could for his eight guineas a week. In his view his son was simply 'no good' and he refused to acknowledge (at least in writing) that he might have been at fault for the way Alexis had turned out. Sappho, however, was anxious to learn as much as she could about the 'queer at times, strange behaviour of our son'. But for Lyward it was a common enough story. As Michael Burn noted from his long discussions with 'Chief': 'The boys who became members of the family at Finchden had begun to live [a] lie about themselves . . . And it had worked. For a time it had worked; until one day the model son, the supposedly contented one, had been discovered stealing or lying . . . and the parents discovered themselves, overnight, living with someone they did not recognise and could not recognise, because they and the boy had never really met.'

In the same letter of 22 April Sappho denies that it was she and Emil who inculcated this notion of not letting people down and blames boarding school. 'For instance, once we asked him why he was being caned so often at St Pauls and he said he could not let his friends down and that we would not understand if he explained.'

This comment suggests that Alexis was prepared to take the blame for misdemeanours whether he'd actually done them or not to win kudos – or was just unlucky at being the one who always got caught but wouldn't 'squeal'. Another possibility was that he was automatically singled out by the particular masters because he was clearly 'not English'.

Emil adds in this letter: ' We never encouraged Alexis' ideas of getting into the Navy English or French – and we don't believe he is sea-minded at all . . . His house master (the only person he really loved at St Pauls) had discussed with Alexis his future studies and they had decided he would take up history and modern languages and work for a scholarship at Oxford or Cambridge . . .

'Then came the disaster of last Autumn [expulsion] and only then came the craving for the Navy "as the only way of saving himself" [which, apparently, is how Alexis expressed it to his parents] . . . I think he tries to deceive himself, he is ambitious and wants to be somebody as soon as possible to see the world.'

That was the last letter Emil ever wrote to George Lyward. On 6 May 1944 he succumbed to a fatal heart attack at the age of seventy-one.

The next day Sappho wrote to Lyward: 'The news I have to send my son today are [sic] very very sad. That is why I am writing to you to break them to him. My dear husband who has not been well for quite a long time has suddenly passed away last night. You can imagine the tragedy of the whole situation. The poor man was so terribly worried about our boy and hoped so much to live long enough to see him grow into a good honest man. I sent Alexis a little parcel yesterday, twenty cigarettes, and wrote to him that his father was not too well, but never dreamt that the end would come so soon. Will you kindly break these sad news to him in your own way which I have no doubt will be the best. I am going to write to him also. I do not wish him to come to London not even for a few days as I'm afraid that the good work you have started with him will get spoilt here. Don't you think this is the best for him?'

Some years later Alexis said that he had a dream the night before his father died. He dreamt they both went up in an aeroplane, but when the plane landed, Alexis was alone. When Chief called Alexis into his office, Alexis knew why, but still cried bitterly for the father he needed so badly. But sadly, according to George Körner, Emil regarded Alexis as 'disloyal'. In Emil's last letter to George (then in the Army) from a nursing home in Reading, where he was recuperating from a prostate operation and completely out of touch with his eldest son, Herman, trapped in Nazi-occupied Paris, he wrote: 'if it wasn't for Sappho and you, George, life wouldn't be worth living'. No mention of Alexis.

In a letter to Crichton-Miller, Lyward relates how Alexis reacted to his father's death. Once he stopped crying, 'he said that he had just had a picture of a church with the sun shining through the windows, very beautiful and reassuring . . . he is glib and rather unctuous, but will do quite well'. In other words, having cried (and thus revealed his true feelings) he had to swiftly cover up with some kind of sentimental and rather unconvincing imagery because this is how he thought he should be acting, or rather how he believed he should come across to Lyward – as somebody who would just stiffen his upper lip and carry on in true 'British' tradition. He couldn't have known that while he was acting out, George Lyward was reading the script.

Crichton-Miller wrote back declaring his complete agreement with Lyward's character analysis, adding in some kind of recognized but nonetheless objectionable psychiatric shorthand that 'the depressing thing to me is the recognition that these qualities are so racial and innate in their origin'.

In his letter of condolence to Sappho, Lyward mentions how sensitive Alexis is: 'no wonder he was so easily influenced when young. He looks as if he is capable of making the most of his chances here. I hope that his father realised that we did not in any way think of Andrew as bad, but only as confused.'

As and when they felt like it, Chief asked the boys to write down any dreams they happened to remember – not as part of any specific therapy, but just because they could be revealing in general conversation. Most of Alexis' seemed to involve car crashes, having to walk along narrow cliff edges and nearly falling, battling against strong currents in rivers and streams and being attacked by snakes. Once he dreamt that his closest friends at Finchden were attacking him. Another time he dreamt that all his teeth were either taken out or came out and were placed on a table in front of him; they were all mouldy and dirty.

Whatever one's view of the revelatory powers of dreams, one dream in particular seemed especially revealing. 'Mr Lyward and I were standing on a very high cliff overlooking the sea. The sea was very heavy and large green waves were clashing against the rocks at the bottom of the cliff. Mr Lyward was telling me to cross a difficult part of the cliff edge. It was a narrow ledge, like a path, about a foot and half in width and covered in shining ice. I decided to cross and started out. When I had got about half way, I stopped for about twenty seconds to regain my breadth and then I went on. After about 15 minutes of struggling not to lose my grip, I got to the other side.'

Sappho was rather concerned that Alexis was not writing to her, but Lyward said that this was par for the course and it would be entirely wrong for him to put any pressure on Alexis to write; and that in fact this was just the sort of thing that resulted in him coming to Finchden in the first place – being forced to 'do the right thing' whether he wanted to or not. If Alexis did write in those circumstances, it would only be out of a sense of duty and the letters would thus be dishonest. 'I can't imagine you would welcome letters in which there was no real Andrew.'

He went on to say that if you leave him alone, 'he will gradually let you into his world where at the moment there is only room for him . . . watch against using words like "he ought", when you really mean "I want".'

And as a postscript he wrote: 'Please don't think this is all

27

unsympathetic, but I want to help you to worry less for your own sake as well as Andrew's.'

In the continuing correspondence between Sappho and Lyward, she agreed that Alexis should be left alone and acknowledged how her own 'wants' could damage his progress. 'I can tell you frankly you have helped me tremendously . . . in future I will try to analyse my feelings before putting them down on paper, thus I hope avoiding being "ticked off" . . . I think a lot about this subject but can say very little.'

For Christmas 1944 Alexis stayed with a friend in Sunderland and went back home for New Year. On 11 Jan 1945 Sappho wrote to Lyward: 'the change in him is so marked that I would not forgive myself if I would even unwillingly hinder your wonderful work in any way. The boy is so happy to be in your care and so full of confidence . . .'

In the monthly report of January 1945 Lyward observed: 'Andrew came back *no worse* [author's emphasis] from his holiday' – as if he expected boys to relapse when outside his immediate control. It may well be that they did, but such a comment is also indicative of the degree to which Finchden fulfilled certain needs within George Lyward himself. Although rather fragile-looking, Chief possessed the ability to reassure parents, empathize with boys and fend off local authority bureaucrats with equal facility while commanding abiding love and respect. The singer Tom Robinson, an ex-Finchden boy from the late 1960s who was befriended by Alexis, says that the most violent, disturbed and frightening boys invariably did as they were asked simply because they didn't want to upset Chief wherever their instincts might have otherwise have led them.

One of Lyward's key 'techniques' for helping boys 'grow' into their calendar age and beyond was to disarm them, to nurture expectance of the unexpected, to make them accept that they couldn't always get their own way, to make them realize that there were few certainties in life, which might be unsettling, but also liberating. As Tom Robinson explains: 'He would wander into breakfast and might say, "Give that boy bacon and eggs" or he might say, "Get back to bed *now* – breakfast started twenty minutes ago. Get to your bed." And you'd go. The most tough, streetwise ex-Borstal boys were in terror of him. He had an iron streak in the centre of his personality. He might decide to give somebody free rein and then call them to heel. Or a boy might be "gated" on some pretext. That boy might run away on the first night. Nothing might happen as a consequence *or* a staff member might drive up alongside him and invite him to get in *or* he might be given a cup of coffee in the staffroom *or* be sent straight to bed *or* dressed down *or* expelled *or* just a word if they looked frightened by the lack of reaction. You wouldn't know what would happen.' All the options for a boy would be carefully considered by Lyward over time – so what might appear as random was calculated.

Of course, Tom Robinson is speaking of a later period and over time Lyward modified his thinking, moving, for example, from a notion of trying to make boys 'fit and well' for the return to 'normal society' they had come from, to acknowledging their right to follow their own path, having gone through a life-redeeming maturation process at Finchden. In some respects a Finchden boy of the 1940s would not have recognized the place twenty years on, but some of the basic methodology went back to its earliest days. Chief applied 'disarmament' to Alexis on at least one occasion when in May 1945 Sappho asked Chief if Alexis could come on holiday with her to Torquay. He told Alexis that there would be a ninety-nine percent chance of this happening, but then refused on the grounds that Alexis must learn that the one percent can also happen. Alexis and his mother were deeply disappointed, but seemed to accept this as all part of the treatment.

As a kind of sweetener perhaps to Sappho, Lyward wrote to her on 12 May 1945, saying 'as a pleasure seeker of some years standing, he cannot be expected to surrender some of his attitudes rapidly, but I believe the seeds of future values are within him'.

Early in 1945 Alexis met George Körner once or twice in Shrewsbury. On 28 February Alexis wrote an awkward letter to him – first telling him about life there and then asking for money. 'I'm now going to do something which I really do not like, but which I feel I have to do. I am going to ask you for money and here is the reason.' Alexis had bet the boy he stayed with at Christmas that the war would be over by the end of February 1945. Obviously it wasn't and Alexis owed the boy five shillings. If he had asked Chief for the money the boy wouldn't have got his money, since the policy was to cancel all existing debts. Alexis felt this would be dishonourable. 'So you can see my reasons are not illegitimate.'

Not only did he ask for it by return, but also said that if George fancied sending him cigarettes and more money this 'will be welcome'. He signed the letter 'Your loving brother Alexis', leading up to the inevitable PS: 'please send the money as soon as possible'.

The periods when Alexis did not write home are those marked in Lyward's view by progress in his psychological development. He wrote on 7 June to Sappho: 'Andrew is coarsening. By this I don't mean anything unpleasant, but rather he is losing the rather unnatural delicacy which stood in the way of him being himself and more honest.'

On 11 September Alexis wrote a note which announced that after due consideration he was going to study agricultural engineering and then mapped out the whole career plan starting with his matriculation in maths which he had already failed, on to Loughborough College for practical work, then university for the theoretical grounding and finally into the world of work.

What is interesting about this plan is that music doesn't feature at all. Certainly Alexis was trying to play at Finchden because of the guitar he had made. He said that he took up guitar because his father found it even more annoying than boogie-woogie piano, regarding it as a 'woman's instrument'. It is quite possible at this stage that either Alexis had his heart set on playing piano or he simply saw music as a relaxation to be indulged in when he chose, free from the admonishments at home.

On 29 September Lyward wrote to Sappho: 'Andrew had been jolted into shedding some of his veneer. We hope to be able to deal with some of the aspects of his more inner life which we could not get at until more recently' – although whether he is referring to a specific incident or simply progress over time is unstated.

Lyward encouraged every form of self-expression, whether it was dream stories, diary recollections or passing thoughts like this one written by Alexis on 8 December 1945: 'I have been rather afraid of dark colours ever since I looked at a picture of Christ in a Bible I had when I was very small. It depicted Christ and the disciples in a boat in a very stormy sea with terrific waves around it. The only patches of light and colour in the whole sea were Christ's face and the clothes and the crests of breaking waves. The disciples faces were all shaded and they were wearing either dark blues or dark reds. The ship was a deep brown colour. After seeing the picture once, whenever I opened the book, I tried to avoid the page on which the picture was printed. Once or twice however, I saw the picture in the book and was so fascinated and terrified by it that I almost literally had to tear myself from it. Even now when I think about it, I feel queer and do now as I write about it.'

The first few months of 1946 appear to have passed without major incident. Alexis was extremely happy at Finchden, and his mother was gaining ever deepening insights into her son's true nature and how Finchden was helping him. Both were perfectly happy for Alexis to stay at Finchden until Chief decided it was time to go. And then tragedy struck.

Sappho Körner was admitted to the French Hospital in Shaftesbury Avenue with acute appendicitis. Peritonitis set in and she died on 26 May 1946, aged forty-eight. Her brother Themi and sister Cali took over as Alexis' legal guardians, heralding the beginning of the end of his stay at Finchden.

The day after his sister died Themi sent a priority telegram to George Lyward requesting that he 'please break the sad news to Alexis'. Heartbroken, Alexis made the journey back to London to Cali's house in Collingham Road, Earls Court, from where, on 30 May, he sent to Chief this letter, written at one-thirty a.m.: 'I tried to get you on the phone, but the operator didn't seem to think it necessary to answer. I'm going to try again in the morning and if I still can't get through I'm going to send a telegram.

'I just cannot get to sleep, so I thought I would unburden myself. The actual writing of this to you is an immeasurable help to me, though I may not say much.

'Well, as you should know, Mum died of peritonitis. It set in almost as soon as she came through the anaesthetic. This was on Wednesday last week . . . everyone thought she would be fine. On Friday the trouble started and they noticed what had happened, but it was too late. Mummy was given 10 or 12 M&B Sulphur injections, but she got worse and the miserable part of it was that she felt it all the time and did not die in comfort but in pain. She died on Saturday at 5 o'clock in the afternoon. At least God might have let her die in peace, but then he had his reason.

'No sooner is my darling dead than George [Körner] starts talking about what he will put aside for me by selling this and that. Can he not wait a bit instead of talking about it in front of granny? [Sappho's mother]. It hurts both granny and myself but I can stand it just. It's so much harder for her. I'm afraid, really afraid that I have found George to be very different from what I thought him to be. We've not argued yet, but if I'm not careful we will. He does not seem to realize that his age does not give him the right to run my life for me. He means so well, but after all I am a human being and 18 years of age. It was not his mother who died last Saturday, it was mine. He does not feel what I feel. He tries to play the part of the big brother trying to look after his poor little brother. There are times when quite inadvertently he goes too far. This afternoon for instance we went to the flat to get some things and he started talking about selling the furniture. Before he could get very far, I stopped him dead by saying whatever else you may do you will not sell the piano among other things.'

Alexis goes on to say that George keeps telling him that he has attained manhood, and comments: 'in some ways he is right, but in others wrong . . . our temperaments do not match and God alone knows if I will ever come to an understanding with him. I do so want to . . .'

Once Alexis had returned to Finchden, Themi Aperguis immediately began writing to Lyward about Alexis' leaving. He had no understanding of why Alexis was there or what Lyward could do for him; in fact he thought the place actually did harm rather than good and when · interviewed for this book simply referred to it as 'that place in Kent'. From the correspondence he had with Lyward, he obviously believed that it was an insult to the family name that Alexis should have to go to such a place. Picking up on George Körner's theme in being mindful of the fact that Alexis was now eighteen, he made a number of references about Alexis 'becoming a man', 'doing his duty' and 'looking to his responsibilities'. Like Emil (and like most fathers whose boys went to Finchden) he could not accept the idea that Alexis' emotional development might lag some way behind the calendar. And, as we have seen, it was that lack of understanding by fathers, dating back to their sons' earliest years, which drove most of them to Finchden in the first place.

Knowing nothing about Lyward's extensive and highly acclaimed skill and experience, Themi regarded his views on bringing up Alexis as just one opinion. While most politely accepting Lyward's right to his own views, Themi believed that he and Cali could do just as well as anybody else.

In his replies Lyward obviously tried to dissuade Themi from taking Alexis away, especially as the young man needed some stability so shortly after the death of his mother. Lyward quoted from one of Sappho's letters in which she makes it clear that Alexis was to stay at Finchden until Lyward thought he was ready to leave. However, albeit for different reasons, both Themi and Lyward did agree that as Alexis was now eligible for his National Service, a spell in the Army would do him some good. Lyward thought that military service would give Alexis some stability and protect him from civilian life for a bit longer; Themi's reasoning was more gung-ho and traditional.

Alexis finally left early in September 1946, as Lyward was reclaiming his house back from the Army and the boys and staff were able to leave Marrington Hall for their rightful home.

Just before Finchden actually moved back to Tenterden on 23 September 1946, Alexis wrote to Lyward from Collingham Road, where he was now living with his Aunt Cali. 'It is now roughly two weeks since I left Finchden and I miss it very much. I am getting on very well at home, but I miss the companionship which I had in Finchden.' He goes on to ask advice about getting deferment from National Service in order to do his matriculation and ends the letter: 'you must surely realise how deeply grateful I am to you and I wish you to know that I have not forgotten your last six words to me – 'Function and c'est moie qui ait vecu' – yours ever Andrew.'

Alexis went to work as an office clerk in Themi's firm – A.G. TH. Avgherino & N. Aperguis, steam ship and insurance brokers, of Bury St, London EC3 – and wrote again to Lyward saying he was bored stiff and learning Spanish in his spare time 'of which there is lots'.

Confounding the analysis of his abilities made at Finchden, he managed to fail his maths again, but his call-up was in any case deferred pending reports from Lyward as to his medical fitness for military service. Alexis wrote to Lyward in April 1947 about his latest deferment, saying again how much he missed Finchden, especially as 'life at home is inclined to be rather difficult and wearing'. One can imagine that Alexis and his family did not exactly see eye to eye on how he should conduct himself, although there were no obvious rows over the matter. Alexis was naturally very disappointed at having had to leave Finchden, Chief and all his friends. Shortly before he left, he had had an altercation with his grandmother about the purchase of a guitar where (to Lyward's delight) Alexis' will prevailed. It was a little victory in a general war of attrition.

But it wasn't simply the generation gap that was causing problems. In April 1947 he wrote to Lyward accusing his family of trying to deny him his inheritance, mentioning shares to the value of £9000 which were 'lost' and a further £25,000 which 'I just managed to save'.

This is very odd and doesn't square with both Emil's and later Sappho's pleading poverty over the fees of eight guineas a week for Finchden. Not only that, as well as the flat in Ealing Village, the Körners had a guest house at 9 Queen's Gate Terrace, South Kensington. George was at one time looking after this property, then a housekeeper (who was apparently dishonest) and then Cali. Thus either Emil simply chose not to spend his money on Alexis, or he (and subsequently Sappho) was unable to realize sufficient funds to deal with the apparent cash-flow crisis. Alexis was living at Queen's Gate Terrace in May 1947 and may subsequently have sold the property to Cali in the late 1950s. All in all the family's business affairs seem shrouded in mystery. It is not at all clear whether or not Alexis was left any money and, if he was, how much and what happened to it.

Alexis became very estranged from George. He was best man at his wedding in 1948; shortly afterwards George and his new wife Dorothy gave Alexis a lift on their way to their holiday in France. They dropped him off in central London and never saw him again. George said he sent Alexis a small cheque for his twenty-first birthday, but received no reply. Interviewed around 1965, Alexis spoke about George without actually mentioning his name: 'I never see him at all because he lives too close . . . he's an accountant – the sort you read about in books', although he freely admitted, 'I'm probably being unfair to him.'

He made a strange (and by his own admission non-existent) distinction between Herman, whom he called his 'half-brother' and George, his 'stepbrother'. He'd obviously built up a romantic picture in his mind about the more remote Herman, living in Paris, who, Alexis claimed, was a French resistance fighter in the war, as opposed to George, who was much closer to home and against whom Alexis held a grudge over money. In one of his Finchden dreams he is sitting in a café with George when a stranger approaches the table. When Alexis realizes it is Herman, 'I flung my arms around him'.

Eventually the Army too embraced Alexis. They accepted a medical report from Lyward saying that Alexis was not suffering from any mental disturbances and in mid 1947 he began two years of National Service.

4

ROBERTA, ROBERTA

Alexis' glimpse of war as a twelve-year-old boy out on the high seas made it seem like one very long Bonfire Night full of glory and excitement. His teenage fixation with the Navy evaporated, but not before he had tried to pass himself off as a French sailor in pre-Finchden days, roaming around Soho on the run from his Notting Hill Gate crammer.

Yet the spirit of danger and adventure was deep within him – something he never lost as an adult; his driving was frightening and on aircraft he would revel in the air turbulence that made others lose their lunch. As a raw recruit in 1947 he wanted to join the Parachute Regiment, but shortly after call-up he was buried beneath a pile of Bren-guns that fell on him as he was travelling in a lorry. As he lay in hospital with a back injury, any hopes he might have harboured of an 'active' spell of National Service were finished.

The Army's assessment of his future revealed his high level of intelligence and they sent him to the Education Corps and from there his fluent German and growing knowledge of music booked him a passage to British Forces Network (BFN) broadcasting in Hamburg.

The city had been devastated by Allied bombing during the baking-hot summer of 1943; Hamburg became a gigantic oven as the fire storms cut through everything in their path. One of the few buildings of significance left standing was the Musikhalle and it was here that BFN had started broadcasting on 27 July 1945.

BFN took over from the Allied Expeditionary Forces Programme and came on air to coincide with the inauguration of the BBC Light Programme. The station's complement was impressive: two hundred staff and three orchestras. Apart from the British forces, the German civilian population were avid listeners, having been deprived of popular music on the radio for the duration of the war. Many famous names in the world of entertainment started out with BFN. An adaptation of *Robin Hood* by Trevor Hill included in the cast: Brian Mathew as King Richard; Cliff Michelmore as Little John; Raymond Baxter as Guy De Gisborn; Geraint Evans as Blondel; Bryan Forbes as the Head of Foresters; and Roger Moore as a forester.

BFN was also a convenient outpost for the aspiringly creative who were not quite A1 enough for 'real' Army life. Like Alexis' bad back, the poor eyesight of actor Nigel Davenport was such that he was able to swap a dose of the infantry for life at BFN.

As well as starting his broadcasting career at BFN doing sports commentaries, Cliff Michelmore was Squadron Leader of the RAF element at BFN and the Deputy Station Director.

Reporting to Michelmore, Alexis was put in charge of the record library. 'In desperation they gave me two stripes and made me an NCO to keep me out of harm's way, so they thought.' Michelmore remembers Alexis 'going in search of jazz along the Reeperbahn'. Alexis also helped on a series of jazz programmes presented by the Queen's cousin, Gerald Lascelles, who broadcast under the name of 'Mr Swing'. Lascelles, a jazz fanatic, had the wherewithal to accumulate a substantial record collection, much of which was flown out to Hamburg to augment the station's meagre jazz collection and passed into Alexis' eager grasp. Alexis' other brush with royalty came during a visit to the station by Princess Margaret, the Queen's sister, to whom Alexis made the priceless comment: 'Hello, I'm Alexis Korner. Who are you?'

But although he now had the golden opportunity to listen to music he liked without getting told off, there was no way that Alexis would be content simply doling out records for other people's shows. His key mentor at BFN was Captain Neville Powley, who took Alexis around with him to meet various German musicians and introduced him to broadcasting techniques, so that he accumulated knowledge in addition to what he had already learnt from doing the 'Mr Swing' programmes. Denied the chance to actually broadcast with BFN, he 'moonlighted' illegally for Nord-West Deutsche Rundfunk (NDR), presenting a programme of jazz records no doubt 'borrowed' from the

BFN library. But although such activity was technically forbidden, it is possible that it was known of but ignored, because in a mid-sixties interview he said that some of the money he earned was donated to the BFN Artists' Fund, 'and [I] was allowed to keep the balance for myself'.

With the balance of his ill-gotten gains, he bought a guitar. 'I really took up the guitar in the Army because I had eight hours a day in which I was doing practically nothing. I started fiddling about with it on the wrong tuning and everything.' Alexis had a dislike for the banjo, but felt hardly more disposed towards the guitar. If his father thought the guitar was a 'woman's instrument', Alexis saw it as simply for 'hillbilly music', not jazz or blues. Thus his first songs on the instrument were 'The Little Red Caboose Behind The Train' and 'Roll Along Covered Wagon, Roll Along'.

It wasn't until May 1949, shortly before his demob, that he caught an inkling of the guitar's potential in the hands of no less a master than Leadbelly (Huddie Ledbetter). Alexis was one of the few people, owing to poor publicity, who turned up at the Paris Lyceum for a Leadbelly concert. In the event, he would not have learnt that much about guitar playing; blues guitarists were always chary about revealing their technique. Robert Johnson would play with his back to the audience, and Leadbelly draped a cloth over the neck. It was in Paris that Leadbelly was diagnosed as suffering from Lou Gehrig's Disease, amyotrophic lateral sclerosis, a degenerative disease of the nerve cells with no known cause or cure. Destined to become the single most important influence on the British and American white folk and blues scenes of the fifties and early sixties, Leadbelly died in New York on 6 December 1949.

By then Alexis was back in London, living at Queen's Gate Terrace, South Kensington. His prowess at sports (mainly rugby) and the bliss of working for BFN combined to ensure that, by his own admission, he had a cushy time in the Army. It also gave him plenty of opportunity for deep thought. There is no doubt that working for BFN changed Alexis' life. Up until then, and during the early part of his National Service, he firmly believed that he was destined to build a serious career in business. He had big ideas. Themi Aperguis and his wife Isobel employed a Swiss au pair, Anne-Marie. Before his call-up, Alexis was frequently in her company and went to see her in Switzerland when she returned there for holidays. He once told her that one day he would own a Rolls-Royce. The developing relationship fizzled out when she went back to Switzerland for good – but even Alexis could not have conceived of owning a Roller by becoming a jazz musician. Yet his time at BFN had given him a glimpse of possibilities as yet undreamt of: the chance of making a living in the world of music.

By day he was working in Themi's office and was highly thought of as somebody who would become successful in shipping. But Alexis had now turned twenty-one, and the pull of the family, which had been so strong, and his desire to please, which had been almost the defining aspect of his character, were both weakening. Finchden and George Lyward had given him 'permission' to follow his own path. In a very real sense Alexis was standing at the crossroads.

From his earnest practising in the Army Alexis emerged 'a bad player, [but] I had apparently got a slightly peculiar sound which attracted some people. So I was offered work at between five and ten bob a night.' His first musical home was the world of traditional or revivalist New Orleans jazz, inspired by the music of Joe 'King' Oliver's Creole Jazz Band with Johnny Dodds, Louis Armstrong and Lil Hardin, and at its height in the early twenties.

In England the music mainly attracted the offspring of the middle classes whose parents had supported socialism and communism in the wake of the 1914–18 war and the General Strike, which for many signalled the moral bankruptcy of capitalism.

The postwar jazz revivalists despised the growing hordes of Teddy Boys tumbling out of south London as aliens from another world and viewed pop singers like Johnnie Ray as phoney commercialism. They found bebop just as unsettling, mainly because they couldn't understand it until they heard Charlie Parker play 'Cool Blues'. Then, for some at any rate, the penny dropped. Instead New Orleans jazz was held up as an 'exemplary art form'. Louis Armstrong notwithstanding, its collective ensemble playing appealed to communal sensibilities over the cult of the individual improvising bebop genius like Parker.

The political pretensions imposed on the music possibly bypassed Alexis at this time, although the anti-capitalist stance of the fans reflected perfectly his antipathy towards his own family and their way of life.

The traditionalists were sentimentalists, wedded to a pastoral view; New Orleans jazz was the outcropping of good honest working-class expression. In *Bomb Culture* Jeff Nuttall pegged them as those for whom 'naivety was equated with honesty, ineptitude was equated with sincerity and merit was gauged in terms of proximity to the animal and the vegetable'. For the revivalists, New Orleans jazz had a purity and an earthiness which was incorruptible. Thus it followed that the clubs established in London to give a platform to the music and the amateur musicians who played there would (in the early days at any rate) be genuinely untainted by commercial considerations.

The first of the traditional bands to make an impact was George Webb's Dixielanders. First formed in 1943, the band brought people crowding in from all over the country to see them play every Monday night at the Red Barn in Bexleyheath, Kent. The band went through a number of changes until in 1947 they signed up a young trumpet player, a newly discharged Army captain named Humphrey Lyttelton. According to Jim Godbolt's *History of British Jazz*, so great was Lyttelton's impact that when he left to form his own band about six months later, the Dixielanders virtually folded. As a former Old Etonian and member of the Brigade of Guards, Lyttelton was attracting the attention of a media somewhat aghast that such an aristocratic figure should be championing 'primitive' black music. Still a semi-professional with a place at Camberwell School of Art, he quickly established his band as the foremost of its type.

Webb himself joined the band in 1948, and in November 1949 they played with Sidney Bechet almost under cover of darkness to escape the Musicians' Union's ludicrous ban on foreign musicians where there was no exchange with British musicians ('All right, guv, we'll take Count Basie if you have Sid Spoons and his Hot Six') and recorded their first record for Parlophone, selling 4000 copies in the first month. The band had a regular spot at the 100 Club in Oxford Street, originally the Swing Club run by Joseph Feldman, who had the premises until 1954, when Lyttelton himself took over. The dustbins outside the club often played host to a swarthy, nattily dressed young man called Korner urgently trying to learn guitar.

The example of Webb and Lyttelton was taken up by amateur bands from all over the country and it was one such band, organized by a trainee actuary called Chris Barber, that Alexis joined in 1949, replacing a young Glaswegian banjo player called Tony Donegan, who had just been called up for National Service.

Chris Barber was born in Welwyn Garden City in Hertfordshire on 17 April 1930. He was at King Alfred School (where his mother was headmistress) at the same time as Alexis, although they never met. Chris was also at St Paul's, but again their paths failed to cross. After leaving school he became a trainee actuary at the Clerical and Medical insurance company, but failed the exams twice. Chris was already an aspiring jazz trombonist, and his employers suggested that as they had wanted a clerk and not a student, he had better take his trombone and go elsewhere. Chris's father was a statistician, but had also been first violinist for the Christ's Hospital School Orchestra in Sussex. He might have been expected to take a dim view of his son's musical taste, but instead supported his musical ambitions and agreed that if Chris could secure a place at music school, he would pay the fees. London's Guildhall School of Music made the all-important offer.

The postwar London and Home Counties jazz scene was so small that all the fans and musicians knew each other, so it wasn't long before Chris and Alexis met up. While the world of the actuary was still at his feet, Chris formed his first amateur band with Alexis. Inevitably, the inspiration for the music was King Oliver; as another band member, pianist Dave Stevens, recalled, Oliver was God. 'If anyone deviated from the Oliver version we had to stop and start again.' But Chris was also a blues fan and so, as he said, 'we had a guitar player'; and that was Alexis, playing a semi-acoustic Hofner.

Down the years, despite being frequently asked, Chris never had any recollection of what Alexis actually sounded like in the band. Apparently it wasn't until 1983 that he approached Alexis during a Dr John concert at the Half Moon pub in Putney to tell him that he'd only just realized that back in 1949 Alexis didn't have an amplifier – so Chris wasn't able to hear him. Retelling the story to Bob Harris in 1983 for a Radio Oxford interview, Alexis went on: 'Nobody could ever hear me in the band, but they all convinced themselves they could feel me. We used to do a half-hour set of R&B – "race blues" it was called then – a piano [Dave Stevens], guitar [Alexis], bass [Chris], drums [Brian Laws] set-up – like the Tampa Red and Bill Broonzy Chicago sessions on Bluebird in the late thirties and early forties. I was given the mike and I used to do single string and people would say, "What's that funny stuff you played in the middle?" '

Chris Barber's first blues record was bought in 1945, 'either Sleepy John Estes or Cow Cow Davenport. I think I got my first Robert Johnson in 1947 which I got in Dobell's shop for seven shillings and sixpence.' By then Alexis was also hooked on country blues. 'Alexis and I used to vie with each other for who got to the Robert Johnson 78s first. He used to buy up every Charlie Patton record he could find.'

One night Alexis was playing an upstairs jazz club called the Galleon in Newport Court, near Leicester Square. Another blues fan was in the audience who sat not so much in awe of his playing, but of his whole appearance and demeanour and, especially among all the pale, spotty oiks trying to play jazz, his sophisticated, exotic good looks. Her name was Roberta Melville. 'A couple of nights later I went to the Greek Cafe in St Giles Circus, where I always used to go. Doug Witton was there from the No 1 Jazz Club in Leicester Square. Alexi came in and Doug introduced me. I never looked at anybody else ever again.' (She always called him Alexi. Some of his musician colleagues and friends also referred to him as Alex.)

Bobbie Melville was born in the Midlands, the daughter of Robert and Lilian Melville. She had a brother who died when he was still a baby. Robert was employed at a steelworks office in Birmingham, but his real love was art, and he eventually wrote at night as an art critic for the *New Statesman*. In 1947 the family moved to London, to the flat which remains Bobbie's London home. An early champion of the British Surrealist movement, Robert worked at Edouard Messens' London Gallery (where he met George Melly, a Messens protégé) and eventually became a partner in the Arthur Jeffries Gallery, where Bobbie later trained as a picture restorer.

The family's politics were on the left and as a child Bobbie was sent to the Beacon Hill school run by Dora Russell and much derided by George Lyward. Bobbie's experience of experimental education was nothing like as positive as Alexis', and she hated it. During the war, as the bombs rained down, she was given the chance to be evacuated to America. Unfortunately, her parents failed to mention the intended destination, simply asking her in the middle of the night if she wanted to go away. She said no, so they sent her instead to St John's Convent School at Alton Towers, Northamptonshire. 'I just could not put up with it; I was so distraught.'

Robert Melville was a music fan who brought Bobbie up on a diet of Bix Beiderbecke and Louis Armstrong. She had one go at emulating Alexis by attempting to steal a Big Joe Williams record. She got caught and never tried again.

Many fans of traditional jazz were, like Bobbie, into classic and big-band city blues, but gradually they began to be aware of country blues as well. 'There was a suggestion that we at the No 1 Jazz Club would lobby Parlophone to reissue blues records and one of the first suggestions was "Black Snake Moan" by Blind Lemon Jefferson. That was the first time I'd come across country blues – before that I'd only known Joe Turner.'

She began collecting blues 78s. 'Early blues or "race" records were thin, ex-juke box records which came as packing around V-discs, big twelve-inch discs of swing music sent to the American Army in Europe.'

Bobbie was also into the dance side of traditional jazz, much frowned upon in some quarters, where the general idea of a good night out down the 'rhythm club' was to sit nodding to records while a worthy sage imparted pearls of wisdom with the correct degree of earnestness. It took the Aussies to shake this up when Graeme Bell's Australian Jazz Band instigated a jazz dance policy at their Leicester Square Jazz Club Monday-night residency – an innovation eagerly embraced by Lyttelton. Many of the venues Bobbie patronized were located above shops and restaurants. As Lyttelton put it in *I Play As I Please*: 'Some of the old guard from the peaceful beer-drinking, pipe-smoking Hot Club of London days turned up as well, determined to make the worst of a bad job and hoping perhaps for the day when the floor would give in, plummeting the dancers into the restaurant below and leaving them perched round the walls to enjoy their jazz in peace.'

Contemptuous of both sets of fans and the musicians they came to see were the modernists, the lovers of bebop, or 'rebop' as it was also known then. For these fans, the largely amateur trad players were 'the blow and hope boys'. Bobbie and her friends held the beboppers in some awe. 'We were quite bumpkin-like compared to them – they were utterly cool and a bit dangerous.'

The audience for bebop was tightly located in London's West End, the territory of 'wide boys', cool and aloof, seekers after the secret and deliberately difficult black jazz of Bird, covetous of hipster chic and the culture of the zoot suit. Many were Jewish lads whose families knew all about discrimination, ghettos and restricted opportunities.

They played or hung around the first club for 'modernists' – Club Eleven. Starting life as Mac's Rehearsal Rooms, a grubby basement at the corner of Windmill Street and Archer Street (where the dance-band musicians gathered looking for work), Club Eleven opened in December 1948. The house musicians were the likes of Lennie Bush, Ronnie Scott and Tony Crombie, some of whom had sampled bebop at the famous

New York clubs like Minton's on 52nd Street. Charlie Parker was their folk hero, whose life and death (in 1955) would assume almost supernatural significance and whose voracious appetites made him every bit as much the Devil's Son as the deepest Delta bluesman.

The would-be beboppers also latched on to their heroes' penchant for chemical entertainment; the club was raided in April 1950 after, in the words of arresting officer Detective Sergeant George Lyle, 'complaints began to be received that Indian hemp was being sold in certain dance clubs in the West End'. Cocaine, morphine and cannabis were recovered, fines dished out and the club closed down.

These working-class roughnecks embraced contemporary popular culture. They weren't interested in looking back, so much as looking black. They hankered after the twilight margins of modern urban life, scorning straight white society in the headlong rush towards 'blackness'.

Alexis, despite being seen as part of the traditional scene, was equally sympathetic to the new music. His wide-open ears led him to find common cause with both musical forms and yet placed him at odds with both camps. 'It was "impossible" for me to like traditional jazz and Charlie Parker and Dizzy Gillespie – it just wasn't allowed.'

He also enjoyed linking himself with the aura of delinquency and sartorial elegance that accompanied the music; Alexis was never part of the beard and sloppy jumper set. Bobbie also encouraged the change away from smart but boring. 'We went to Alexander's and got him his bird's-eye drape [so called because of the small dotted pattern in the cloth] and he had his hair cut in a DA in no time flat.'

Harold Pendleton, who was to open the original Marquee Club with Chris Barber, remembers Bobbie at that time as 'a very early feminist, a tough lady with a male name, outspoken, stared you straight in the face. There was nothing demure about Bobbie.' And then Alexis came on to the scene. 'I met her "dago" boyfriend – that was my first impression of him; strange, wild, smoking black cigarettes, grew his hair shaggy for those days. Demonstrably a foreigner and weird. He looked like a Balkan terrorist.'

Trixie Stevens, wife of pianist Dave Stevens, knew Alexis before she met Bobbie. 'My first impression was that he was weird – he didn't fit into any category and had this strange family background. We were all slightly puzzled as to who or what he was.'

Alexis and Bobbie were married at Kensington Register Office on 27

March 1951 and went to Paris for their honeymoon. Bobbie says that her mother, Lilian, 'was a bit worried about me marrying a musician, but she came to love him after she calmed down'. 'Musician' was how Alexis presented himself, even though he was still working in Themi's office and only playing for pennies anywhere he could. Over time, Alexis and Robert in particular grew very close; they shared a love of music, modern art, fine books and both were *bons viveurs* appreciative of good food and wine. Lilian Melville could be fierce and domineering, but Alexis had found a family where he could feel at home. His other new-found family was the community of musicians.

He parted company with Chris Barber and joined a small group with Leeds-born trumpet player Dicky Hawdon, whose brilliant career started in the Yorkshire Jazz Band. In the early days, the band would come to London at weekends and play at the 100 Club and Cooks Ferry Inn. 'I was at college and the other guys were doing something else,' says Dicky. 'There was nothing professional about it at all. I met Alexis because he was a friend of Dave and Trixie Stevens. When Barbara and I moved to London in 1950 we became very friendly with Bobbie and Alexis. We were all thick as thieves, Alexis was lovely. His French was immaculate, it used to impress us no end. As a guitarist he was better than the average banjo player in a Dixieland band in those days.'

Alexis and Dicky decided to try to cut a demo disc. Dicky explains: 'We went into a studio in Denmark Street. We wanted to get a broadcast on Jazz Club. We did an audition and didn't get one, which pissed us off no end, probably because we didn't have a drummer.' That disc, of which there is probably only one in existence, was Alexis' earliest recording with Dicky Hawdon on trumpet, pianist Dave Stevens, Colin Thompson on clarinet and soprano and Denny Coffey on bass, playing 'Sportin' Life', previously recorded by, among many others, Sonny Terry and Brownie McGhee, and 'Monday Date'.

'We had a nice band,' says Dicky, 'we were lovely mates and we had a ball. But I really wanted to do it for a living, I was absolutely hell-bent on being a professional musician, whereas I never felt Alexis did. I thought he was a bit of a dilettante. As a band we never got any serious work, apart from Sundays, so in despair I joined Chris Barber.'

No slave to traditionalism, Dicky went on to play with Don Rendell, Tubby Hayes, John Dankworth and Terry Lightfoot, as well as leading his own bands. Switching to an academic career, Dicky Hawdon eventually became a professor at Leeds College of Music.

It is probably fair to say that in 1951 Alexis did not harbour a burning ambition to become a professional musician, although he was certainly rapidly tiring of life in the City. Bobbie relates that his shipping career came to an end ostensibly over a jacket. It was one of those signal moments when a trivial annoyance suddenly throws into sharp relief a myriad of deeper frustrations and unhappiness. 'He finally left there when they wouldn't let him wear his corduroy jacket on a Saturday morning. That was absolutely the last straw. He'd put up with everything else, but the jacket was it.'

When Bobbie first knew Alexis and heard of his complete antipathy towards his family, she rather dismissed its vehemence as typical of many family relationships. But the more she got to know the family the more she realized that they were desperately trying to 'hang on to' Alexis and steer him towards the life they thought he should live. With Bobbie, he was going to jazz clubs, being a musician, wearing 'wild' clothes and, worst of all, not working in the family business.

'I was really bad news for the family,' says Bobbie. 'I remember Alexi's Aunt Cali [Themi's sister] shrieking in a heavy Greek accent, "Blood is thicker than water!!" Alexi tried to break with the family completely. But I mistakenly thought, oh no, we don't want to do that. So we tried to get on with them, but we just had nothing in common. The Aperguis family in Greece were communists. During the time of the Colonels second time round, the Aperguis came to England and wanted to see Alexi because they'd been told that Alexi and his wife were communists. In fact, it was simply the worst description that the family could think of to describe us – and these poor disappointed Greeks took it literally.'

Having started off married life in a bed and breakfast in Leinster Square, Bayswater, they now had their own Regency flat in nearby Norfolk Crescent. They needed to find the rent. For Alexis, having left Themi's firm and virtually cut family ties altogether, the question was: Now what? The need for a swift answer was made all the more acute by the arrival of their daughter Sappho in July 1952.

Alexis flitted from one job to another trying to make ends meet. 'I remember once,' recalls Bobbie, 'he went for a job at a feather-hat company – it was one of the few jobs he actually turned down – usually, they turned him down. And the man actually ran down the street after Alexi shouting, "Mr Korner, you have missed the bus." '

Alexis' first job in the music business came in 1953, when he worked briefly for Emile Shalit, who founded the record label Melodisc. Shalit was one of the more shady operatives in a business which has cornered the market in sharks – a species to which Alexis seemed repeatedly drawn down the years.

Shalit, who died in 1983, registered Melodisc as a company in 1950. He had connections with Savoy Records in the USA and possibly Vogue in France as well. The company's first recordings in Britain were the Bechet–Lyttelton sessions. Shalit also leased records from other companies, often distributing material to which he had no rights, especially in the field of fifties and sixties Jamaican music. He was dealing in markets that hardly anybody else touched, so that most of his sleights of hand went unnoticed, although, according to John Cowley, a leading expert on calypso, Max Jones of *Melody Maker* always regarded Shalit as 'the biggest crook of them all'.

But in 1953 it was Shalit who claimed to be the aggrieved party when he sued his Melodisc partner, John Chilkes, over claims that Chilkes had tried illegally to obtain an equal share of the company while Shalit was out of the country. Shalit won the case, but the judge was totally unimpressed with him as a witness and granted him only a small proportion of the costs. In the period immediately after the case, Alexis' name appears on Melodisc documentation as the company secretary, although the association appears to have been relatively short-lived.

Tagged as 'lovable rogue' rather than 'crook' was another employer of Alexis, Sinclair Traill, the long-time editor of *Jazz Journal*. A friend of Gerald Lascelles, 'Mr Swing' from Alexis' British Forces Network days, Traill was described by George Melly in *Owning Up* as having 'protruding blue eyes, Air Force moustache, casual throwaway manner and a legendary reluctance to stand his round'. He was somewhat seedy, but with a charm which got him through life's obstacles. Before he died of a heart attack in 1981, Traill's life was littered with tales of his double dealings, but he was usually spoken of with great affection, although Bobbie, with a child to look after, didn't necessarily buy into the legend – especially when it came to the housekeeping. 'Alexi had to keep getting subs on his salary, which he thought was £3 a week. When it came to pay day, it turned out to be £3 a month because it was only part-time.'

Nor was she enamoured of Traill's 'generosity' in lieu of hard cash. 'Sinclair thought it all right because he got free cinema tickets and took Alexi to cinema shows in the afternoon. It used to infuriate me because Alexi would go off to the pictures and I couldn't go. I remember leaping up and down on the balcony and shouting, "Well, if you must go with your fish-faced friend . . ." He once made a great play of the fact that he'd invited Princess Margaret to his wedding. Of course, it didn't register that anybody can invite Princess Margaret to their wedding – it doesn't mean to say she is going to come.'

Alexis dipped in and out of the music scene, coming round to the view that playing unamplified and consequently unheard guitar in a trad-jazz band really wasn't for him and becoming increasingly disillusioned with the in-fighting between the traditional and modernist camps which so infected London's tiny jazz scene. Alexis never took the staunch purist view; although he became close to a musician for whom the word 'purist' might have been invented.

Ken Colyer, born on 18 April 1928, was just a day older than Alexis. In contrast to the likes of Alexis, Humphrey Lyttelton and Chris Barber, Colyer was solid working-class. He played trumpet alongside his brother Bill on washboard, and together they founded the Crane River Jazz Band in 1949. Named after a muddy trickle that ran into the Grand Union Canal west of London, it was one of the first British bands to embrace the spirit of Bunk Johnson's New Orleans traditional jazz, as distinct from that form of British traditional jazz which was reviving the genre (Lyttelton and others) rather than attempting to recreate one aspect of it. Taking all opportunities to emphasize their own humble background, the Colyers bound themselves both politically and spiritually to New Orleans jazz, preaching at length on its historical and social roots enmeshed in the saga of the black American diaspora.

Like Alexis, Ken and Bill were smitten by the thought of a life at sea – except they did something about it. Ken had tried to join the Merchant Navy at fourteen, and was, not surprisingly, turned down. However, after a succession of labouring jobs he joined a ship in Glasgow in 1945 and stayed at sea, learning trumpet, until 1948, when he returned to a life of manual labour in Cranford, Middlesex. It was after forming the Crane River Jazz Band the following year that he met up with Alexis on the circuit and they became friends.

Ken and Bill would often go round to Norfolk Crescent to play and talk. Bill swished brushes across a suitcase to keep the noise down, Alexis and Ken played acoustic guitars and they were often joined by a mysterious American who used to hang around, never seeming to do any work. He turned out to be a major American painter, Ralston Crawford, whose nephew, Danny Adler, would be in Rocket 88, a band Alexis guested with in the late seventies.

The song Alexis and his friends most often jammed on was 'Midnight Special'. This was attributed to Leadbelly, who integrated traditional material into the song, which he had written while an inmate at the Central State Farm prison, known as Sugarland, near Houston, Texas. The 'Midnight Special' was a Southern Pacific train that ran from Houston to the west via San Antonio. For Alexis, learning this song and its antecedents was the start of a lifelong interest in the history of train songs in American folk music.

The style in which Alexis and the Colyers sang the song became known as 'skiffle', although it is unclear if that was the name used by Ken Colyer when their talk came round to this popular black 'rent-party music' of the twenties and thirties.

Skiffle, spasm or hokum-style music was essentially a jazz-band rhythm section with the voice carrying the melody instead of the brass frontline. The instrumentation suggests its exponents were poor people who couldn't afford proper instruments. One of the earliest spasm bands came from New Orleans; it was part of Doc Malney's Minstrel Show and was led by a musician known as 'Stale Bread', who played zither, with 'Cajun' on harp, 'Slew Foot Pete' on cigar box guitar, a bass player using half a barrel and 'Warm Gravy' on a cheese-box banjo. In 1896 these immensely popular musicians were New Orleans's answer to Oasis.

This kind of rough-and-ready music and its Heath Robinson instruments probably travelled with the Southern black migrants who moved up North in droves or may have simply developed independently in the black ghettos of New York and Chicago. In any event, rent-party music played on jugs, bottles, washboards, paper and comb, kazoos and packing-crate basses could be heard all over the cities of the northern USA as poor people desperately tried to keep their heads above water. The name skiffle probably denoted no more rigid a musical form than the expression 'jam session', which is basically what happened – jams around blues, gospel, old work songs, ballads and snatches of British folk. One thing is for sure: nobody argued over what to call it – they just did it.

The name 'skiffle' appears on an obscure Paramount sampler of 1929, but it seems that nobody bothered to record it seriously until about 1948, when a Harlem newspaper editor called Dan Burley made some piano recordings of the songs he had heard at rent parties in his younger days. Called the Dan Burley Skiffle Boys, the group featured Brownie

McGhee on guitar and Pops Foster on bass, who had played with King Oliver, Kid Ory and Sidney Bechet. Skiffle was possibly first heard in England as early as 1947 with the Original London Blue Blowers. The Colyers picked up on the music shortly after and featured skiffle within the Crane River Jazz Band.

Ken wanted to form a proper band. But first he had a divine mission to perform. He had to go to New Orleans to revel in the well-spring of all his inspiration, to walk its streets, soak up its sounds. He rejoined the Merchant Navy and it took him a year and a journey halfway round the world before he finally docked in the city of his dreams during October 1952.

He broke every social code in the book by playing live and recording with black musicians until the authorities finally found a way to get rid of him when he overstayed his visitor's permit. He was deported in the spring of 1953 after spending a month in jail.

Meanwhile Chris Barber had turned professional and formed a co-operative band including future Korner sideman Jim Bray on bass and drummer Ron Bowden, plus Lonnie Donegan (Tony Donegan had renamed himself after supporting guitarist Lonnie Johnson in London in 1950) and Monty Sunshine. On his return to England, Colyer joined the band. But he was too dominant a personality to fit in with the idea of co-operative working and when he tried to sack Donegan and Ron Bowden in May 1954, everybody else 'left' (or he was sacked – depending on who is telling the story) and Colyer found himself out on a limb.

While Ken Colyer was still in the band they decided to introduce skiffle into the set. Alexis was part of this line-up, with Chris on bass, Bill Colyer on washboard and Lonnie Donegan, although Donegan maintains he never played on stage with Alexis. As well as guitar and mandolin, Alexis very briefly took up harmonica, 'for a couple of weeks . . . as I was one of the first and one of the worst harmonica players in the country. We dropped that one very quickly.' Alexis claimed he soon dropped the Chris Barber version of skiffle altogether because he couldn't stand Lonnie Donegan shifting the music towards 'country weepies' as he called them, in the style of the Carter Family.

Just two months after Colyer had gone, Chris went into the studio with Lonnie, Ron, himself on bass and Beryl Bryden guesting on washboard, to record a number of songs as the Lonnie Donegan Skiffle Group. One song, 'Rock Island Line', by Leadbelly was released as a single in 1956 and became an incredible success on both sides of the Atlantic. The skiffle craze was born.

In June 1954 Colyer formed his own band and included Alexis in the 'skiffle section' of the band's stage repertoire. The Ken Colyer Skiffle Group recorded seven tracks for Decca over the next twelve months, with Alexis on either guitar or mandolin. But in the same way that Alexis began to feel alienated within trad jazz because of its antipathy to bebop, so he similarly drifted away from skiffle, partly because it was becoming a pop phenomenon, but more crucially because he wanted to be a solo country-blues player. He had one small problem to overcome first: it was about time he learnt to play the guitar properly. 'I was getting away with murder for years playing an open tuning of my own that nobody could quite work out. It was OK for jazz tunes because it was an open B-flat tuning and fine for E-flat and things like that. But when it came to country blues, it was absolutely useless. To be a country-blues player I knew I had to retune and I didn't want to do that.'

He hadn't reckoned with Bobbie, who had a deep love for country blues and wanted her husband to get to grips with it. 'She went out and bought a guitar and said, "You're not retuning this one, you'd better learn how to play it now." But I couldn't work my thumb independently from my fingers.' So Bobbie actually worked Alexis' thumb, while he concentrated on the rest until he had enough control for her to let go.

Having turned his back on what meagre income was to be derived in 1955 from playing skiffle, and with his serendipitous part-time work earning just as little and a wife and child to support, Alexis had to face harsh reality. On 31 May 1955 he joined the BBC as a trainee studio manager. A regular job.

5

BLACK, BROWN AND WHITE

A lexis joined the BBC's Training Reserve department. This was the beginning of commercial television and the BBC was losing staff in droves. Lord Reith, the architect of the organization's paternalism, had given up the directorship in 1938, but his spirit lived on. In its own heavily patronizing, bureaucratic way, the BBC was not a bad employer: as with the Civil Service, once you were in you could expect a job for life. So it was a major shock for the higher-ups when staff actually deserted Auntie Beeb for the nasty world of commercialism and they found themselves needing a hefty recruitment drive to fill the gaps.

They advertised for studio managers largely among students and the press, looking for those with some experience in theatre, music and allied arts who might have the potential to become producers. This was a new breed of studio manager; until then the jobs had been filled by technicians rather than the arty crowd who were now pushing at the gates.

The BBC had three main buildings, all in London. Broadcasting House, in Portland Place, was the home of domestic radio. Two others housed the General Overseas Service (later renamed the World Service): Bush House, in the Aldwych, for European and Latin-American broadcasts and 200 Oxford Street for the Middle East, Asia and Africa. Trainees spent six weeks at each site before choosing the area they wished to work in.

New entrants were divided up into small groups to train together. There were ten new entrants for Alexis' intake, divided into one group of four and another group of six: Alexis and five women.

The studio manager's job was to ensure that the programme was switched into the right network, make sure all the broadcasters were there, do the wavelength announcement, play the signature tune, balance the microphones and play the discs. One of the trainees who joined at the same time as Alexis was Chris Bell, who recalls that these discs were the width of car wheels.

'There were no tape inserts for music, interviews and so on; all the inserts were on 16rpm discs with about four minutes on each side. You had a bank of "grams" or turntables – huge, square machines standing at waist height – and you had to line up the appropriate recording, stop the mechanism and start up again when required. If you were doing a half-hour documentary, you might have seventeen or eighteen little inserts – that meant a lot of editing and you had to learn to edit on disc. Sometimes you had to do "jump cuts" [more than one insert on the same disc], so you marked up the bits you wanted in yellow pencil so you could see them visually. You might have to jump from the end of one sentence to a yellow mark a bit further on and come in on exactly the right word.'

Anybody who has 'bunny-hopped' across a record trying to hit the right track, let alone the right note, can appreciate what a skill this was – especially if you were on the night shift, it was two o'clock in the morning and you were in charge of a programme in Urdu. You wouldn't have had the foggiest idea if you'd hit the right spot unless you got an anguished look from the Indian broadcaster on the other side of the glass.

What did it take to be a good studio manager? Chris Bell says: 'You needed to be relaxed and patient – the work was high pressure because much of it was live, you had to be alert the whole time, quick reacting, make sure the programme started and finished on a particular second.'

You also had to be something of a diplomat, as another of Alexis' colleagues, Madalena Fagandini, explains: 'You had to know who hated who, like the Hungarians, Bulgarians and Romanians, and keep one lot out until the other lot had left the studio.'

Alexis thrived in this environment; by all accounts he was very good at the technical side of the job and got on well with all his colleagues. He was much more at home away from the stiff regime imposed on employees at Broadcasting House. At the other establishments staff were working for a part of the BBC that most of the population knew nothing about and the 'unEnglish' ambience helped undermine BBC formalities.

Based at Bush House and 200 Oxford Street were many interesting, high-flying refugee intellectuals from various repressive regimes. Alexis related well to their sense of displacement and his polished intellect and command of languages made him well respected in such circles. Words like 'charming', 'congenial' and 'very sociable' occur repeatedly in the memories of those he trained with and under. Another is 'unconventional'.

Despite working in the more *laissez-faire* outposts of the BBC, Alexis still looked 'exotic and unusual', as Chris Bell puts it, in the company of his Oxbridge-type colleagues. Their dress sense was by and large conventional for the BBC of the 1950s, whereas Alexis in his fancy shirts and leather trousers was hauled before a Head Office preacher on more than one occasion. His response, according to one friend, Pete King, was: 'Unless they pay me more, I can't afford different clothes.' He could afford, however, to indulge his penchant for classic cars and was the proud owner of first a Clyno and then a Delage, much envied by his friends. Alexis was never eccentric or outlandish in his behaviour – he just let his foreign good looks, his clothes, his long hair and the cigarettes rolled in liquorice paper (sometimes with that little something extra added) make all the necessary style statements. And then there was the music.

His associates were somewhat in awe of his knowledge, taste and skill. Viv Perry was one of the older studio managers, a highly skilled technician in his own right who taught Alexis and his fellow trainees what being a studio manager was all about. 'On night duty when we had the odd half-hour between programmes, we would adjourn to Studio 3 or 4, which had pianos. Alex would start playing jazz like I never heard before. At other times he would try and teach me guitar, which was pretty hopeless. Just occasionally if I started to play Bach or Schubert on the piano while he lit up a joint, he'd join in and he could play classics when he felt that way inclined. I have even heard him play flamenco like a veteran. I could have listened to him all night.'

Most of his friends knew of his interest in music, but he didn't exactly flaunt the depth of his knowledge or involvement. In 1956 Chris Bell was asked to produce a review for the BBC's amateur dramatic group, who were trying to raise money for Hungarian refugees displaced by the Soviet invasion. 'I asked Alexis if he would come along and play, sing or whatever it was he did. He agreed. I'd written this protest song about blacks in the southern states and we had a crooner who liked the song and said he'd sing it. I tried to get Alexis along to rehearse it, but he wouldn't say that he hated it or that it was awful – he just kept putting it off. Two days before the first performance, he rang up in a very muffled voice saying that the doctor had confined him to bed and there was no way he could play and how bad he felt about it and so on. It was only years later that I realized Alexis' music was the blues and I thought how tactful he'd been to get himself out of accompanying that song.'

Nineteen fifty-six was also the year of Suez, and Alexis almost caused a diplomatic incident. Being buried underground at 200 Oxford Street on the night shift was reminiscent of a John le Carré novel – broadcasts by foreign emigrés, many in exile, emanating from dimly lit studios in a Babel of foreign languages and travelling on the night airwaves to faraway places. The young studio managers took on a lot of responsibility, because at night there were few people to refer to if there were problems. Night-shift workers often came to informal arrangements about taking turns to sleep in the windowless basement conference room.

At four a.m. every morning the BBC General Overseas Service began the daily broadcasts to the Arab world with a set piece from the Koran, played on those huge discs. One night Chris Bell and Alexis were on duty together. 'Alexis had very bad toothache and he'd taken some sleeping pills or something and gone down to the basement room for some sleep. It was his job that night to play the Koran at four a.m. and he took the discs with him. With only three people on and so much to do, nobody was checking up on anybody else. Four a.m. comes: no Alexis, no Koran. He was fast asleep in the basement, door locked, discs under the camp bed. Anybody listening to the BBC during this very sensitive time with a war going on between Britain and Egypt would have immediately thought that no Koran signalled a new development in British foreign policy. Alexis got into a lot of trouble over that, but because of his great charm he somehow wormed his way out of it.'

Although politics could not interfere with the way the BBC worked, there was great tension at 200 Oxford Street because many Arabs worked there. Meanwhile the Hebrew Service and the BBC were trying to explain to the rest of the world why Britain seemed to be siding with France and Israel against Egypt.

Out of hours Chris and Alexis would go on demonstrations against the Suez campaign – a good opportunity for the 'naughty boy' in Alexis to go walkabout. 'One day in the studio managers' common room,

Alexis very quietly produced these blue stickers which said, "Chelsea and Westminster Young Conservatives Say Fight Against the Suez War". He said he'd had these printed up as a form of black propaganda and he wanted me to come round with him after work and stick these up all over the place. So they went up on bus stops, in tube stations, everywhere.'

But their protest was not simply a product of youth, as Chris explains. 'You couldn't be in the World Service without a reasonable understanding of world events and an interest in current affairs.' And working with so many different nationalities, not all of them well disposed to Britain, allowed Alexis and his colleagues to hear the other side and take a world view beyond what the BBC itself and the print media chose to serve up as objective reporting.

Yet despite his interest in what was going on around him politically and (apart from the odd lapse) his professional approach to the work, it was clear to his friends that this was just a stopping-off point for Alexis. Broadcaster Gordon Snell, another contemporary of Alexis, observes: 'You never thought he'd want to go up the BBC ladder. He was sort of perched there, almost doing the BBC a favour. He was terribly urbane and quite detached from the work – he did it efficiently and courteously, but it was obvious he wasn't going to be there very long. Even within our group which was pretty restless, keen to move up in the BBC, he was a maverick, you felt he was just drifting in as a way to earn money.'

And that was a pretty accurate assessment of the situation. The outside pull was always music. According to one friend: 'There were times when he had a gig and he had to change his hours and it began to happen rather a lot.' Not least when Alexis met a gruff, no-nonsense character from west London called Cyril Davies.

During 1956 Cyril Davies had been running the London Skiffle Club upstairs at the Roundhouse pub in Wardour Street, Soho. Although 'Rock Island Line' had been a major chart success early that year, the craze hadn't taken off enough for there to be much distinction between skiffle, blues and folk. There certainly weren't discrete audiences for the different genres and the very few people like Alexis who wanted to promote black American music were trying to sing and play like Leadbelly. In that respect Cyril Davies was something special. Born in 1932, he was of Welsh origin but had been brought up in Denham, Buckinghamshire. He met his wife, Marie, in Uxbridge and they were married in 1953. By trade Cyril was a panel-beater; he had his own yard in South Harrow guarded by one of the hounds from hell. Cyril had a fearsome reputation for his hair-trigger temper and there were few, even in his cut-throat business, who would tangle with him.

But towards the ladies he exuded charm and the kind of old-world chivalry which went in hand in hand with honest villainy. In fact, Cyril would erupt if anybody used bad language in front of a woman; it was something he could not abide. One day he was standing in a queue for fish and chips carrying a brand-new twelve-string guitar hand made by the guitar makers Grimshaw. Ahead of him, some louts were making a nuisance of themselves and swearing loudly. There were women waiting to be served. Cyril remonstrated with them to stop and when they wouldn't, he just brained one with his new guitar, sending splinters of wood all over the pavement.

Cyril's musical career started in a trad band, playing banjo in Steve Lane's Southern Stompers, but his forte was twelve-string guitar, although he is actually best remembered for his harmonica playing. What he really wanted to do was play country blues. He was absolutely fixated with Leadbelly and, although the sparse and poorly recorded surviving records really don't do him justice, his rendition of Leadbelly songs was spine-chilling. This talent, taken together with his solid working-class background, tough exterior and underworld acquaintances, makes him probably the most authentic bluesman Britain has ever produced. This is certainly the view of blues writer Paul Oliver: 'without exception, the only white singer I ever met who seemed to me to be an absolute blues singer in personality was Cyril Davies. His background, his compulsive personality was just like those black singers I subsequently met.'

Socially and temperamentally, Alexis and Cyril had nothing in common; Alexis later categorized his relationship with Cyril as 'a great working mismatch'. What they shared was a driving passion to promote black blues. Once skiffle took off, the club had been doing great business, open three of the four Thursdays in every month. 'Then one day, Cyril said to me, "I'm fed up with all this skiffle rubbish, I want to open a blues club, will you run it with me?" I said yes. One week we shut down with a full house – the next we opened the Barrelhouse Blues Club and three people turned up.' Which is a fair indicator of the potential audience for American country blues at that time.

As we have seen, the likes of Chris Barber, Bobbie and Alexis had been picking up on country blues since the late 1940s, buying the few releases available in Britain. But in the earliest days of hunting out elusive records, nobody knew anything about the music, its socio-cultural roots, the musical tradition it came from or anything about the lives of the musicians themselves. The earliest response to the music by individual white listeners here was purely emotional. The blues most familiar to whites was the 'classic blues' of Bessie Smith, Ma Rainey and Louis Armstrong. During the war Paul Oliver heard some black American GIs setting up camp in Suffolk having just entered the conflict. He hid behind a hedge with his friend Stan, who had brought him especially to experience the sound of the blues.

'We stayed behind the hedge, getting cold. I was getting impatient too, when suddenly the air seemed split by the most eerie sounds. The two men were singing, swooping, undulating, unintelligible words; and the back of my neck tingled. "They're singing a blues," Stan hissed at me. It was the strangest, most compelling singing I'd ever heard.'

Ottilie Patterson, one of the very few top-class women blues singers Britain has produced, tells a similar story of being struck to the core. 'The first time I heard Bessie singing "Reckless Blues" I was transfixed. I thought I was melting. It was almost orgasmic. All those sad sounds, all those blues sounds I was looking for . . . I thought Bessie was marvellous, but when I first heard the "race" thing, I thought, this goes further and deeper. It turned out to be Robert Johnson's "Dust My Broom".'

The British music press began to take some interest in the subject just after the war. In 1946 Max Jones wrote an article 'On Blues' for Albert McCarthy's *Yearbook of Jazz* and with Rex Harris started a 'Collector's Corner' column in *Melody Maker*. There were articles and discographical listings for such artists as Blind Lemon Jefferson – whose risqué 'Black Snake Moan' had been championed by Bobbie Korner – Peetie Wheatstraw, Barbecue Bob and Leroy Carr. Contributors to the column included Albert McCarthy and Charles Fox, who was to play such a big part in the life of the Korner family. In December 1951 folklorist Alan Lomax presented *The Art of the Negro* on the BBC Third Programme, and the last programme in the series of three was 'Blues in the Mississippi Night', with recordings by Sleepy John Estes, Robert Johnson, John Lee Hooker and Muddy Waters.

The first black-American solo singer to come to Britain was Josh White, in July 1950. Although he left home as a boy to be 'the eyes' for Blind Lemon Jefferson and Blind Blake, White's style was more grounded in English and Irish folk and gospel, which probably accounted for his wider popularity. He even performed as a New York cabaret artist in the 1940s, but was also deeply committed to singing about the injustices visited upon the black community. According to Val Wilmer, due to anti-communist witch-hunts White was forced to drop the word 'comrade' from a Spanish Civil War song. Playing at the Feldman Club (later the 100 Club) at 100 Oxford Street, he refused to sing 'Free and Equal Blues' and 'Strange Fruit' because whenever he sang them in public he found himself in trouble with the 'Feds' when he returned home. Apparently, while in England he sang these songs at a private party and word still got back to the States.

Singer and broadcaster Wally Whyton, one time leader of the Vipers, a highly successful skiffle group which evolved into the Shadows, saw Josh White at the Shepherd's Bush Empire. 'I was floored; he was a smooth-talking, beautiful black man, white trousers, this great shirt, flashing guitar style. I was absolutely entranced. Out the front there was this showcase with a picture of him. It was open so I pulled the picture off and took it to the stage door. He came out with this beautiful blonde girl and I said, "Would you mind signing this for me?" "Where did you get that? I've only just had these taken."

'Years later I had this series in 1963 at the BBC called *Folk Room*. Josh and his daughter Dorothy were on the show. I told him about the photo and he had a good laugh then he said: "Can you snap your fingers?"

' "Yes."

' "Can you do it in three–four time?"

' "Yes."

' "Right, take this tempo."

' "Yeah, easy."

'He let me do that for about twenty seconds and then carried on into the song. After about three minutes I could feel this muscle beginning to seize up. *And he knew it.*'

Guitarist and singer Lonnie Johnson had come to Britain as early as 1917, with a New Orleans review show. He came again in 1952, by which time his work with Louis Armstrong and Duke Ellington had marked him out as one of the prime architects of jazz guitar. He played the Royal Festival Hall, backed by Tony Donegan and his Jazz Band. From that day on, Tony became Lonnie.

It must have been immensely puzzling for the early blues visitors to Britain. First, they had to come in as 'variety' acts to skirt around the Musicians' Union's ban and secondly, sophisticated musicians like

Lonnie Johnson had to revert to more traditional, even arcane blues forms that were going out of favour in their own country, in order to please white fans. But if, as Humphrey Lyttelton once put it, the blues walked backwards into Britain, it arrived in the hand luggage of the most influential bluesman ever to have whisky for breakfast in an English kitchen: William Lee Conley, better known as Big Bill Broonzy.

Born in 1893 in Mississippi and raised in Arkansas, Broonzy went to Chicago in 1920 and within ten years was one of the most prolific artists on the 'race record' and club and rent-party scene while at the same time keeping a farm going in his home state during the quiet times and working in various city jobs in factories, on the railways and as a hotel janitor. Contemporary photos, which always show him immaculately dressed, bear witness to more disposable income than many of his neighbours and fellow musicians. In 1938, his first choice, Robert Johnson, dead and his second, Blind Boy Fuller, in jail, producer John Hammond came knocking to ask Bill to take part in a Carnegie Hall pageant called 'From Spirituals to Swing'. Broonzy had developed a smooth, crisp, urban style both in New York and also for Chicago's famous Bluebird label. One remarkable song, 'How You Want It Done', recorded in New York in 1932, was shot through with what can only be described as rock 'n' roll riffs. During the 1940s he was to play with almost a jazz line-up, featuring himself on electric guitar. Yet Broonzy was presented to the white audiences at Carnegie Hall as 'a sharecropper from Arkansas, one of the great country blues singers'.

In August 1951 Broonzy was invited to the Hot Club de France by its president, Hugues Panassié. This time he found himself tagged 'The Last of the Mississippi Blues Singers', so he obligingly presented a programme of 'down home blues' for patrons at this bastion of orthodox jazz. British jazz promoter Bert Wilcox saw Broonzy on tour in Germany and brought him to London in September 1951 to play a 'recital of blues, folk songs and ballads' at the Kingsway Hall in front of what *Melody Maker* described as a 'small, but discerning and enthusiastic audience'. The same review praised Wilcox for having the 'courage' to bring Broonzy over. Such were the expectations that one review described the singer's naturally stiff-legged gait as the clear legacy of shifting bales of cotton.

With the help of money from Chris Barber's agent, Broonzy was back in 1954 and again in October 1955 to record thirteen tracks at Pye, whose staff then included a very young Joe Meek, with an 'all-star' jazz group including drummer Phil Seaman, Bruce Turner, Kenny Graham and Benny Green. Allowing for the fact that 'a session is a session', and whether you like the music or not, this particular line-up neatly emphasizes that while the fans made hard-and-fast distinctions between genres, musicians generally did not. All these guys were 'modernists', yet saxophonist Bruce Turner became closely associated with Britain's burgeoning folk scene, while Kenny Graham and Phil Seamen were both early champions of traditional African and Cuban music.

It was during Broonzy's 1955 visit that Alexis eventually met him. 'I got as close to worshipping Bill Broonzy as I've ever worshipped anyone in my somewhat unworshipful life.' A relationship seemed to develop where Alexis was keen to learn, but still with that old kick against being told what to do, even if the advice came from a master bluesman. 'When you worship someone you invest them with all sorts of qualities which you expect them to live up to. And when they don't, sometimes you get very heavy scenes. Also Bill was old enough to be my Dad and he treated me rather like my Dad, only I liked Bill better than I'd ever liked my Dad. And it made more problems, you know.'

But when Broonzy first came, Alexis was full of trepidation about talking to him. 'I was much too shy to go and talk to people then. But Max Jones persuaded me to go and talk to him I thought, I can't talk to Bill Broonzy, I've got his records. How can I ring him and talk to him? I mean he's made gramophone records, he plays the blues, he's an incredible man . . . I was really almost pissing myself when I had to pick up the phone and dial him and say, "Hallo, is that Mr Broonzy? I'm Alexis Korner . . ." My wife was propping me up, it was a terrible scene altogether.'

Alexis then had to prepare himself for 'the visit' of Bill to their house in Molyneux Street, off the Edgware Road. 'Having sweated steadily for some twenty-four hours, and carefully hidden my guitar, I felt prepared to meet Big Bill Broonzy. By eight o'clock in the evening my wife, who had been viewing my mental and physical preparations with amused exasperation, began to show some concern at my rapidly declining state of health. Whilst I had not yet begun to twitch, this development seemed imminent and it was the sound of the doorbell which finally startled me back to the realization that it was necessary for me to maintain some pretence of normal sanity. I trickled down to the hall and opened the front door . . . I am told I introduced myself quite coherently although I wonder if my first words, whatever they might have been, had anything to do with the look of slight suspicion which remained with Bill for the next hour or so. Soon, however, everyone relaxed and by the end of the evening we were all laughing heartily at Bill's jokes.'

A few days later Broonzy moved in with Alexis, Bobbie and Sappho. He used to sing Sappho, now three and a half years old, to sleep, but what amazed Alexis was that, 'he would never, ever go in without practising first. He would sit in his room and he'd practise the two songs he was going to sing her. And what's more, he would practise alternate verses, in case he forgot the right ones. So he was carrying around in his head two sets of verses for "Trouble In Mind" and two sets of verses for "In The Evening When The Sun Goes Down". He had some amazing click where, if he forgot the original sets of verses, he would just automatically click into the other set – and I never knew how he did that.

'We found out things about him like he really preferred cocoa to whisky last thing at night. He didn't always want to fall into bed totally out of his skull. Some nights he liked to sit and talk after a gig and drink some cocoa and then go to bed. It's quite a fact, though, isn't it – all these blues giants, they always lush themselves to death and to find one who actually liked cocoa, it was something else.'

Also 'something else' were the breakfasts that Broonzy consumed which Bobbie cooked for him. 'He had two pork chops and six eggs, tomatoes, fried potatoes, gravy, anything.' Not that all European cuisine was to his liking; faced by 1950s British Rail fare, which demanded 'chips with everything', he said, 'Well then, you'd better bring me whisky and chips', and his response to the French penchant for horse was: 'Where I come from we don't eat horses, we ride 'em.'

Hiding his guitar from Bill Broonzy was evidence of just how self-conscious Alexis was about his playing, how much he wanted to get it right. For Paul Oliver, this showed in Alexis' playing when he first saw him at a folk club called The Good Earth in Gerrard Street. 'Alexis was playing endless choruses of Leadbelly's "Yellow Girl". Later he sang some blues which were good and effective and a bit of a surprise because I hadn't heard any English people play blues up to then.' But Paul says he often felt nervous for Alexis watching him perform. 'He always seemed to me to be tense, biting his lip, clenching his teeth and clawing at the guitar. You wondered what would happen if he broke a string.'

Wally Whyton came to know Alexis very well, first around the club scene in the 1950s and then through their association on the 1960s children's TV programme, *Five O'Clock Club*. 'I spoke to Bill Broonzy once and we were talking about Alexis and he said in his folksy kind of way: "The only thing wrong with Alexis is that he plays all the right notes." Bill had the idea that with the blues there's something about being a dirty player rather than a clean player, that sometimes you put in a discord and I think Bill felt that Alexis had anglicized the music, which to some extent he had.'

For Alexis, any kind of criticism from a black bluesman, especially from one of the few men he ever respected in his life, was going to be hard to take. Wally recalls: 'Years later I told Alexis this and he got really angry – it was the only time I ever saw him angry: "Oh, he'd say anything, silly old sod."'

Cyril Davies's performance style was very different. Cyril was a man with limited horizons, with none of Alexis' background or education, totally absorbed in playing the blues, passionate, hard-driving, but always relaxed, never tense – the composure that comes with natural talent. Paul Oliver imagines that if Cyril broke a string, 'he'd just laugh it off'.

Nineteen fifty-seven was the year of Broonzy's longest visit, when British fans and musicians came to know this tall, urbane blues artist with his deep, sonorous voice, cool style and homespun philosophy. At this distance and with the blues so accessible since the late 1960s, it is difficult to imagine the impact that Broonzy had on those who had scratched around since the mid forties buying up the music of those they never thought they would see on stage. The slightly younger generation of music fans who idolized Ken Colyer and Chris Barber and were forming their own trad bands to play Broonzy songs were equally in awe. In some of the provincial towns where Broonzy toured, they had hardly ever seen a black man, let alone one who played the blues.

Nobody really knew how many of the pre-war blues artists were alive. Broonzy's billing in the press and sleeve-notes to his records written by Alexis suggested he was the last of the line. Although Broonzy had been before, 'Rock Island Line' and the skiffle boom had helped promote a greater interest in the blues although still on a small scale. And now for the embryonic blues audience came the real thing. Like Charlie Parker, Big Bill Broonzy became a role model for the whites who rather desperately wanted to be black. A story circulated on the jazz scene of the man who went into Charing Cross Hospital to see if they had injections to turn his white skin black.

Broonzy offered to take Chris Barber's singer and wife-to-be, Ottilie Patterson, out to lunch. Many white girls during the 1950s would have felt very self-conscious about walking down Oxford Street on the arm of a tall, handsome, elegant black man, 'but not me, I was the proudest wee girl in the world, he was just a dream come true. It was so thrilling. He said, "Do you mind being seen with me?" I could have wept.'

Over lunch with Ottilie at the Great Royal Chinese restaurant, Bill offered his philosophy of the blues. 'He'd just finished his drink and held up the glass he'd been drinking from and said: "That's not just a glass. I could fill that with whisky and make a man drunk. I could fill it with water and save a man's life. Or I could break that glass and kill a man. It's not just a glass. And when you're writing the blues, it's not just an ordinary thing." '

Broonzy was one of the first of the visiting bluesmen to play at Alexis and Cyril's London Blues and Barrelhouse Club at the Roundhouse pub, an elongated upstairs room holding about 125 people, although on some nights there were more people waiting to play than pay. For the early birds, there were seats in front of the stage which had a piano to one side and a large mirror on the wall behind. A guest would open the evening about seven-thirty, then Cyril on twelve-string and Alexis often on mandolin would play as a duo, and as the evening wore on, other musicians would be invited up.

Sitting on the stage after hours, or perhaps at Britain's first folk club, the Ballad and Blues Club above the Princess Louise pub in Holborn, Broonzy would hold master-classes. A dozen bad guitarists would try to play one of his most popular songs, 'Black, Brown and White Blues', without having any idea what was really behind it. The chorus of the song was 'If you're white, you're all right/If you're brown, stick around/But if you're black, get back.' Broonzy knew all about racism and sang a number of songs highlighting its evils. He could spot English racists (including some on the jazz scene, of all places) within a few moments of striking up a conversation and then he would simply ignore them. His worst moment came in Nottingham, when he arrived with Bert Wilcox and the Chris Barber band and the hotel management refused to let him in.

Broonzy told a rather fanciful version of his life story to the Belgian writer Yannick Bruynoghe, and Trixie Stevens recalls some of these cosy reminiscences. 'He was a story-teller *par excellence* – he'd sit and tell you lies for hours on end.' Blues musicians were no different from any other entertainers: quick to put down or somehow undermine their rivals. Bobbie and the others would soak up information such as 'where to send the flowers for Sleepy John Estes' grave, except he wasn't dead. And we were heartbroken when Bill told us about how Bukka White had been killed by prison guards in the penitentiary. Until he came on tour.'

When such tales were being told nobody had much to go on. In the sleeve-notes for a 1957 Broonzy EP on Vogue, Alexis wrote that he was 'the only blues singer of the old school left today', presumably in ignorance not only of the other 'dearly departed' singers on the verge of rediscovery, but also of Broonzy's alter ego as a city slicker. Broonzy was no fool: he knew that once he had come, others would follow, especially those singers who were now regarded, in his words, as 'old fogies' but who could find a new audience in Britain.

In contrast to the half-empty Methodist preaching hall in 1951 (Paul Oliver reckoned about forty people turned up) Bill played to a packed Festival Hall in February 1957. On stage with him was Brother John Sellers, a folk–gospel singer who joined Broonzy's tour from the Continent, where he'd been touring and recording in France and Belgium. Mahalia Jackson had rescued Brother John from a Chicago brothel, where he'd been dumped as a child by his mother. He became Mahalia's surrogate son and sang in her church. Unashamedly camp, Brother John complained bitterly when asked to do a film in France about authentic southern folk and blues. They asked him to wield a hammer while performing work songs. He thought it would be artificial, made of paper or rubber. Instead they produced a twenty-eight-pound sledgehammer. He told *Melody Maker*: 'I had to lift this thing and sing. I'm telling you it was no joke.'

Brother John's British début was marred by a faulty microphone, although he was still warmly applauded. His repertoire included Memphis Slim's 'Every Day I Have The Blues', 'Motherless Child' and 'House Of The Rising Sun'.

Writer Max Jones was less enamoured of Brother John's backing musicians, who included Alexis playing the biggest gig of his life to date: 'one song [by Brother John] was accompanied by Alex Korner playing a borrowed guitar; others by Korner, pianist Dave Stevens and drummer Colin Bowden and the rest by Korner, Stevens and the entire Ken Colyer band. All the backings sounded under-rehearsed and some were dire. Indeed, it is best to draw a veil over that part of the proceedings.'

In fact by the time Alexis and friends had strutted their stuff, Bill only had time to do four songs before 'watch-watching Harold Pendleton of the National Jazz Federation' brought the evening to a rapid conclusion.

Chris Barber was the only professional musician at the time with a deep enough love of the blues and the financial wherewithal to take the trouble to locate American blues musicians and arrange (through his agent) for them to tour England. After Broonzy came Sister Rosetta Tharpe. While Broonzy spared English sensibilities by leaving his electric guitar at home, Rosetta Tharpe made no such concessions.

Despite being a gospel singer with a staunch religious background, Rosetta Tharpe was an entertainer. When Val Wilmer saw her in concert, she was 'wearing a tight green satin dress . . . and auburn or golden coloured wigs, playing a white guitar' described as a 'modified Gibson SG'. This account appears in Val's engaging and richly detailed autobiography *Mama Said There'd Be Days Like This,* published by the Women's Press in 1989, but others have Tharpe playing both a Telecaster and a Strat. When she came in November 1957 she was backed by Chris Barber's band and sang duets with Ottilie Patterson, playing twenty-one concerts to packed houses in London and Birmingham. Her repertoire was a mixture of gospel, blues, jazz and pop songs, but the electric guitar gave much of her set an almost rock 'n' roll feel. This was most obvious on her solo numbers, and of course brought criticism from *Melody Maker,* which complained of long-admired guitar playing 'transformed through a jangle box into a shambles of slurring sound'. And despite being an eventual champion of electric guitar, Alexis himself was not (with some justification) beyond bemoaning the lack of finesse that power can inflict; writing the blues entries for *Jazz on Record 1960,* he observed: 'unhappily some years ago, Sister Rosetta Tharpe went all electric, at least her guitar did. Since then we have had no opportunity to hear her exciting acoustic solo work anymore.'

Rosetta Tharpe never equated religion with abstinence; Chris Barber's drummer, Graham Burbidge, remembers seeing her 'disappearing into a hotel room with this little promoter under her arm. We'd go off to various nightclubs after we'd been playing. She liked to drink, but because she was a gospel singer she couldn't really be seen drinking. She'd order a glass of milk in a little girly voice and, of course, she'd got a bottle of scotch in her handbag. The milk got browner and browner as the evening wore on.'

Because she was a well-known concert artist in the USA, playing to

white as well as black audiences, Tharpe was easy to get to because all
the agents knew her. The same applied to a duo, both singers, one a
blind harp player, the other a guitarist: Saunders 'Sonny Terry' Terrell
and Walter 'Brownie' McGhee. They started out as protégés of Blind
Boy Fuller, Brownie played in the Dan Burley Skiffle Boys and both
were active in the New York political-cum-folk scene of the forties
that circled around Leadbelly. But in the fifties they were Broadway
performers, most notably in the original production of *Cat On A Hot
Tin Roof* by Tennessee Williams. *Melody Maker* announced their six-week
tour supported by Chris Barber starting in Brighton on 25 April 1958.

For the uninitiated, *Melody Maker* published a short article about the
duo by Alexis which appeared on his thirtieth birthday and marked
his début as a journalist. He proclaimed them as masters of their art,
but identified Brownie McGhee as the more sophisticated of the two.
'Brownie's singing and playing are at times reminiscent of [Blind Boy]
Fuller, but the highly individual rhythmic emphases show that Brownie
learned and did not simply copy. His mastery of the guitar permits him
to perform the hard swoops, from top to bottom of the fingerboard and
gives a controlled accent to his outstanding rhythm work.'

Such was the rarity of the genuine article that for most people Big Bill
Broonzy was the blues, but 'this is not what will be heard from Sonny
Terry and Brownie McGhee, for there are many different ways of playing
and singing the blues'. Brownie McGhee was a particular influence on
Alexis' guitar style and when the duo played the Roundhouse club, Alexis
could be seen to one side of the stage, leaning on the wall and watching
thoughtfully as Brownie thundered through his set.

Inevitably, Sonny and Brownie were entertained at Alexis' house.
Little Sappho had inherited from both parents a singular talent for
saying exactly what she thought when she thought it. Once she had
walked into where Bill Broonzy was sleeping, his huge frame hanging
over the end of the spare bed. Bill was woken by a three-year-old gazing
adoringly at his feet and saying: 'Bill, you've got the lovcliest feet I've
ever seen – they're dark brown on top and pink on the bottom.' When
Sonny arrived, she walked up to him, put her hands on his knees and
said in a loud voice: 'Daddy, why is it so hard to like somebody who
is ugly?' There was a moment's tense, embarrassed silence then the
visitors broke up laughing. On occasion, being around Sonny could
be a spooky experience. Chris Barber's drummer, Graham Burbidge,
was travelling in a car with him, and recalls that 'he was supposed to

be entirely blind, the car in front stops suddenly and the brake lights go on and Sonny says, "Slow down." ' However, in their private dealings with each other there was little mystery and not much laughter. Alexis said that he and Cyril could hate each other's guts and still make good music together and so it was with Sonny and Brownie. Their partnership continued until 1982, four years before Sonny died, in March 1986, and still they would in turn sidle up to a sound man and whisper: 'I don't wanna hear that sonofabitch out the monitor.'

Towards the end of 1957, about six months before they arrived in Britain, Sonny and Brownie took over from Bill Broonzy, who had fallen ill on his European tour. Broonzy was flown back to Chicago for a series of operations on his throat and it was feared that he would never sing again. In December *Melody Maker* reported that he was 'happily recovering', but a story filed from Chicago the following February, headlined 'The whisper of Big Bill Broonzy', told a less optimistic tale. The reporter Bernie Asbell said that Broonzy looked healthy enough until he spoke, but 'when he opens his mouth to talk, Big Bill Broonzy isn't there'. He received lots of 'get well' letters from friends in England and right across Europe. However élitist the blues scene might have been outside the USA, Bill was clearly pleased that the music was being taken seriously. 'People here in the United States have forgotten what the real blues sound like and when it's done right, the people think it sounds wrong. These fellows singing folk music in the night clubs, and with dance bands, they're all right, but it's not blues.

'When a fellow is always thinking about whether his shirt looks just right, man he can't be thinking about the blues. The blues is when a man feels that there's a lot of trouble today, but tomorrow's going to be better. Maybe today we got it too good and folks are afraid tomorrow's going to be worse. That's being scared. It's not the blues.'

For Broonzy, tomorrow was going to be worse: he wasn't working, it is doubtful if he was seeing much if anything in royalty payments from his music and there were mounting hospital bills to pay. So he was especially pleased to receive a letter from Alexis and Dave Stevens informing him of a benefit concert they were planning. They had asked whether he might be fit enough to come over. He obviously wanted to, but the doctors said no.

The story of the Broonzy benefit concert twisted itself into what Chris Barber tactfully describes as an example of the 'typical paranoid mistrustfulness you get in this business'. In fact two concerts were announced. The first was at the London Coliseum on 9 March 1958. Dave Stevens says that Alexis was the driving force behind this one, but it didn't involve many of the musicians who had actually played with Bill or knew him particularly well. Humphrey Lyttleton was the exception in a bill comprising modern jazz artists like Cleo Lane, John Dankworth, Don Rendell, Mick Mulligan and skiffle bands like the Vipers and Johnny Duncan. Alexis found an organization who agreed to sell tickets, print posters and do the publicity.

Six days later, at the Dominion Theatre in Tottenham Court Road, came another concert, organized by Chris Barber and Harold Pendleton of the National Jazz Federation, who led a committee of organizers which included Charles Fox and Sinclair Traill. On the bill for the Dominion concert were Chris, Ken Colyer, Lonnie Donegan, Ottilie Patterson and others who had close associations with Broonzy. Bobbie Korner remembers Alexis 'biting the bullet' (because Alexis and Lonnie had fallen out) by going backstage at a Donegan variety show and asking him to appear. This he did, but not at the concert being organized by Alexis.

Why Alexis involved himself in a concert so clearly at a distance from Bill (although all the participating musicians admired his work and were only too keen to help) is something of a mystery. Harold Pendleton claims that Alexis had told him that he was going with the other concert because it was in some way to his 'personal advantage'. They had a big row in Pendleton's office; in his view the other concert organizers were simply crooks using musicians and the excuse of a benefit concert to get a foothold in the music business and Alexis should not have given them credence. Pendleton says he actually threw Alexis out of his office and so began a long period of hostility between the two that was only partially resolved a few months before Alexis died.

Pendleton relates a lighter side to the Dominion concert: 'the place was packed, not a seat left and Buddy Holly comes to the stage saying that he really wants to get in to see Donegan. I told him there wasn't any room, but I gave him my seat next to my aged mum. Afterwards I said to her: "Do you know who that was? Buddy Holly." "That's nice dear, who is he?" '

Both concerts went ahead as planned. *Melody Maker* of 10 May 1958 published the financial reckoning for both concerts; it totalled £1066 8s 6d, with '£500 already sent to Bill Broonzy'. Fund treasurer Dave Stevens says that as far as he was concerned the Coliseum concert organizers weren't necessarily crooks, 'but I was a bit concerned at the amount they had deducted for expenses before they sent us the cheque'.

At the time the only public acknowledgement of any financial problems were the Bank of England currency restrictions, which meant that the transfer of funds to Broonzy's wife was piecemeal. Sadly, by August it wasn't just hospital bills that needed paying; there was a funeral to be arranged. Bill Broonzy died of cancer on the 14th of that month, aged sixty-five. Dave Stevens, who had kept in close contact with Broonzy, received a heart-breaking letter from him a few weeks before he died. The optimism of his previous letters was gone. 'Please don't think hard of me for not writing you all. I can't see, I'm almost blind and my writing is not good. I am so nervous.' He added: 'I really need the other money for the bills.'

His friends and admirers remember him towering above them and weighing in at over fourteen stone. Wally Whyton was one of the many witnesses to his physical capacities. 'He'd play this blues bar in Düsseldorf for eight hours. He'd get a break from eleven-forty until midnight and then go on until four. I sat with him in this club when they brought up a baking tray of potatoes and a whole chicken. He pulled a bottle of scotch out of his overcoat and ate and drank the lot.' When Broonzy died, he weighed barely six stone.

In his autobiography, *Big Bill Blues*, published in 1955, Broonzy had dictated his own epitaph: 'When you write about me, please don't say I'm a jazz musician. Don't say I'm a musician or a guitar player. Just write Big Bill was a well-known blues singer and player and has recorded 260 songs from 1925 to 1952. He was a happy man when he was drunk and played with women. He was liked by all the blues singers, some would get a little jealous sometimes, but Bill would buy a bottle of whisky and they all would start laughing and playing again.'

Broonzy was buried in Chicago; nine friends were the pallbearers – the man at the front, hands behind him clasped tightly on the coffin, owed much to him for introducing him to the music club scene on Chicago's South Side in the mid forties. As Bill Broonzy was laid to rest, his friend Muddy Waters took over virtually unchallenged as the king of the Chicago blues scene.

But Muddy's career had taken a dip. Up until 1956 he had a string of hits in the *Billboard* R&B charts – in his best year, 1954, he had three records in the Top Ten, including 'Hoochie Coochie Man' and 'I Just

Want To Make Love To You'. After 'Mannish Boy' in 1956, the hits dried up as Chess concentrated their efforts on the embryonic rock 'n' roll market with Chuck Berry and Bo Diddley. They lost interest in Muddy and he in turn became disillusioned with the music. He was still playing seven nights a week, but more inclined to 'sit back' in the band and let his pianist brother-in-law Otis Spann and harmonica player James Cotton carry more of the show.

Meanwhile in February 1958, the Modern Jazz Quartet came to England and toured the country with Chris Barber. MJQ pianist John Lewis and Chris got talking about how successful Sonny Terry, Bill Broonzy and the others had been over here. John immediately suggested they bring in Muddy Waters. Chris had a few records but 'he [Muddy] was a sort of figure that you'd think: do you write to him care of the first swamp on the left, you know? He's a bit like that. Once you know more about it, you realize it was not like that at all. Rather sophisticated enterprise altogether, you see?'

Muddy was found, not in a Mississippi ditch, but deep in heart of black Chicago at his regular haunt, Smitty's Corner, on 35th and Indiana. In August 1958 *Melody Maker* announced that Muddy would make his British début at the Leeds Festival in October. Right at the end of his life Bill Broonzy was able to give his friend another helping hand by stating for *Melody Maker*: 'Muddy's real. See the way he plays guitar? Mississippi style – not the big city way.' He also called him 'the finest Mississippi blues singer'.

In hindsight, perhaps Bill's accolades weren't as helpful as he might have hoped. Broonzy was canny enough to know what the British expected of their blues stars and possibly phrased his comments accordingly. Muddy, on the other hand, had been used to delivering high-voltage, shuddering, violent music, grounded in the deepest blues that Mississippi could offer but presented streetwise in a sharp suit with a screaming-white Telecaster.

The coolness of the reception afforded Muddy Waters in 1958 has turned frostier with retelling over the years. It was true that with Otis Spann by his side and backed by Chris Barber's rhythm section, the applause for him at Leeds was less than ecstatic. But as Max Jones reported for *Melody Maker*, at St Pancras Town Hall it was 'hot and strong'. Some people did find it all too much, but Jones's review was full of praise for both Muddy and Otis Spann: 'it was tough, unpolite, strongly rhythmic music, often very loud, but with some light and shade in each number such as you could have danced to with confidence'. In fact, his playing was rather more tentative and restrained than his records suggested because he'd hardly played much in the preceding months. He was giving over more of his performance to singing and the lyrical content rather than self-accompaniment, and this situation was compounded by an accident to his left hand which forced him to stop playing altogether for a while.

In London, he dropped by the Blues and Barrelhouse Club to sit in with Alexis and Cyril for the customary bottle of whisky. He visited the Korners' house and, with Sappho on his knee, listened to Alexis' records and discussed the music. On a subsequent visit he brought along for Sappho a classic little red dress. He also brought his acoustic guitar. Just before he left in October 1958, he told Max Jones that his one regret was that nobody had warned him about English tastes in the blues. 'Now I know that people in England like soft guitar and the old blues. Back home they want to hear the guitar ring out . . . next time I come I'll learn some old songs first.' In 1960 he did just as he'd promised; but by his third visit in 1963 Alexis was taking city blues all over the country and the electric revolution in pop was building up a head of steam. Parts of the audience were disappointed with the acoustic set. More confusion for Muddy Waters.

During 1959 Alexis had two articles on Muddy published, one in *Jazz Review* and the other in a magazine on folk music edited by A L Lloyd. The intelligence and erudition of his writing combined to put him in the forefront of blues writers, alongside Paul Oliver.

The second article was the more extensive and began by explaining how Alan Lomax came in search of Robert Johnson and instead discovered McKinley Morganfield, who was to take the name Muddy Waters, on a plantation in Stovalls, Mississippi. Alexis described the early Library of Congress recordings and then compared the singing and playing styles of Muddy Waters and Robert Johnson, styles which differed more than they coincided. He quoted Lomax, who says about Johnson on the sleeve-notes to the earliest recordings that 'Muddy Waters never saw him'.

Years later Alexis said that he couldn't conceive of the blues without Robert Johnson. In tune with many other musicians and commentators, he believed Johnson had made the music as sophisticated as it was ever likely to become. But he also swallowed at least part of the gospel of St Robert handed down by John Hammond, Alan Lomax and a slew of white writers ever since. One cannot deny the importance of Robert Johnson, but we are fed with the notion that he was the well-spring from which the whole of the blues, not to mention rock 'n' roll, is supposed to have been derived – an unbroken line of development from Robert Johnson to Robert Plant. One wonders just how much of an icon he would have been had he not lived hard and died young in mysterious circumstances; if instead, he had lived out his life in crushing poverty, to be 'rediscovered' in the 1960s, herded round some rock festivals making no money, finally succumbing to alcoholism or just plain old age in the 1970s.

In his article Alexis points out that Muddy copied Johnson's guitar phrasing 'in only a rudimentary way', that 'their different weight of voice and method of delivery make confusion impossible' and highlights the voice phrasing as intentionally irregular in Johnson, but more predictable in Muddy Waters, and so on.

As he was the first to admit, in keeping with all blues enthusiasts of the day (and many more since) there was an element of the purist about Alexis. But in the same way that he had wide-open ears when it came to jazz, he took the view that the blues wasn't just about a handful of Chicago recordings set down between 1945 and the late 1950s. Later he would happily tag as the blues 'anything from Louis Jordan to Martha and the Vandellas'.

Nor did he have much truck with the notion of regarding the blues as exclusively a 'folk music' and thus attributing to a very disparate group of individual musicians the burden of speaking for the 'black community' as a whole. The blues tackled social and political issues, but also dealt with a side of life involving violence, sex, abuse of women, drugs and drinking that many in the black community would want to distance themselves from, whatever their social standing. In many respects the blues was no more 'representative' of black America as a whole than rock 'n' roll or country music was of WASP society.

Studied from an anthropological perspective, the blues is often denied an identity as pop music, but over the years Alexis was at pains to counter this view. 'We [i.e. he and Cyril Davies] were convinced that blues was world pop music and it was ridiculous to suggest that it was just for a few people with esoteric tastes. It wasn't that, it was pop music and we were going to make it back to what it had been . . . the first million-selling blues record had been in the States in the twenties, so don't tell me it wasn't pop music.' An overly academic perspective also runs the risk of inadvertently patronizing the performers. Alexis himself was somewhat guilty of this when he wrote of Bill Broonzy in *Melody Maker* that he 'is from another world than ours and it is with his own people that he will always be happiest – knowing them, he is secure in the knowledge that they know him'.

So readers of his Muddy Waters article in which he went on to regret the singer's 'urbanization' might have seen a fellow traveller in a duffel coat. But for Alexis, it was much more to do with the music than the rosy glow of supposed nostalgia or purity of spirit. He saw Muddy's music as becoming 'at once more ambitious and less subtle' and suggested that Johnson and Broonzy were more subtle than Muddy as singers because the form then was more 'formal and precise'. He recognized that in the postwar period of 'reactionary primitivism' Muddy had to swim with the tide: 'the audiences have grown younger and, to complete the disruption, America has "invented" the teenager. The effect on the blues has been enormous and, in a world which has steadily increased its audible volume of living, the music has become harsher and louder.'

The main victim here, Alexis felt, was Muddy's voice, which (on the most recent recordings then available in Britain) he thought had been coarsened with 'obsessive echo' to heighten the 'voodoo' effect – the idea being to boost sales in the face of rock 'n' roll by restating the primitive aspects of the music'. Which is where the dance steps came in. Alexis remarked on how much Muddy was eschewing guitar to focus on the singing enhanced by visual performance.

'No one who saw Muddy at the Roundhouse last September could fail to realize that the visual effect of his singing makes a lasting impression, and that the songs now seem incomplete without the contortions. Furthermore, it is fair to assume the need for a change in technique, to suit his 'dancing style'. It is one thing to stand up and sing a note and another to produce this note with one leg twisted in the air and the stomach muscles tightly contracted. So the notes have become shorter and the tendency to shout more pronounced. But when Muddy sings one of the older blues . . . one can hear immediately that much of his earlier style remains, and the enormous masculinity of his voice almost dwarfs the vicious guitar playing. It is at times like these that one understands Bill Broonzy's high opinion of Muddy's singing.'

For Alexis the shouting singing style was 'a matter of taste', but he was pleased to be able to report that if Muddy – in Alexis' opinion – had lost something in pursuit of record sales, more recent songs such as

'Hoochie Coochie Man' and 'Still A Fool' had, if anything, gained in poetic character and expressiveness.

For his part, Muddy believed that he'd toned down the dancing because, as he told *Melody Maker*, otherwise 'I guess they'd figure I was following behind Presley or something.' He went on: 'but that's always been there in southern blues'. Here is where Alexis' knowledge and that of most other early blues writers let them down. Much of what was generally condemned as pandering to modern commercial tastes had been in the music since its inception. When Hendrix played with his teeth or behind his head, it was part of a blues tradition going back at least as far as Charley Patton and Tommy Johnson. Playing outdoors to crowds of noisy, inattentive people or trying to catch the eye of a pretty girl, you had to do something out of the ordinary.

What Alexis was describing was a blues artist in transition, firmly rooted in southern blues traditions with a record of urban commercial success behind him, trying to update his performance to meet the expectations of younger audiences. But, in the late fifties and early sixties, he failed. The relationship between black blues musicians, both the urban stars with fading careers and the 'rediscovered' pre-war artists like Skip James, and the white music business, audience and musicians was a complex mixture of adoration, patronage, envy, 'ownership' and crude exploitation. But simply put, Muddy's fortunes and those of B. B., Freddie and Albert King, Howlin' Wolf and many others were revived by white champions of the music such as Alexis, Cyril and then John Mayall in Britain and Paul Butterfield in the USA.

But the early road to international recognition was laid out by Chris Barber. Other bluesmen, many of them pianists, heard what was happening in England and came for a taste of the adulation they were lacking at home. New Orleans-born Eurreal 'Little Brother' Montgomery came in from Chicago and wanted Val Wilmer to take pictures of him outside Buckingham Palace so that he could send them home to show he'd made it. He recorded an album with Ken Colyer; Alexis played guitar on two of the tracks and wrote the sleeve-notes: 'The two most striking things about Little Brother are his music and his craving for seafood. I know nobody who can eat more shrimps and rice with such relish.' Rufus 'Speckled Red' Perryman, a bald, freckled albino, thumped out old-style barrelhouse piano down at the Roundhouse. Little Brother remembered a professional boxer following him around the US South wanting to make it as a pianist. As Champion

Jack Dupree, he succeeded and became such a firm favourite in Europe as an entertainer [rather than any kind of virtuoso musician] that he moved first to Switzerland then Sweden and eventually settled down to live in Halifax with his English wife. Dupree was a wonderful cook of Creole food. American musicians would often insist that their itinerary was arranged so they could pass by Champion Jack's house to get some real Louisiana gumbo inside them.

Dupree and the Korners became firm friends. Alexis played on his album *Natural and Soulful Blues* and on many of his gigs, but Jack could never quite get his head around the name. Bobbie went with Alexis once to see Jack playing in a club. 'He was doing this long, rambling thing where he played piano and talked. At one point, to our absolute amazement, he said: "There's a man over there, he's in the audience, and I want to tell you that when I first came to England, he made me so welcome and it was the first time I'd eaten in a white man's home. He's here tonight, please give a big hand to ELKS KRONER!!" '

Peter 'Memphis Slim' Chatman became another emigré in Europe. He was already highly successful in Chicago, with a blues standard 'Every Day I Have The Blues' under his belt, when Alan Lomax sent a message to England via Max Jones at *Melody Maker* saying: 'Now that I have seen Memphis Slim in person, I can assure you – and everyone in Britain – that he would be an asset to any programme.' *Melody Maker* printed Chatman's address in Chicago and so began a trail of visits to Europe, often in the company of Willie Dixon and Matt 'Guitar' Murphy. Eventually he toured mainly as a solo artist and lived in some splendour in Paris (complete with Rolls-Royce), where he died in 1988. Alexis and drummer Stan Grieg recorded several sides with Memphis Slim in 1960, although Alexis' over-respectful Martin acoustic can hardly be heard.

Josh White, Bill Broonzy, Muddy Waters, Champion Jack Dupree and Memphis Slim blew away many of the enduring stereotypes of the 'poor boy, long long way from home'. But one visitor was less than comfortable in his new surroundings. Jesse Fuller, nicknamed 'Lone Cat', was not a blues artist in the accepted sense. He had come out of the tent-show tradition as a one-man band playing twelve-string guitar and a unique six-string foot-operated bass called a fotdella plus kazoo, harmonica, microphone on a harness and a hi-hat played with the left foot. Influential white-American folk singer Ramblin' Jack Elliott made Fuller's 'San Francisco Bay Blues' a highlight of his set, giving Fuller an entrée into US TV in the fifties. Dylan later cited him as a major influence and copied the neck harness idea.

But when Fuller came to England he was a troubled man. Val Wilmer had been looking forward to meeting him, but found him cynical and dissatisfied. He was also nursing an ulcer and wished to be back home. He was even a 'lone cat' in what Val fondly imagined was his own milieu. She witnessed a reluctant Rosetta Tharpe agreeing to be photographed with Fuller, not wishing to be associated with what was clearly viewed as 'old-time down-home music'. But Val was able to make some connection with him; in 1959 she worked up a series of letters he sent her into one of her first published articles.

However, when Fuller stayed with the Korners, he was far more ill at ease. Bobbie got the impression that he was either unused to being in a white man's house or simply uncomfortable. 'He wouldn't eat our food. He'd say: "Oh, that looks nice, will you buy me some. He must have been in turmoil, he just didn't seem to know what to do." '

Alexis was very much 'in the scene' in the mid to late fifties, playing at the Roundhouse, entertaining and writing about visiting bluesmen, recording with them and penning the sleeve-notes for their albums. In the early fifties he hadn't given the impression of seriously hankering after the life of a professional musician. He had held down respectable jobs, had an eye for clothes and cars and, compared with the rat-holes many jazz musicians inhabited, had a decent roof over his head. To somebody like Lonnie Donegan, who says he went round to Alexis' flat in Norfolk Crescent to listen to expensive import records that Donegan couldn't afford, making it in the business was life or death – do it or starve.

But as the years went by, and especially after meeting Cyril, Alexis became very single-minded about pursuing a career in music. Eventually the pull was too great and in January 1957, against all the dictates of common sense, he left the BBC.

6

SKIFFLE OR SCUFFLE?

Alexis' decision to leave his full-time job with the BBC can be regarded as either brave or entirely irresponsible because by now he and Bobbie had not only Sappho, who was nearly five, but a son, Nico, born in July 1956 and another baby due in June – Damian.

Bobbie knew how single-minded Alexis had become about music. To her credit, she was keen for him to succeed because she was a great devotee herself, but as she admits: 'I was pretty horrified when Alexis became a professional musician because of the insecurity. We could never find the money for rent. It was a terrible struggle. I wasn't resentful, because I did like the music – it was very much my life as well. But we were constantly worried about money.'

Poverty is a relative concept; Lonnie Donegan viewed Alexis as 'well off' compared with himself, who had been brought up in London's East End. As children neither Alexis nor Bobbie had been materially deprived, but as parents with a growing family and an unreliable income, the going was evidently rough.

The Korners had moved from the flat in Norfolk Crescent to a house in Molyneux Street, near the Edgware Road, and then to a house in nearby Linden Gardens, which, according to Bobbie and others, was haunted. 'You would often get the feeling of somebody watching you and you'd hear footsteps walking across the floor upstairs when you knew that nobody else was there.'

They shared their house with Bill Colyer and his wife. This was supposed to be a temporary arrangement, but then Bill's wife had a baby. Much to Bobbie's annoyance, 'they stayed and stayed and in the end we really fell out with them'. Once they had gone, they still needed a lodger. Jazz critic and broadcaster Charles Fox moved in and stayed with the family for over thirty years until he died suddenly of a heart attack in 1991.

Fox was raised in Dorset on a diet of jazz and cricket, which remained undying passions throughout his life. When he left school he went to work in a travel agency in Bournemouth, a job made redundant by the war. For health reasons he saw out the conflict as an engineering draughtsman while reeling off letters about his jazz heroes to the editors of music magazines. Other writing followed: record sleeve-notes, freelance journalism, a children's novel and a spell at Reuters. He was an early pioneer of jazz poetry with Christopher Logue, long before its brief flurry of fame in the early sixties with Pete Brown and Michael Horovitz.

For Bobbie, Charles was 'the one stabilizing influence' in a household which became increasingly chaotic over the years. He was a bachelor in the 'old-fashioned' sense; he had his own room into which he could hardly squeeze for all the books, records and papers. But he never ate with the family, and always went out to local cafés and restaurants.

Trixie Stevens regarded the Korners as 'the perfect married couple – obviously they had their spats, but if any two people epitomized what marriage was all about, it was Bobbie and Alexis'. There was certainly much humour in the early days when the children were young. Trixie was there one Christmas, and remembers: 'Sappho was very whiny and miserable; Bobbie said to Alexis, "Could you have her on your lap please?" So he had Sappho on his knee while he was trying to fix the Xmas lights. And then she said, "Could you hold Nico?" And then it was, "Oh Alexi" . . . at which point he said, "Why don't you just stick the plug up my arse? I'm sure I'll have enough power to light the tree as well." That was typical of the kind of exchanges they'd have. They were very funny together.'

As for 'spats', Bobbie clearly felt unhappy at being left at home while Alexis went off to the cinema with Sinclair Traill in lieu of wages. The early days of motherhood were tough, with Alexis working in the day and trying to find gigs by night. Sappho spent a lot of time with her grandmother Lilian and with Trixie, who was only too willing to help out, as she explains: 'She would come and spend weekends and days with me when she was a baby. I was a second mother to Sappho.' Robert and Lilian Melville, Bobbie's parents, were also on hand, not far away in their Gower Mews flat, off Tottenham Court Road. Sappho's memories of early childhood are dim, but mainly centre around time spent with her grandparents, 'the pushchair they took me around in and the smell of their flat'.

But with the arrival of Nico and Damian, and before Alexis went on the road with a band, they enjoyed a relatively settled family life which suited Bobbie's views of how the children should be brought up: 'They had a wonderful time and he was a nice father.' Being a musician, rather than read bedtime stories he sang his kids to sleep with old railway songs like 'Casey Jones' and 'Wreck Of The Old '97'.

However, once liberated from the BBC, Alexis had to patch together some kind of living. He was a regular contributor to the music press, earned a few pounds from gigs and sessions and spent a brief period as an A&R man at Decca and other labels. He also wanted to record in his own right.

In February 1957 Alexis Korner's Breakdown Group with Cyril Davies plus Terry Plant on string bass and Mike Collins on washboard recorded tracks for Doug Dobell's 77 label (his record shop was at 77 Charing Cross Road) seven of which were later released under the title *Blues from The Roundhouse*. Songs like 'Skip To My Lou' and 'Boll Weevil' were very close to skiffle, using similar instrumentation.

Five months later he was back in the studio, this time for Decca (recording a session for its subsidiary label, Tempo, specializing in jazz, folk and blues), who coerced him despite much protest into renaming the line-up (with Chris Capon as a new bassist plus Dave Stevens on piano) the Alexis Korner Skiffle Group. Sleepy John Estes' 'I Ain't Gonna Worry No More', Big Maceo's 'Kid Man' and 'County Jail', were hardly derived from skiffle, although Cyril doing Leadbelly's version of 'Easy Rider' might have been closer to the mark. To add to the confusion, the record was titled *Blues At The Roundhouse Vol 1*.

At that time skiffle was probably at its peak, just about to tip over the hill into oblivion as rock 'n' roll took over. Skiffle was arguably one of the most important musical genres ever to emerge in Britain. This may have been an even greater legacy to lay at the feet of Chris Barber (and Ken Colyer) than that of bringing over the American blues stars. Barber and Colyer were genuine pop stars of their day: audiences flocked to see trad jazz and were introduced to skiffle in the intervals. These interval line-ups, with Chris Barber and Ken Colyer together and then separately, included Alexis, Lonnie Donegan, pianist Johnny Parker, Bill Colyer, bassist Micky Ashman and George Melly and were very influential. Skiffle created an environment which assisted in the acceptance of blues music by introducing the works of Broonzy and Leadbelly to a young audience and from it came the English folk scene on one side and on the other commercial rock 'n' roll and pop. The Quarrymen became the Beatles, the Vipers became the Shadows while Lonnie Donegan was the first British guitar hero. Skiffle's use of simple, often home-made, instruments enabled young people from every walk of life to make music.

Hand in hand with skiffle went coffee bars, equally important as the first venues where young people could play. Wally Whyton explains: 'It was the coffee bars that made it all happen. Before then if you were a young kid, you either went to youth clubs, if you had one locally, and they depended very much on the wardens who'd say, "no music, no this, no that" and they were absolute gauleiters when it came to what went on in their clubs. There wasn't much going on in the pubs either (assuming you could get in) except on Saturday night, when you'd have somebody on the piano for some kind of music-hall knees-up.

'Coffee places were the first places where you could hang about for an evening, spend a shilling on a coffee, go in at nine and come out at eleven, nobody bothered you, nobody said you had to have a second cup of coffee. It meant that you met strangers and socialized with them.

'"What do you do?"

'"Oh, I'm in advertising. I play the guitar."

'"Oh really, I play as well. What about bringing it down next Wednesday?" '

Coffee bars spread out from Soho in the early 1950s. The Moka in Frith Street opened its doors in 1953 and was the first with a proper espresso machine. On the corner of Berwick Street and D'Arblay Street was the House of Sam Widges, with a jazz place in the basement called the Pad and, nearby on Old Compton Street, the Heaven and Hell. These were mainly patronized by the beatnik–bebop jazz set. The first coffee bars to attract the skiffle crowd were the Skiffle Cellar at 49 Greek Street and the Breadbasket in Cleveland Street, both haunts of Alexis in his earliest scuffling days on solo guitar. Most famous of all, the 2Is in Old Compton Street played host to a clutch of future rock 'n' rollers and pop stars, notably Screaming Lord Sutch and Tommy Steele.

But many of the original leading lights of the skiffle world were fed up with the form itself. Cyril and Alexis had tired of it very quickly and ditched skiffle at the Roundhouse pub when Carter Family songs began to creep in. Then Charles McDevitt's 'Freight Train', sung by Nancy Whiskey, got to number five in the charts in April 1957, followed by Johnny Duncan's 'Last Train To San Fernando', which did even better, reaching number two in July. The metamorphosis from black Chicago rent-party music to white Appalachian bluegrass was complete. Chris Barber was now seriously considering dropping skiffle from his sets altogether, while in the wake of two Top Ten skiffle hits, Alexis was doing battle with Tempo over the name of the band.

White appropriation was not the only problem with skiffle. Aside from the chart success, there were still many hundreds of skiffle bands up and down the country. A statistic of the time claimed that every third male teenager was in a skiffle band. But those who were attempting to preserve the music's integrity were, with their imposition of 'codes of conduct', causing it to become ossified. The best example of this was a book on skiffle by Brian Bird published in 1958. There was a section on running a local jazz club, debating whether or not you should allocate a period in the evening to records and actually allow people to bring in their own. Bird nevertheless exhorted the chairman or secretary to adopt 'vigilance' and a 'certain supervision over the records played'. He quoted a salutary experience from his local club, 'when a near riot was only just avoided when a certain young girl put on a Elvis Presley record and insisted on playing it right through'.

As for playing skiffle, this loose-limbed, free-and-easy, good-time party music, Bird offered formal advice on clothes, mannerisms, how and where to stand on the stage and keeping the washboard in line. 'The instruments should be well kept and it is permissible to paint the box bass and washboard . . . A skiffle group should present a number in a sincere unaffected manner. There should be no striving for theatrical effects and it is not necessary to wear startling costumes or adopt dramatic poses when playing.'

Bird was a true champion of the music, emphasizing what he saw as its sincerity, its lack of pretension, its folk roots and its links with ordinary people. But the misty-eyed vision of British teenagers finding their pre-industrial roots was not to be realized. It wasn't long after the book was published that skiffle was dead in the water, sunk by the stronger, more raucous images and sounds of rock 'n' roll.

But the music did not die without sparking off another of those internecine wars on the British music scene which had already seen the revivalists slugging it out with the traditionalists, both doing battle with the modernists, American blues versus English folk, country blues versus urban blues, acoustic versus electric – and still to come – can the white man sing the blues in the first place? Now it was skiffle – folk music or pap?

Lonnie Donegan wrote a foreword to Bird's book in which he said: 'it was necessary for someone to trace its story as a genuine development of folk music and to establish its legitimate position within the jazz movement.'

But Alexis and others believed strongly that by 'going variety', far from reviving an old folk form, Donegan had entirely 'sold out'. And it still rankles with Donegan today: 'It was an awfully simple and rather pathetically English situation which is the English hate success – mine was accidental. I was doing exactly the same thing as Alexis Korner and Chris Barber and suddenly some DJ played "Rock Island Line" on the radio and whoosh – you've got a hit record. And all those who didn't have a hit record stand over this side of the room and throw stones at those who did. I guess Alexis was one of those.

'And when it came to songs like "My Old Man's A Dustman", what the folkies overlooked is that it is a pure, pure English folk song, originally heard in Liverpool as 'My Old Man's A Fireman On The Oder Shipping Line'. When I was researching it for publishing purposes you could trace it to the 1914–18 war and then to the school playground, where I picked it up when I was about four or five.

'What I did was to rewrite some of the comedy lines, just to make the comedy current because you couldn't sing about putting bullets up people's arses on the BBC. And this was considered my cardinal sin. I had blackened the name of skiffle, but if you get some of those records from the 1930s, you'll also find they were totally commercial, comedy songs done in as jokey a way as blacks living in Chicago could manage.

'I thought I was going to be the King of English Folk Music and I became a man without a country – and it was very upsetting at the time. I considered all these people my friends and they would cross the road – they didn't want to know.'

Alexis also felt that Donegan should not have taken the writing credits for 'Rock Island Line' or 'Have A Drink On Me', although many subsequent songs of Alexis were quite legitimately credited 'Trad arr. Korner'. Nor did he think Lonnie could sing very well, a view he actually expressed on sleeve-notes for a Chris Barber album when Lonnie was in the band. Small wonder that when he wanted Lonnie to appear in his Broonzy benefit as a guaranteed crowd-puller, Alexis approached him with some trepidation.

Their row over skiffle blew up in a series of articles in *Melody Maker* spread over two years from 1956 to 1958. Alexis kicked off with 'Skiffle is Piffle' in July 1956, by which time he had stopped playing skiffle himself while Cyril Davies was forming the idea of running a 'proper' blues club. In the wake of 'Rock Island Line', Alexis derided attempts to sing what was essentially an instrumental music and also the whole notion of playing it before an audience at all: '. . . it is a private music. To produce "skiffle sessions" as regular interval spots at jazz clubs and worse still, to produce these same sessions at concerts is complete nonsense. On both these scores British Skiffle – as I think it had better be known – is so far out of line that it bears but a superficial resemblance to the music which inspired it.

'With some exceptions, notably the skiffles at Greek Street in 1952 and early 1953 and on occasion, the Johnny Parker Group with the Humphrey Lyttelton band, this vocal trend has completely swamped the skiffle movement . . . It is with shame and considerable regret that I have to admit my part as one of the originators of the movement; a movement which has become the joy of community songsters and a fair source of income for half the dilettante three chord thumpers in London.

'British skiffle is, most certainly, a commercial success, but musically it rarely exceeds the mediocre and is, in general, so abysmally low that it defies proper musical judgement.'

The debate continued in March 1957 with a *Melody Maker* panel giving their views under the headline 'Skiffle: music or menace?' Lonnie Donegan struck back: 'Let's be brutally frank about the critics of skiffle, the men who held up their hands in pious horror and wrote articles declaring to the world that art was being prostituted. One such article "Skiffle is Piffle" appeared in the *Melody Maker* last summer. And what is its author doing today? [Donegan couldn't bring himself to name Alexis.] Playing in skiffle groups. Look for all the other critical neo-folklorists and you'll find them among the three-chord guitarists. They're on the skiffle wagon today because it pays off.'

Back came Alexis with a letter to the editor, printed in the next issue. 'As the author of "Skiffle is Piffle" may I point out that I am not "playing with skiffle groups". I am playing with the same guitarist (Cyril) and washboard player (Mike Collins) as at the time of writing the article.

'I have since played a concert with Ken Colyer, two or three sessions with Jack Elliott and Darrell Adams (strictly hillbilly) and an occasional session with Bob Kelly (strictly Chicago race blues).

'But the main point in my article was not that all skifflers were "prostituting an art". It was that they were too inept, musically to do so – "dilettante tub thumpers" – and this still holds good.'

This semantic ping-pong indicates just how confusing the notion of skiffle had become. The instrumentation and the sounds of skiffle were being applied to everything from Leadbelly to proto-rock 'n' roll and pop music, simply because it was fashionable. Hence Alexis' assertion that although he was playing in a group with the classic skiffle instrument, a washboard, he still wasn't playing skiffle.

He also won the battle over the name he would record under for Tempo Records. In April 1958 he recorded an EP, *Blues At The Roundhouse Vol 2*, as Alexis Korner's Blues Incorporated, although at the time there was no thought of having a working band. The choice of material would have been more to Cyril's liking: three of the four tracks were credited to Leadbelly.

Had it happened, it would have been most interesting to see how Alexis would have reacted to his own 'Rock Island Line' success, but in the event he would not record with his own group for another four years. From about 1958 to 1960 he began to drift away from Cyril and the Roundhouse and play around the embryonic folk scene happening at different venues. His relationship with Cyril was always on-off. 'We'd split up because we got on each other's nerves as people though we still admired each other as musicians. Cyril got this bug that you had to live it to understand it and therefore wanted to do everything that Leadbelly had done – several GBH charges – he hadn't actually got himself involved with a murder, but it was that kind of thinking and I couldn't take it all. By then he was reading paperbacks on Al Capone, you know, he was really sinking, sinking right down to that essential sort of thing.'

For Alexis, the need to play was overpowering. Alongside his Thursday night sessions at the Roundhouse, he had already played a number of solo and duet sessions at the Ballad and Blues Club; a filthy basement dive at the back of Charing Cross Station called the Gyre and Gimble; the Topic Folk Club; and Bunjies in Denmark Street with American

Emil Korner, circa 1893.

Sappho Korner, 1928.

Alexis Korner, child of the blues.

Alexis and Sappho, circa 1933.

Early Dicky Hawden Band with Dave Stevens on piano, 1951.
(Credit: George Harrison)

Alexis and bassist Denny Coffee, Dicky Hawden Band, 1951. (Credit: George Harrison)

Sonny Terry and Brownie McGhee, with Alexis on mandolin, the Barrelhouse and Blues Club at The Roundhouse pub, 1958. *(Credit: Terry Cryer)*

Alexis and National Steel, The Roundhouse pub, 1958. *(Credit: Terry Cryer)*

Vintage car blues. *(Credit: Marc Sharratt)*

Chris Barber Band with Ottilie Patterson, early 1960s.

lexis and Cyril Davies.

Eric Clapton bought a Kay guitar after seeing Alexis play one.

The beginning of so much ... with Charlie Watts on drums.

A classic Blues Incorporated shot (from left to right): Dave Stevens, Dick Heckstall-Smith, Alexis Korner, Jack Bruce, Mick Jagger, Cyril Davies, Charlie Watts (obscured, on drums).

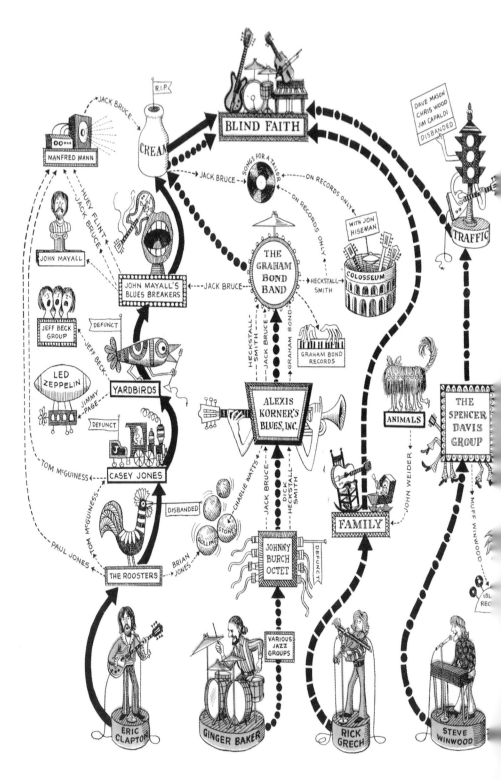

A *Life* magazine family tree. (*Credit: Flora*)

folk singers like Ramblin' Jack Elliott, who was a big influence on the mid-fifties folk scene. He learnt to play from a milkman, ran away from home to Brooklyn, got a job in a rodeo and sang with Woody Guthrie for four years.

Alexis also appeared with more traditional British folk singers like Ewan McColl, Alex Campbell (whom Cyril once threw down the stairs of the Roundhouse for swearing in front of a woman), Professor John Hasted and a merchant seaman named Red Sullivan who would sing unaccompanied on the bomb site opposite the 2Is coffee bar.

Although Alexis was never going to be any sort of political activist, the politics of the British folk scene suited his temperament. Key folklorists like A. L. ('Bert') Lloyd, who published Alexis' article on Muddy Waters, and Ewan McColl, and important upcoming figures like writer Karl Dallas were all members of the Communist Party. Topic Records was founded by the Workers' Music Association and the early jazz societies like Max Jones' Jazz Appreciation Society and, in its first incarnation, the Jazz Sociological Society all had left-wing or CP affiliations. In fact it was difficult to be part of the folk-blues scene and not be caught up in left-wing politics. All the musicians were regularly involved in benefit concerts. In the wake of the 1958 Notting Hill race riot, for example, Karl Dallas organized a benefit at the Skiffle Cellar for the Stars Campaign for Interracial Friendship. Alexis was on the bill and all his life he made a point of being available for charity gigs.

Alexis also hired himself out for trendy parties. 'You'd have to play the whole night by yourself. I used to play five or six hours. I played the blues, but I also played music for dancing and just odd things like that. Used to pick up nearly £25 a night, which was OK. You worked maybe one or two nights a week – you worked for your bread – you were expected to be a dance band, cabaret and everything else at the same time.'

Outside of the tight circle of West End clubs, there was really only the Troubadour in Old Brompton Road, Earls Court. The co-organizer of the club was Anthea Joseph. She came from an upper-middle-class bohemian milieu. Her father was a journalist, her mother, a former girlfriend of Bert Lloyd, was a classicist who enjoyed all forms of music. T. S. Eliot, Bertrand Russell, the Freuds and Dylan Thomas were all friends of the family, which could trace its ancestry back to Owen Glendower on one side and the Borgias on the other. After running several folk clubs, including the Troubadour, she had a distinguished career in the music business and became a close friend of Alexis, whom she first saw from a distance in 1956.

'I was sixteen years old and up in London for half-term weekend and went to Collet's to buy a record I wanted. I walked into the shop, all gawky and angles, and there was this absolutely gorgeous man buying some records. This exquisite creature was talking to the owner Jill Cook in a voice like bitter chocolate – tight black curly hair, a waisted tan jacket down to the knees, check trousers and beautiful hand-made boots. I didn't know who he was, all I knew was that he was gorgeous. I never forgot him – you couldn't.'

Coming from rural Suffolk, Anthea was eager to sample the club scene of London's young artistic community. She summoned up enough courage to go into the Partisan coffee bar in Carlisle Street, haunt of painters, poets, writers, singers and musicians and the characters of Soho: Red Sullivan, Quentin Crisp in green velvet jacket and make-up, Gypsy Larry, Ironfoot Jack and the Countess. 'I was so terrified, it took me three weeks to decide to go in. Alexis turned up one day and I realized this was the man from Collet's. I asked Red Sullivan, "Who's that?" "Oh, that's Alexis Korner." "*That's* Alexis Korner?" Because I had heard about him but never met him. He invited me to the Roundhouse that very evening.'

Anthea was at the Roundhouse the night the police arrived. 'There was a shadow on the wall and Alexis stopped the band and said, "Everybody empty their pockets, it's the law." There was this rattling sound on the floor, blues, black bombers, God knows what. "We've come to see if you got drugs?" "What? Us?" They went round searching pockets, oblivious to the crunching sounds beneath their feet. Alexis was trying very hard not to grin.'

James Moyes, a young artist who came to London in 1958 in search of the blues, recalls: 'I briefly met a carpenter called Ron who made guitars and lived on a barge and said there are two people you have to meet: one is Davy Graham and the other is Alexis Korner.' James found out about the Roundhouse and 'I met all the people there who were having lessons from Alexis.'

Tentative as his own self-confidence might have been, Alexis had a strong intuitive grasp of music which had its roots right back in his childhood. Giving guitar lessons was yet another way of clawing in a few pounds. But much to Bobbie's despair, Alexis and his money were easily parted. 'He wasn't terribly interested in money, he couldn't be bothered and that was genuine. He'd have it and spend it. He didn't think about how much he would earn. It wasn't the main thing. He must have had a heck of a lot of money go through his hands, but God knows where it went.' Where it didn't go was in making the mortgage payments on their Molyneux Street house, which was repossessed. The ghost of Linden Gardens (and windows you couldn't open) drove them out of their next home, and by March 1959 they had moved to a flat in Burnham Court in Moscow Road, Bayswater. It was here that James came for his guitar lessons.

James learnt much from Alexis. 'He was willing to spend any amount of time with anyone who was interested to inform and inspire them as much as he could. I think I learnt how to listen from Alexis. He could play a record three times and because of his academic music background, he could listen to music in layers.'

But despite his theoretical knowledge, Alexis was technically limited and eventually the pupil became as competent as the teacher. 'I think Bobbie heard me playing one day and thought it was Alexis. After that, he didn't want to give me any more lessons.'

It was at a party given by Jack Elliott that James introduced Alexis to Davy Graham, one of Britain's finest-ever acoustic guitarists, a musical polymath whose music has blended folk idioms from all over the world. He was the star of Anthea's Troubadour club; a large poster of him hung on the wall. James observed the relationship between the two men. 'It was very interesting. Alexis had been a very good mandolin player, but he came late to the guitar. When he started he was playing in open tuning and had to work quite hard at a time when there wasn't a lot of time – it wasn't as if he was single, living by himself and able to practise three or four hours a day. To a certain extent he protected his insecurities as a guitarist by his immense musicality. I think he found it very frustrating to relate to someone like Davy – here was this guitar phenomenon who was totally indiscriminate – he could play anything he heard – and on the other side a man of great taste who was struggling to play guitar.'

So much did Alexis respect Davy's talent that he asked him to form a regular partnership to replace the one he had with Cyril. For about a year they were the backing duo for an Australian singer, Shirley Abicair, and together they performed many times on TV and radio. Alexis and Davy also recorded an EP together for the Topic label called *3/4 AD*, produced by Bill Leader literally in his front room. For Davy, 'it was tremendously exciting for me to make a record', but he admits they had a strange relationship: 'I couldn't help feeling Alexis and I were like the main characters in *Of Mice and Men* – me the big lummox and Alexis the little guy with the brains. All I could do was shut up and play some interesting chords. I couldn't contradict him, just couldn't, and he captivated me for that reason. He wouldn't tolerate pretension, just wouldn't tolerate it, and I wanted to develop the same finesse of character.' And when it came to playing, 'I had the facility, he had the intensity – passion compensating for technique.'

Alexis was pursuing his music on all available fronts – writing, playing and recording, but he did have another passion: broadcasting. His time in the Army had whetted his appetite and he knew he was on to something when doing the links as a studio manager: he had been ticked off for having too sexy a voice for the BBC.

From the mid fifties, Teddy Warwick had been a record programme producer. He says: 'There were some jazz presenters at the time, but I decided to cast the net a bit wider and look for other people. I was introduced to [Alexis] and it was obvious he had a good broadcasting voice, I could hear that just by talking to him. He had the confidence to be a broadcaster and the knowledge. On jazz programmes you had to use people who knew their subject.' Alexis' début on domestic radio was *Jazz Session* on Network Three, broadcast between six-fifteen and six forty-five p.m. on 4 June 1958. The fee was ten guineas to 'select records, write script and present on microphone'.

From then on Alexis began receiving regular fees as a freelance broadcaster. He presented jazz and blues on both domestic and overseas radio and scripted his own series such as *The Louis Armstrong Story*, inserted into a magazine programme *Tonight At Six* on the Light Programme. He developed his skills as a sympathetic, knowledgeable interviewer of musicians. One of his first guests was New Orleans trombonist Kid Ory, on the Home Service's *Today* programme on 14 October 1959. However, he had to learn to restrain his natural tendency to dominate proceedings. His producer, Elizabeth Brewer, wrote to him saying: 'It was splendid to be able to have Kid Ory in the programme . . . but the general consensus of opinion was rather too much information had come from you rather than him. Could you guard against this when interviewing Champion Jack du Pris [sic] for us which we should indeed like you to do if you are not averse to it being done on a "without commitment" basis.'

Alexis' interviewees ranged from Josh White to Count Basie, Miles

Davis to Cliff Richard. But the meeting that had most impact on him was Charles Mingus in the summer of 1961.

If there was a recipe for the music that Alexis was to aspire to, it was one part Muddy Waters, one part Bill Broonzy and the final ingredient, Charles Mingus. One of the most important composers of black music this century, Mingus was deeply concerned to express the social condition of the black community in America and found an ideal vehicle in the blues as a root music, a common denominator to help explore the black experience. One album he entitled *Blues and Roots* and another, with Eric Dolphy, *Folk Forms*. Like Miles Davis, who had also been entertained by the Korners, Mingus responded to Alexis' unEnglish 'hip' demeanour and felt more at ease than he might otherwise have done with the usual over-reverential white journalist, whom he would have despised. Alexis and Bobbie took Charles to a local Indian restaurant. 'Up to then,' says Bobbie, 'this place had been an excellent restaurant and then they changed the chef and it was awful. Mingus was fantastic, a great sense of humour and the poor waiters had to suffer us collapsing with laughter as one plate of dreadful food after another was served up. Alexis told Mingus's biographer, Brian Priestley: 'and at the end of the evening he wanted this cup of coffee with cream, and the Indian waiter came up to him, "I'm afraid we have no cream, sir." And he said, "Whadya mean, you got no cream? Well, send someone out to go and fetch some." "At this time of night, sir, I'm afraid we can't get any cream." "You got ice cream?" [*pause*] "Yes, we have ice cream." "Well, melt it!" And I actually said to him, "You're getting a bit heavy," and he said, "Who, me? Some of my best friends . . .", pointing at the waiter.'

Mingus was in the UK to make a film, which seems to have been cut short when the press lady he was after refused to sleep with him and he broke down her hotel room door brandishing a gun. Alexis did record an interview with Mingus, but as he said 'fuck' every second word, the BBC wouldn't broadcast it. But in between the obscenities, Mingus left Alexis with his notion of 'Rotary Perception'. He had objected to the word 'jazz' because every time he had heard the word in England it was attached to music like Acker Bilk's 'Stranger on the Shore' that he did not regard as jazz at all. Alexis tried to press Mingus on what his music should be called, if not jazz. 'Call it Rotary Perception,' said Mingus. Alexis duly went away and had a T-shirt printed up with the legend blazoned across the front. In fact the name derived not so much from Mingus's disgust with what passed for jazz in Britain, but from a concept based on swirling, circular rhythmic patterns. As he told British critic Kitty Grime for *Jazz News* during his visit, he thought that jazz had been held back 'by people who think that everything must be in the "heard" or obvious pulse'. But imagine circles around the beat and you have Rotary Perception: 'the notes can fall at any point within the circle so that the original feeling of the beat is not disturbed. If anyone in the group lost confidence, one of the quartet can hit the beat again.'

Alexis didn't confine himself to music programmes and interviews. He had a regular slot on a magazine programme, *Roundabout*, called 'Korner's Corner', where he had three to four minutes to expound on anything he liked from sport to Green Shield trading stamps, and another spot devoted to motoring. He did one-off programmes like *Portrait of a Southern Penitentiary*, based on his self-taught knowledge of American history, did various programmes about London, and used his language skills to present Schools Intermediate German programmes. In fact, Alexis became very active in children's radio, doing book reviews, a six-week series called *The Great American Railroad* and then another entitled *Gold Fever*. He wrote his own scripts, edited his own tapes, narrated and where appropriate added guitar accompaniments. Under the pseudonym Nick Wheatstraw – because of his contract with Tempo Records – he had recorded classic American ballads with Alan Lomax. 'Nick' came from Nico, his son's name, while 'Wheatstraw' derived from his German surname's connotation of wheat production. He also recorded an album of children's songs with Ramblin' Jack Elliott at the Lansdowne Studios in 1959.

But blues was where Alexis felt he had found a niche, as musician, journalist and broadcaster, and it was a position he rather jealously guarded. The very first book on the blues was Sam Charters's *Country Blues*, published in New York in 1959. But hard on its heels was Paul Oliver's *Blues Fell This Morning*, which appeared the following year. Looking back, Paul Oliver feels that Alexis was 'very ambitious and rather conceited and it was probably why I didn't get to know them [the Korners] better. Bobbie I liked very much, but with Alexis I had this discomfort. I did a television programme in the early days, something Alexis was hosting. I'd been invited to do a talk and I also used to do very rapid drawings. The idea was that as we hadn't got photographs [of bluesmen] in those days, I would do contextual drawings as I talked. They had it down to introduce me as "Paul Oliver, the blues writer".

Alexis scrubbed this out and had put, "The artist Paul Oliver who has an interest in blues", which he had no right to do.

'He knew I was working on "Blues Fell This Morning", as everybody did, because I'd travel across London to hear one record. In fact, the first time I went to Alexis' house was to hear his copy of Skip James's "I'm so Glad" on Paramount 78. Well, the first review of it was Alexis on the BBC and it was very cutting, starting off, "This is not the book we expected . . ." Charles Fox was also grudging at first, but in later years he came round to saying what a remarkable achievement it was.'

Back out in clubland, Alexis was getting thick with Cyril once more. The Roundhouse was still doing well, but the programme was essentially country blues with odd 'brave' presentations of electric guitar courtesy of Brownie McGhee. Initially, Alexis was ambivalent about electric guitar, not so much because of associations with nasty, greasy rock 'n' roll (the trad, folk and skiffle view), but because he preferred the subtleties and intricacies of acoustic playing, which became simplified and coarsened under power. He'd already written unfavourably about Rosetta Tharpe's switch and told Brownie McGhee (to his later regret) that he'd kill his career in the UK if he carried on playing electric. Yet Alexis had been playing around with electric guitar even back in the Army days. 'We had a sort of Benny Goodman quartet thing going at BFN in Hamburg . . . we just used to sit and play after hours [and] I was into electric guitar then – it was a diabolical pickup, but in 1946/47 you didn't get very good pickups.' He had arguments with Broonzy, who'd been playing electric for years. It was Broonzy who turned Alexis on to Muddy Waters and also suggested he listen to Elmore James. The right true path was illuminated when Alexis and Cyril heard Muddy Waters in 1958 and from then on Cyril in particular was absolutely determined that he wanted to recreate the Muddy Waters Chicago sound in London. Alexis definitely wanted to go electric, but had a more open-ended view of the blues and wasn't necessarily committed to Cyril's precise vision.

However, it was all academic because the club and pub circuit was in the grip of trad-jazz promoters who hated the thought of electric anything. Nor were the Roundhouse regulars at the leading edge of radical thinking despite their love of a minority music. James Moyes recalls turning up for Thursday nights of blues where you couldn't really tell the difference between the students and the bank managers. 'Everyone wore long grey flannel trousers and Harris tweed jackets with a shirt and tie. Polo-necked sweaters were a hip item of clothing.' They were not exactly overjoyed when Alexis and Cyril started plugging into a tiny ten-watt amplifier, and the manager of the place even less so.

Meanwhile, in October 1959 Chris Barber and his band had made the dream trip to Chicago and sought out Muddy Waters at Smitty's Corner. This was deep in the black ghetto, and at two a.m. no taxi driver would take them there. Eventually they found it; drummer Graham Burbidge and the others went in. 'Of course it was a black club and the whole place went deathly quiet and then Muddy spotted us and called out, "My man" and once that happened the whole place went wild. We had a big jam session on stage with Muddy and Little Walter.' Ottilie Patterson went up to sing full of fear and trepidation, and brought the house down, people coming up afterwards asking for autographs. There could have been no finer accolade for her abilities as a blues singer.

Chris was overwhelmed by the sheer power of the classic Muddy Waters band and was determined to try to find a way to present this music back home. Supporting Muddy again when he toured England in 1960 only confirmed his belief in what needed to be done. The only way was to repeat the skiffle experience with interval slots in his own band at the Marquee. But he had to do it by degrees in order to gain acceptance.

Founded in April 1958 by Harold Pendleton, director of the National Jazz Federation, the Marquee was located in the basement of the Academy Cinema in Oxford Street. As a co-director of the NJF, Chris Barber was also closely associated with the club and played there regularly. Chris approached Alexis in the late summer of 1961 and Alexis rejoined the band to play alongside Ottilie Patterson when she sang the occasional Muddy Waters number.

Alexis toured with the Barber band and appeared with Chris when he backed Muddy's young harp player, Jimmy Cotton, on a two-EP set. The records received mixed reviews. Peter Clayton, for *Jazz News*, commended a 'tightly-knit group sound from Alexis' guitar, Chris Barber's very excellent bass and Keith Scott's rolling, confident piano'. Val Wilmer, writing for *Jazz News & Review*, was less impressed, particularly with Alexis, who, she felt, 'has had so many opportunities to grasp what the blues is all about, but his stiff phrasing and ever so slightly lagging beat indicate that some seeds fell on stony ground somewhere'.

Alexis was pleased to be given the opportunity by Chris to play the music he loved in the way he wanted, and the money came in handy as well. And yet the attitude of trad promoters and all those who decried electric blues as a popular music form, along with the in-fighting which abused the whole notion of 'pop', still rankled. Alexis reached for the typewriter and wrote 'Notes on the Blues', published in *Jazz News* in October 1961.

'The world is brim-full of reactionaries. The Anti-Establishment group has already established its own set of rules; in a short time these will have crystallized into a set of clichés just as ponderous as those of The Establishment. Often one tends to resign from one group in order to join the other, but so far as this concerns the world of Folk Music, I have simply resigned from groups with hard and fast rules . . . [one] tendency is to imply that "commercial" is synonymous with "bad".

'In the blues one can find a great deal of commercial music. Some of it rises to greatness without detracting from the financial advantages. The important singers of the '20s and '30s may not have made fortunes by current standards, but taking all their circumstances into account, Blind Lemon Jefferson, Leroy Carr, Ma Rainey and Bessie Smith had no need to scuffle for a living. They were catering for a market which was prepared to pay good money for good music. If a song sounded right, it was right; it didn't matter where it originated.'

He went on to talk about the prejudice in music which is 'at the root of these ridiculous quarrels which regularly split both the world of folk music and the world of jazz . . . So much drivel, so often. A successful formula is found for a particular audience and, too often, rather than risk financial loss, this formula is never varied . . . the music system plods on and on, dragging in young people who could have relatively open minds. "You must not use electric guitar" one person will say "or you'll lose your audience". "You must be socially significant or you are nothing" will whisper another.

' "Catholicism in taste? What are you thinking of?" says a third. "Come and join OUR GROUP. We're the only ones who really understand," says No 4. No wonder folk music is not getting anywhere fast. So long as audiences and promoters continue to further this type of thinking we shall produce nothing of real moment. As long as we deny the value of the "pop" song (remembering that "pop" is an abbreviation of "popular") we can only go on churning out material to a standardized pattern . . .'

Blues singers, said Alexis, thought nothing of copying and imitating whatever they thought sounded good, including English folk music, while keeping their own sense of freedom and discipline. He acknowledged that the newer jazz fans suffered from less prejudice; the real problem lay with the trad promoters, who had a tight grip on what kind of music would be heard in the clubs.

But Alexis did have some support in the jazz world. His article was followed in the next issue of *Jazz News* by Peter Clayton's 'Trad and Alexis Korner'. Clayton applauded the Barber band for moving away from the strict confines of trad: 'The band's latest and perhaps biggest single forward stride has been the inclusion in some of its appearances of Alexis Korner. Korner's switch to amplified guitar has bleached the hair of some of the purists and ethnicians, but it has given the normal run of his listeners a chance to hear him properly almost for the first time, since for years he has been unkindly served on record by unsympathetic balance. At long last he has emerged as a brilliant guitarist in the Rhythm and Blues idiom after years of working away in comparative obscurity in small clubs and as accompanist to visiting blues artists.

'His development as a guitarist has been consistent and logical. He has merely followed, like a film in quick succession, some of the course of American blues guitar playing, from the country to the town, from the sophisticated primitiveness of Scrapper Blackwell to the electrified abandon of the later, urban Muddy Waters. In his career at The Roundhouse, in the small clubs and with visiting performers, most of the stages have been passed through, and now, after a period of absorbing and developing, he has reached the point where he can give something of his own . . .'

The success of playing a limited amount of blues with Chris Barber encouraged Alexis, much against Bobbie's wishes, to consider forming a permanent band. She might have spent much of her time at home looking after the children, but she was shrewd enough to envisage the horrors of being a band leader. But, as ever, Alexis was not to be denied and he revived the name Blues Incorporated from the 1958 Tempo recording period. Ironically, Bobbie was one of the two people credited with thinking up the name in the first place, the other being Chris Barber's manager, Phil Robertson.

Blues Incorporated was a concept for an 'anonymous' band in which any group of musicians could play. Alexis didn't even want his name in the title, but it quickly became clear that it needed a personal identity and so Alexis Korner's Blues Incorporated was born. But Alexis stuck to the idea, even if he lost the argument over the name. Blues Inc, as it was inevitably called, was not a band with a neat linear membership ripe for the Pete Frame treatment. Next to his phone, Alexis built up a card index with sections for drummers, bass players, pianists and so on. There were periods when the band had a core membership, otherwise it was a revolving door admitting whoever was available on the night.

One of the earliest press mentions of the band appeared in *Jazz News*, announcing that it would be joining the stage with Acker Bilk in Ipswich on 10 December 1961. The line-up that night included pianist–drummer Stan Grieg, who backed Memphis Slim, Alexis, vocalist Ron McKay and Danny Craig on drums. But as yet no Cyril.

Cyril Davies was still playing the Roundhouse regularly, now in the company of a young blues guitarist, Geoff Bradford. Like Alexis', Geoff's early introduction to popular music was boogie-woogie; he learnt to play piano by copying the boogie-woogie greats on old 78s. Skiffle was hot when Geoff was doing his National Service and as his role model he swapped Meade Lux Lewis for Lonnie Donegan. Geoff began turning up at the Roundhouse and became acquainted first with Keith Scott, with whom he did Leroy Carr–Scrapper Blackwell-style duets, and then Cyril. Geoff's National Steel guitar was a sharp counterpoint to Cyril's twelve-string and they played hard against each other.

Alexis hadn't seen Cyril for a few months, but he knew that he would be very keen on the idea of forming an electric blues band. Further discussions were held with Chris Barber and Harold Pendleton and it was agreed that rather than Alexis simply going on for a few numbers, he should do the whole interval in his own right. On Wednesday 3 January 1962 he took the stage at the Marquee with Chris, his trumpeter Pat Halcox, and Cyril, who relinquished guitar in favour of harmonica and built his reputation as a player of the first rank.

Alexis began to talk up the harp as a popular instrument with an article for *Jazz News*, 'The Harmonica and the Blues'. 'There was a time when the harmonica was very popular. It was cheap, compact and portable. It was, in fact, ideal for the home music-maker. Harmonica bands were all the rage and one would often find three or four friends enjoying a musical soirée at which they would perform arrangements of famous overtures, marches, and light orchestral compositions . . . It was the diatonic harmonica, the common mouth organ, which was really popular.

'. . . the ordinary suck and blow instrument was ideally suited to the Blues. The sound was more intense, a better match [than the more expensive chromatic version] for the incisive tones of jug bands and country blues singers. In the hands of a good player, the harmonica could produce an astoundingly wide range of dynamics and tone colour. One has but to hear recordings by Noah Lewis, Will Shade, Sonny Terry, Sonny Boy Williamson and Little Walter to realize how personally different each of these players makes his harmonica sound.'

Alexis detailed the role of the harmonica in the history of the jug band, where personal improvisation was deemed unnecessary if the authenticity of the idiom might be compromised. He suggested that it was Sonny Boy Williamson who inaugurated a radical shift in blues harp playing to the more horn-like sound of jump blues and of course, ushered in the era of the 'harp hero'. Blues harmonica playing had arrived – even Presley was recording with it.

And in a wonderfully prescient conclusion several months before 'Love Me Do' was released and well in advance of the Rolling Stones, the Yardbirds and the Pretty Things, Alexis posed the question: 'Who knows what may happen next . . . a real R&B hit complete with electric harmonica and guitar [in] the Top Twenty?'

If Alexis was going to persevere with the idea of a band of his own, he would need to build up his own personnel. One remarkable feature of the emerging band was that every time it got a press mention the line-up was different and so, perhaps unsurprisingly, wrongly cited. The first announcement of a permanent band came in *Jazz News* on the same day that the Marquee sessions started; it was 'to include Keith Scott (harmonica/vocal), Malcolm Cecil (bass), Danny Craig (drums) plus a pianist to be announced later'. For Keith Scott, of course, read Cyril Davies. Keith himself was acknowledged by his peers as one of the finest blues pianists in the country. Malcolm Cecil incidentally went on to produce Stevie Wonder, so right from the start Alexis had a vision that his band would be home to the best musicians around, as well as giving opportunities to those on the way up.

By the time *Jazz News* published the first review of a Blues Inc gig a month later, the drummer and bass player had been replaced by Colin Bowden and Graham Beazley respectively, and there was a new vocalist, Andy Wren. The review itself, by Alexis' champion Peter Clayton and headlined 'From Chicago to Croydon', may have been literally a world exclusive – the first coverage of a white R&B show.

' "Forty days and forty nights" caught Acker Bilk's audience unawares when Alexis Korner decided to use it to open his spot in the programme at the Civic Hall, Croydon on January 19th. Blues Incorporated, Korner's new group, with which he hopes to stir up interest in contemporary Chicago-style Rhythm and Blues, was playing its first date in the London area and it had a curious effect on an audience basically suspicious of the guitar in general and the electric guitar in particular.

'Alexis Korner himself having decided to go the whole hog, gallantly used a rather glamorous looking solid. With him he had harmonica, piano, bass, drums and a singer named Andy Wren, who is handicapped at the moment by having to try to revise history and evolve R&B from a rock 'n' roll approach. As yet he lacks the technique which Muddy Waters' subtle music demands, and for a crowd which looks upon Acker's very good band as the Whole Truth, he came too close to some Elvisisms for their liking. Somebody, whose voice was stronger than his grasp of history, shouted "We came to a jazz concert!" But we gathered later that Blues Inc aroused a good deal of genuine interest also and that the rather thoughtless yelling that occasionally came from a certain section of the audience led to some bitter later scuffles.

'Alexis found the whole thing encouraging. "An Acker Bilk audience is probably the toughest of the lot. They come to hear Acker, and if King Oliver himself were suddenly to be reincarnated and given the first half of the show, they'd probably want their money back. Modern R&B is practically unknown in this country, but I think that a lot of people will soon be at home with it."

'The group is not quite a group yet, but it has in Cyril Davies a very exciting harmonica player. He also had the whole audience with him – with no dissenters when he sang "Hoochie Coochie Man". Keith Scott, who has done a lot of solo work at the Colyer Club, was on piano, rolling a good mean blues sound behind his leader's percussive hit parade guitar work. Colin Bowden was on drums, and while supplying the necessary drive, created undue monotony by clamping his foot firmly on the pedal of his hi-hat cymbals and bashing away on the upper one for most of the set.'

Alexis might have found the event 'encouraging', but probably only insofar as the band didn't get bottled off because later we read: '*Jazz News* found him unduly saddened by the mixed reception; he need not have been, for the group did precisely what it set out to do. Alexis Korner played in an unfamiliar but thoroughly authentic way, giving a noisy unstable but powerful lead. Croydon and Chicago are poles apart, but there's no reason why the gap shouldn't be narrowed.'

More than anybody, Alexis knew that he didn't have 'quite a group yet'; no more is heard of Andy Wren as far as the history of Blues Inc is concerned. Colin Bowden's claim to fame rests on the fact that he was probably the first of Alexis' sidemen to get a rubber cheque. Around the time of the Croydon gig, the band recorded Billy Boy Arnold's 'She Fooled Me', which appeared on the Alexis compilation album *Bootleg Him*. Keith Scott was on that session, and remembers: 'Colin broke a snare-drum skin and obviously couldn't continue until he had a replacement. So we stopped to enable him to go out to a local music shop, but he was virtually broke and so Alexis loaned him a cheque. When Colin went to collect the skin from the shop he found that the cheque had bounced.' It was the first of many stories involving Alexis and money: creative accounting and trying to make ends meet as a band leader.

Early in 1962 the band was represented by David Bilk, who wrote to the Light Entertainment division of the BBC to get an audition for the band. They were invited to appear at Audition Studio 2 at Aeolian Hall in New Bond Street on 28 February. The response was encouraging, said the BBC. 'We are pleased to inform you that the performance received favourable reports and they have now been added to the list of those available for broadcasting.

'We must add however that this does not mean that offers of engagements will automatically follow . . . Mr Korner will no doubt realise that for a specialized group such as this, there is only a limited amount of use, and bookings if any are likely to be few and far between.'

Meanwhile Alexis was still changing the line-up, trying to get the right mix; the card index was building up and would soon reach the point where he was more like a modern football manager amassing an interchangeable squad of players than a band leader. For the BBC audition, Alexis had Keith, Cyril and Graham Beazley; a different drummer, Derek Manfredi. himself a replacement for another unknown, Denny Hutchinson, plus a new singer, Art Wood.

Art recalls: 'I used to have a band called the Art Wood Combo, which was a nine-piece band doing arranged swing stuff plus R&B. We played the Viaduct Club in Hanwell. The Roundhouse was only Thursday nights, so Cyril Davies did the interval at the Viaduct, doing Muddy Waters stuff on electric guitar for Colin Kingwell's Jazz Bandits with my brother Ted on drums. One day he said, "Art, I like your voice, will you come and sing in my new band I'm forming with Alexis Korner?" The

Combo was coming to an end anyway because it was moving towards rock 'n' roll, which a lot of the band didn't want. But to me that was mind-blowing to be invited to sing by Cyril Davies, because he was a good singer as well.'

Alexis went down to the Troubadour one night to sit in with a Thelonious Monk-inspired modern jazz quartet. The drummer was a young commercial artist named Charlie Watts. He remembers: 'This man came in wearing Rupert Bear trousers and carrying an amplifier, which he put above my head. It was only about six inches square, hardly an amp at all, but I still hated it. I thought, bloody hell — noise. Then I went to Denmark for the company I was working for and I kept getting messages from this mate of mine who was piano player for Screaming Lord Sutch saying this man Alexis Korner was trying to get in touch with me.' Eventually they spoke on the phone and Alexis invited Charlie to rehearsals. Charlie brought along a string bassist friend, Andy Hoogenboom, who in turn brought a friend of his from art college, a girl named Shirley, who became Charlie's wife. 'I can see it all now, the first time I met my wife, the first time I met the wonderful Cyril Davies, who had a God-given talent. It all happened that one time. That was Alexis for you.'

It was only a matter of weeks for the intervals with the Barber band to become a problem for everybody. Alexis wanted to play for longer and sometimes they did when the crowd wouldn't let them go and it began to spill over into Chris's own set. Art was at rehearsals one day at the Marquee. 'Cyril and Alexis said that we have to find our own club instead of doing intervals. Anybody got any ideas? Now I already knew about the Ealing Club from when I was at Ealing Art School. It was a trad-jazz place, underneath the ABC tearoom opposite Ealing Broadway Station. It was a drinking club in the afternoon, but jazz in the evening. The musicians called it the Moist Hoist because of all the condensation that dripped on them from the street pavement lights above. The bands would put a tarpaulin across the top of the stage to catch the water.'

Alexis said to Art: 'Let's go and have a look at it.' Art had a motorcycle and sidecar, so 'I took Cyril in the sidecar, who did the whole journey standing up with Alexis in the back and we went down there. They had a chat with the guy, had a look around and the deal was no rent, we took the door and he took the booze. And that's how the Ealing Club was born.'

7

RED, WHITE AND BLUES

When Keith Richard bumped into Mick Jagger on a train bound for Sidcup in Kent, they were both nineteen years old and hadn't seen each other since primary school. Keith was enrolled at Sidcup Art College, Mick at the London School of Economics. They discovered a shared interest in blues and R&B. Mick had a band, Little Boy Blue and the Blue Boys, and a mouth-watering collection of import albums under his arm bearing the talismanic names of Chuck Berry and Little Walter. Keith was Dartford's own guitar-slinger with attitude; by the time he got off the train, a get-together had been arranged.

A friend introduced Eric Burdon to the music of Gene Vincent, Johnny Burnette, Chuck Berry and Little Richard. At a local jazz club in Newcastle, Eric was called up to sing with Mighty Joe Young's Jazz Band. They took off on Count Basie, Joe Turner and Jimmy Witherspoon, and the crowd loved it. Eric hitched all the way to Paris to hear Ray Charles; when he first heard the name Alexis Korner, 'I didn't know if it was a name or a place.'

Another art-school drop-out was slumming around Kingston in south-west London, missing the last train home from Waterloo and sleeping on the platform. Soaking up blues from records bought at Dobell's in Charing Cross Road, he played constantly, until this lost soul, who lurked alone on the edge of the playground knowing he was different, became Eric Clapton.

Only sixteen years old but already impossibly tall, 'Long' John Baldry moved around the Soho club scene, singing at Ewan McColl's Ballad and Blues Club, the Skiffle Cellar, the Gyre and Gimble and the Roundhouse, where in 1957 he met Alexis and Cyril. Everybody knew he was exceptional; James Moyes believed he was as good a singer as Davy Graham was a guitarist: 'John had a gift to imitate vocally anything he heard. He had this magic effect on a room full of people, he'd produce these spooky sounds like they were coming off an Alan Lomax field recording, but then he used to take the piss out of himself afterwards and camp it up.'

Although they were great trad jazz fans, it was Muddy Waters rather than trad jazz that brought Brian Jones and Richard Hattrell together. Richard was the local blues buff and during the interval of a Kenny Ball gig at the Cheltenham Rotunda, Brian approached Richard and asked him for a list of Muddy Waters recordings. Richard obliged and back came Brian wanting to know all about Elmore James.

Brian and Richard were trapped by the stifling respectability of Cheltenham, a town steeped in shire-county conservatism. Brian had done his best to ruffle feathers; he led a rebellion at school against the prefects, got his fourteen-year-old girlfriend pregnant, dropped out of school, hung around coffee bars, worked on the buses and flexed his short but strong body as a lifeguard, piling outrage upon outrage for his bewildered parents. He played in local jazz groups and rock 'n' roll bands, both on guitar and on sax, and found a friend and deep admirer in Richard Hattrell. Richard's alienation had entirely different roots. A fragile, sensitive soul, he lost himself in music to escape from the crushing expectations of his overbearing father, a former Army colonel.

When their 'stay out till all hours' lifestyle got too much for their families, Richard and Brian shared a flat at 73 Prestbury Road in Cheltenham, running 'rent parties' to keep themselves solvent, making money both from the entrance fee and from taking the empties back to the off-licence. According to Richard, they persuaded Muddy Waters, Sonny Terry, Brownie McGhee and others to come by and play for a drink.

The Chris Barber band with Alexis played Cheltenham Town Hall in the autumn of 1961. When Chris announced to the audience a set by Alexis Korner, only Richard and Brian cheered; they knew of Alexis from his radio broadcasts and interviews with top blues and jazz stars – nobody else in the hall had a clue who he was. After the concert they went backstage and introduced themselves. Alexis told them about getting a blues scene together in London. They went down regularly to

London until Brian decided that his last gasp at pleasing his parents by becoming an architect just wasn't working out, and he left home for good. Alexis had always promised a floor to sleep on if he came, and proved as good as his word.

By the time Paul Jones prematurely left Oxford University in June 1961, he had already attempted R&B with his own band, Thunder Odin's Big Secret, a jazz line-up trying to do Ray Charles and Jimmy Witherspoon. Brian Jones, roaming the country like a gypsy once he'd left home, happened to catch Paul's band in Oxford. They sat and talked about this blues thing. 'I was amazed,' says Paul, 'that anybody else was into it. I thought I was the only one.'

Keith, Mick, Brian, Eric, John Baldry and Paul Jones were part of the advance guard of the British blues boom, brought up on a mixture of rock 'n' roll and R&B, rather than trad and bebop. Although most of these musicians rapidly took R&B down a commercial route, the sweet crooners and pop singers of the fifties held nothing for them.

Through articles written by Alexis and others, radio interviews with visiting blues musicians and the books by Sam Charters, Paul Oliver and so on, they certainly knew more about the history than the first, even smaller group of fans. Eric Burdon, at school in sight of the Newcastle shipyards, soaked up just as much as semi-detached suburban Mick Jagger. But they didn't carry the purist flag quite so high, they weren't necessarily into the cult of authenticity wedded to a political ethos of brotherhood with the oppressed black community in America. Certainly hipster chic and the love affair with black America continued unabated. Few of this crowd would have heard of Jack Kerouac – he was more for the beatnik poets and jazz freaks. Yet they would have heartily endorsed Kerouac's dream of being black, 'feeling that the best the white world had to offer me was not enough ecstasy for me, not enough life, joy, kicks, darkness, music, not enough night'.

Chuck Berry's lyrics put the workaday experience of young people into popular music for the first time – driving to school, problems with teachers, fickle girlfriends. The new breed picked up on the possibilities of personal expression in rock 'n' roll, but also bought into the universal themes expressed in the blues. One was obviously sex, not simply the implications of rock 'n' roll, let alone the syrupy love songs of pop, but the blow-by-blow *Karma Sutra* lyrics of both country and urban blues, with no laundering of intent. Mick Jagger heard the blues as 'very direct, it didn't beat about the bush, didn't have the "prettiness" of pop of that period, it spoke from a different depth'.

Another persistent theme was alienation, the world of the outsider, the misfit. Because of their love affair with the 'Devil's Music', the bluesmen were often wanderers of the waste in their own land; jumping trains, drinking, womanizing, and spending time in jail for crimes of violence. Much of what the blues singers expressed was simply their own personal sense of 'otherness' as much as social commentary.

Eric Clapton, quoted in Chris Sandford's biography *Edge of Darkness* (Gollancz, 1994), offers one of the few insights into what the blues actually meant for a white boy, beyond the simple how and when of discovery. 'I felt through my youth that my back was against the wall and that the only way to survive was with dignity, pride and courage. I heard that in certain forms of music and I heard it most of all in the blues, because it was always an individual. It was one man and his guitar versus the world. It wasn't a company or a band or a group. When it came down to it, it was one guy who was completely alone and had no options, no alternatives other than just to sing and play to ease his pains. And that echoed what I felt.'

The music they all came looking for when they saw the advert in *New Musical Express* announcing a gig by a British blues band was exciting, urgent, loud – a glorious secret shared only by the lucky few. And smack in the middle, standing on the stage of the Ealing Club on St Patrick's Night, 17 March, 1962, with cigar, shaggy black hair, tartan trousers, swarthy features, sweat rag round his head, almost looking black himself, was Alexis, the bridge between two worlds.

Going down the stairs into the club, the first thing Keith Richard recalls hearing is: 'Alexis calling, "Dooji Wooji".' He was sitting playing with Cyril, Keith Scott, Charlie, Andy Hoogenboom and Art. What struck me was the beat of the drums, before you saw the band you heard it. And visually there was Alexis looking very exotic. The club was packed, which impressed me; we thought we were the only ones into it. There was a bar, lots of girls, we had a great time and we started to go there regularly. The second or third time we went, Alexis said, "There's somebody here who plays slide guitar like Elmore James and his name is Brian Jones." And there's this little blond kid sitting on Alexis' stool playing Alexis' guitar.'

The jockeying for position among the singers was intense. Desperate for a chance to play, blues wannabes dispatched tapes to 'the Man'; Mick sent a tape of Little Boy Blue and the Blue Boys slaughtering 'Reelin'' and Rockin', 'Bright Lights Big City' and 'Around and Around'. After their conversation in Oxford, Brian Jones and Paul Jones made a tape with Ben Palmer on piano, who later played with Eric Clapton and Tom McGuinness in the Roosters. Alexis never said anything about either tape when he met the individuals concerned, although pianist and Stones founder-member Ian Stewart was heard to remark that Brian's tape was 'a bit grim'.

Eric Burdon, in his autobiography *I Used To Be An Animal, But I'm Alright Now* (Faber, 1985), recalled that he was eager for a chance. 'I got up enough courage during the interval to walk up to Alexis, who was leaning against the bar, and tell him I had hitch-hiked all the way down from Newcastle to see the band. He was quite pleased at this. I asked if there was a possibility of singing with him. We discussed some songs I could try, and he put his arm around my shoulder then wandered off towards the stage to begin the second set.

'I stood in the front row clutching a beer, anxiously waiting to be beckoned on stage. Standing next to me was a tall, skinny, short-haired full-mouthed schoolboy singing along with the music and moving in time with the rhythm. Jam-time came around. We both jumped up on stage.

'Alexis was diplomatic. "How about you two singing together?" Alexis pushed his glasses back, as the sweat poured down onto the rag tied around his forehead. The audience yelled and screamed, "Come on, let's go. Get it on!"

' "Do you know, 'I Ain't Got You'?" I asked.

' "Sure," said the buck-toothed youngster next to me on the stage. "The Billy Boy Arnold thing? Sure I know it."

'Alexis nodded. "By the way, meet Mick, Mick Jagger. This is Eric Burdon from Newcastle." '

One hallmark of Alexis' character which so many have commented on was a genuine desire to see young people fulfil their musical potential, invariably in the face of parental protest that being a musician was not a real job. He created an environment both at Ealing and in his own home where blues became as much a refuge for the dispossessed, the misfits and the rebels as Finchden had been; an environment where the music could perhaps speak to a different kind of deprivation. Alexis was a missionary for George Lyward's belief that some needed 'permission' to be their own person. And, like Lyward, he achieved this through a benign form of personality cult, a need to feel at the centre of a universe, however small that might be.

Bobbie too played her part, a well of calm in the eye of the music-business storm in which so many eager, but gullible young men got caught up during the sixties. 'We had a family and we lived in central London. It's all right going round to someone's "pad", but if they haven't got any bread and they've run out of milk, there's something to be said for going round to a place where they've got all these things. And there was always somebody in for these young men far from home.'

The Burnham Court flat in Moscow Road became a drop-in centre for young musicians who did their tour of duty on the Korners' sofa. When Brian Jones worked in the carpet department at Whiteley's department store, in nearby Queensway, he was often round for tea. John Baldry recalls 'the Sunday-afternoon ritual of rich fruit cake with Malmsey wine'. Charlie Watts fell in love with what most people coming from the provinces or suburban London felt was the Korners' lifestyle – bohemian yet comforting. 'We were very young and didn't bother about things or houses or we lived with our parents. But they had "the pad" with the iguana and in the hallway they had this old cigarette machine. Bobbie was Portobello Road market, that was her. And if you went into Charles Fox's room, the walls were full of records. And the hip thing was to have them going round the floor as well. All the records had been sent in by record companies and I thought it was the hippest thing in the world. The whole Alexis set-up was very glamorous to me, something I really wanted to be a part of whether it was musicians, painters or whatever.'

Coming from an artistic background herself, Anthea Joseph recalls that her eyes popped as she walked around their flat. 'You'd go round the walls and say, "Hey, wait a minute, that's a Chagall" and [there were] first editions of practically everything you could think of.'

James Moyes was one of the first of many to regard the Korners as surrogate parents. 'What I got from spending time with them was at least I could ask the questions even if I had an excruciating time with the answers. And there was always something very alternative about Alexis. It was one of the things that I found attractive about the family. Beside music, I was interested in painting and they were both very well informed. Their experience of life was very rich and cosmopolitan.'

★   ★   ★

Almost as soon as Blues Incorporated was underway, the vision changed. Or rather Alexis became more explicit about what kind of band he had in mind. Cyril's idea was a straightforward, no-nonsense recreation of the 1956 Muddy Waters Band, and for the first few sessions at the Ealing Club that's what they delivered. But on the first night, they also played Duke Ellington's 'Dooji Wooji', which should have rung alarm bells with Cyril.

One night Alexis was at the Troubadour, attempting to sit in and play blues guitar with a bunch of bebop musicians who did their level best to freeze him out. Impervious to cold glances and bad vibes, Alexis outlasted them all. At the end, he introduced himself to the only sax player left, Dick Heckstall-Smith. Phone numbers were exchanged and they parted company.

A few weeks later Alexis invited Dick to rehearsals at the Roundhouse. In his autobiography, *The Safest Place In The World*, Dick tried to answer the question of why he moved from the modern jazz scene, where he had started out in the mid fifties, to blues and R&B. The quick answer might have been money, except that in the spring of 1962, there was virtually nothing to be made from playing blues in England. Dick explained it like this: 'The kind of jazz I like – the kind of music I like – is strong, pushy, forward, full blooded, free of self-imposed restrictions. It takes risks. It is not in the least afraid. It battles its way through to expression. It is full of mistakes, but couldn't care a jot about them because it knows that mistakes are its life-blood . . . It shows no mercy for half measures. It doesn't care about good taste. But this is not to say it can't be beautiful. Its beauty is that of strength triumphing over ugliness.'

He felt there was just too much 'good taste' on the British jazz scene, everyone sitting quietly and assessing the music instead of having a good time. 'I found what I was missing in Blues Incorporated and its audiences.'

Eric Burdon expresses a similar view: 'Music in action is taking a band on the stage, calling the key and taking off without a detailed expectation of what is going to happen, but knowing that the musicians are good enough to carry it off.'

With Alexis' vision of Blues Inc, music would be open to chance, lots of gaps to allow for something that might turn out exceptionally bad, but something else that was brilliant. This meant that firstly, Alexis was not going to allow any rigidity, such as sticking to a particular formula, even if it was Muddy Waters. Secondly, he knew he needed the best musicians around him – as Eric Burdon said, only the best can make this fluid policy work, and Alexis also needed to feed from the best to improve his own playing.

But he had to contend with Cyril and if there was one thing Cyril could not abide it was saxophones. Dick turned up for rehearsals as arranged – he was first there. The rest drifted in and then Cyril arrived: 'ignoring the good-natured shouts of "Hello, Cyril!" he made his way straight to the decrepit upright piano in the corner of the room and upended his briefcase over the top of it. An enormous number of harmonicas flowed out, rather like a liquid, and he cursed roundly and obscenely.' And the object of his cursing was the presence of a sax in the room; Dick took it personally at first, but he soon realized that Cyril 'liked my playing – he just didn't like what it was played on'.

Meanwhile word had got back to Harold Pendleton at the Marquee about the success of the Ealing Club. He already knew the band was popular, because of the Wednesday-night spots Alexis had done with the Barber band. He went down to see for himself and offered Alexis Thursday nights – impossible to fill the club then as it was just before pay day.

The Ealing Club was packed every Saturday night, fans paying a pound just to get in and see the last number. On the first night at the Marquee, 3 May 1962, the whole of the Ealing Club turned up, about a tenth of what the Marquee could hold, but within weeks the joint was jumping. Alexis did quite nicely because of the deal he'd struck with Harold to take on the worst night of the week. The people turned up for the music, certainly, but the fortuitous switch to more Thursday pay-days helped audience figures enormously.

The parade of eager young singers was causing problems for Art Wood, supposedly the band's lead vocalist. Alexis had been very helpful to Art. 'He used to come round my house and bring me the songs to sing for the next night and we'd have a rehearsal, just me and Alexis, and he'd tell me how to sing something – on certain words. One of the songs was "I Feel So Good". I'd sing the way I'd normally do it and he said, "NO!" And he showed me how to sing it in a completely different way and then I'd understand what he was getting at. He was a great teacher to us up-and-coming "trying to be nasty" blues singers.

'But in the end I got blown out. One night I was getting less and less singing time. Alexis said to me, "Art, Cyril's told me you're not nasty enough to be a blues singer." "What do I have to do to be nasty?" "He said you've got to have that edge and bit of raw spitefulness about you which you haven't got." '

When it came to encouraging raw talent, Cyril was not so accommodating. Left to him, the history of British rock might have been quite different. Art Wood watched him in action. 'If you were a guitar player or a drummer, you might get a couple of numbers, if you can't sing, "get stuffed" and if you wanted to play harmonica, "fuck off". Mick Jagger asked him once how to bend notes. "Get a pair of fuckin' pliers." '

Cyril was no less intolerant of the audience, especially anybody who put their feet on the stage when he was playing, let alone clamber up beside him. Art recalls: 'One night at the Marquee a bloke tried to get on stage and get the mike off Cyril and Cyril said, "I wouldn't do that if I were you." The bloke kept on going, "Come on everybody, let's have a sing-song." Cyril said, "Don't do that" and took the mike off him. The bloke jumped on Cyril's back and Cyril just got hold of him and threw him into the crowd.'

Since the late sixties bands have gone on tour to promote new albums. But during the early part of the decade records tended to support live performance. Alexis regarded records as aural calling-cards that you sent off to the promoters to get the next gig. As Blues Incorporated had never recorded before and was not heard on radio, the marketing ploy was to set the recording in a live context. Therefore the album recorded in June 1962 and released in November that year, when the band's popularity was at its height, was called *R&B from the Marquee* even though it was recorded at Decca's West Hampstead studios.

Unlike most band leaders, Alexis was always willing to let young musicians come up on stage for a jam. But his grace and favour understandably dried up when it came to studio work. For recording the all-important first album, Alexis needed seasoned professional musicians – and these had to be jazz musicians: there was nobody else. Alexis called Chris Barber's drummer, Graham Burbidge, who had taken lessons in the finer arts of blues drumming from Muddy Waters's drummer, Francis Clay. 'Alexis asked me to do the session for the album because in his exact words he didn't think Charlie was "up to it".' Charlie himself admits: 'Cyril taught me Chicago blues, but I didn't really understand it until I started to play with Keith Richard.'

Andy Hoogenboom's place was taken by John Dankworth's bassist, Spike Heatley, who, Graham says, 'made me more jazzy where I would have been more stark, angular and bluesy. But Spike was playing this wonderful modern, rolling bass and on the album I was caught between two stools.'

Keith Scott had been replaced on piano by Alexis' close friend Dave Stevens. But Dave was a full-time chartered accountant and couldn't get away for the sessions, and anyway Keith was by far the more experienced player, so Alexis called him back for the recording. In fact Keith and Dave interchanged over the summer until Johnny Parker came in on piano at the end of August. According to John Baldry, he had Mick Jagger's flu to thank for being the lead vocalist alongside Cyril. Apparently Keith Scott had a great voice likened by Art Wood to Hoagy Carmichael, but Keith 'would only sing in rehearsal'.

Charles Fox wrote about the recording session for *Jazz News*. The band started at ten a.m. on what turned out to be a hot June day, and by the time Charles turned up they had five tracks in the can. 'A recording session demands patience even more than genius. First you spend what seems like hours getting a good balance. Often it means splitting musicians up, putting some on their own behind screens, destroying the physical unity of the group. Here, however, everybody is in touch.

'Only Keith Scott, the pianist, has any troubles. He has to turn his head right round to see when the singer stops – for there's no amplification inside the studio.

'Cyril Davies makes the platform beneath him shudder and shake as he plays harmonica, then sings "I've Got My Mojo Working". Around another microphone sit Long John Baldry, Dick Heckstall-Smith and on-looking guitarist Jim Sullivan exchanging ginger biscuits and shouting responses.

'On this title the bass guitar is being used, played by Teddy Wadmore. The group's regular bassist Spike Heatley, seizes the chance to catch forty winks in a corner.

'A snatch of conversation filters from the control room:

' "Well, what the hell is a Mojo, anyway?"

'Halfway through the afternoon they all troop off to the canteen for tea.

'The last stretch is always the toughest. Bottles get raised slightly more often. Dick Heckstall-Smith crouches over his tenor sax, a cross between Sonny Rollins and the eagle outside the American Embassy. Alexis Korner sits placidly, guitar resting on his tartan trousers ("The pattern," he insists, "was chosen to blend with our cat's fur").

'Surrealism creeps into most human activities. This time it enters during the third "take" of "Finkle's Cafe", just as the tenor sax and guitar are swapping phrases. Despite the glowing red light, the studio door opens and in walks a little girl dressed in grey. It's like Alice arriving at the Mad Hatter's Tea Party.

'The end, of course, like most finales, has a quality of anti-climax. Yet fifteen titles – good for one day, more than enough for an LP – have been put on tape. Now for the handing out of money, the packing up of instruments, the telephoning for taxis.

'Jack Good, the A&R man, a City-type bowler jammed on his Byronic head, looses his last shaft of repartee, then strides out of the control room. Drums are trundled, bottles are discarded. Nobody can quite believe that outside it's still 73 in the shade.'

As a Cambridge graduate, Dick Heckstall-Smith retained a number of contacts in the university. In late June, Dick was booked for a modern jazz gig in Cambridge as part of the May Ball celebration. With no line-up of his own, he used trumpeter Bert Courtley's band plus a red-headed drummer called Peter 'Ginger' Baker. Dick played with Ginger at every opportunity; he was loud, uncompromising and a disciple of the legendary Phil Seamen. He had come up through the London jazz circuit, having been sacked by half the band leaders for arguing and ridiculed by the other half for aping Seamen. He even looked like him.

At the end of the first set, a wee Scots lad came up, said he played bass and asked to sit in. He refused to accept the inevitable brush-off and returned later only to rip through every single evil time change that Dick and Ginger could come up with to embarrass him. Jack Bruce had led an even more peripatetic life than Alexis: twelve primary schools in Scotland, Canada and America, and eventually back home to the Royal Scottish Academy to study music. Six months was all he could take; by the age of seventeen, in 1960, he was playing the intervals with the Freddie Riley Trio in Glasgow. He went to Italy with a band from Coventry and then a place was found for him in Jim McHarg's Scotsville Jazz Band. To create the place, the musicians obligingly sacked the bass player – Jim McHarg. They were in Cambridge when Jack happened to wander into a cellar club.

Dick was determined to get Jack into Blues Incorporated, and Alexis agreed. Jack, however, was unimpressed when he caught the band at the Marquee. 'I didn't know anything about blues really at that time and it sounded to me like rock 'n' roll.' But Jack signed up – he was in London to make it as a professional musician and at that stage in your career you don't turn down work.

Dick was also instrumental in signing up Ronnie Jones, a black-American gospel singer stationed with the USAF in England. 'Alexis really wanted me to sing in the band,' recalls Jones. 'He told me he would pay my rail fare from the base and give me £3 each time so that I didn't have to spend my Air Force pay. Shortly after I started the money went up to £5.' Which meant he did better than some of the others. Ronnie laughs when he recalls that 'we did a gig in Birmingham where I got half a crown, but Jack got a quid because he was a professional'.

The only permanent singer up to that point had been John Baldry. Art Wood left early on, while Mick, Eric Burdon, Paul Jones were only occasional guests; others, like Rod Stewart and Eric Clapton, were even more fleeting. Dick remembers Eric as 'this pale, sulky kid' who came on stage with a mike and no guitar, sang a couple of songs and fled.

It didn't take Mick long to realize that although Blues Inc were playing blues, it wasn't the sort of blues he and Keith had in mind, 'apart from when Cyril played the harmonica. A lot of it didn't sound like blues to me, a lot of free form with solos.' Talking about the serried ranks of singers lining up by the side of the stage, he says: 'we'd all sing the same bloody songs; we'd all have a turn singing "Got My Mojo Working" or whatever it was. It was the Muddy Waters that went down best. When Keith and I got up and did our two numbers, the crowd went bananas – it was quite obvious they liked that kind of music.'

Alexis – and even more so Cyril – may well have taken the view that Mick's very visual performance hogged just a little too much of the limelight. 'I couldn't get a regular gig with the only blues band in the country,' Mick says. 'He didn't really want a singer who would take over the front line. It was like the old big bands where you had the singer who would come up and croon a couple of numbers and then the "real thing" would happen and the band leader would take over.'

Nor was Alexis really in step with Mick and Keith musically. 'When we used to do our little Chuck Berry bit, Keith would get up and plug his guitar in and we'd go leaping in. I don't think Alexis could keep up with this because after a couple of weeks, just as we got up there, he'd go "bap" with his thumb pick on the bottom string and break it on purpose. "You just carry on, cock." He did this on a couple of occasions so we knew it was a fake.' However, Alexis frequently broke strings because he hammered so hard trying to increase volume.

The crunch for Mick came with Blues Inc's radio début on *Jazz Club*, Thursday 12 July 1962. This coincided with the Thursday-night residency at the Marquee. To keep it open for Alexis, John Baldry put a band together. This left Alexis needing a vocalist for the radio show and rather than choose Mick, he called up Art Wood. Alexis claimed he wanted Mick as well, but that the BBC would not pay for an extra vocalist. The final contract read: 'Forty pounds, seven shillings for the services of six musicians including Arthur Wood as vocalist and the personal appearance of Alexis Korner as leader.' Mick heard about the radio date; in his Stones biography Philip Norman suggests that Mick didn't mind not going on the BBC, but talking to Mick now, over thirty years later, one senses a residue of bitterness: 'The BBC was such a big thing in those days, getting on the BBC was like going to heaven. "God they've got the BBC – am I gonna go?" And of course, I didn't get to go. Sometimes with Alexis it was like playing 12th man.' It transpired that Art didn't do the session either. In the end the vocals were shared by Alexis and Cyril.

Instead Alexis suggested to Harold Pendleton that he should allow the new band formed by Brian, Mick and Keith to do the interval for John Baldry – not Little Boy Blue and the Blue Boys, but the Rolling Stones. 'I hope they don't think we're a rock 'n' roll band,' Mick told *Jazz News*. Mick says he never knew where he was with Alexis; one minute he was not giving Mick, Keith and Brian a chance to play the Blues Inc intervals as much as they wanted and edging Mick out of a broadcast; the next he was talking them up and arranging showcase gigs.

Brian Jones had advertised in *Jazz News* inviting musicians to come for an audition at the Bricklayers' Arms in Soho. Geoff Bradford showed up, so did a Scots pianist called Ian Stewart, Mick and Keith and Dick Taylor, a bass-player friend of Keith's. Geoff soon fell out with Keith and left, and there was no drummer. Brian chose the name and brought in drummer Mick Avory to fill in for the night. Dick Taylor recalled that on the very first night of the band's history, 'before we'd played a note we could feel the hostility'. Not that the press reception for Blues Inc was much better; *Melody Maker* commented tersely: 'Rather a messy BBC "Jazz Club" debut for Alexis Korner's Blues Inc last Thursday with very suspect tuning and internal balance.'

Charlie Watts had been the regular drummer for live gigs, but he had a good job in advertising and was loath to give it up to turn professional; nor, in his eternally self-effacing way, did he think he was much good. He also knew that Dick wanted Ginger in the band. Ginger came down to the Marquee one Thursday night and sat in. From that moment Charlie was actively encouraging Alexis to keep Ginger. 'When we'd finished playing we used to see the Johnny Burch Octet with Dick, Graham Bond, Ginger and Jack. Ginger had this incredible sound and you could hear this thing that Jack and Ginger had between them – and I didn't want to get in the way of that.' By the end of July, Ginger was in the band and forging what became a tempestuous relationship with Jack Bruce, and rock's most famous rhythm partnership.

As far as Cyril was concerned, with the arrival first of Dick and now Ginger his vision of the band was being diluted. Cyril made it pretty clear to Ginger that 'he didn't want a jazz player coming in, but after the first rehearsal at the Marquee, he came up to me afterwards and said, "I've got to be honest, I didn't want you in the band, but hearing you play, fuckin' welcome." ' From Dick, Jack and Ginger's point of view, they were moving both to a freer musical policy under Alexis than was possible in modern jazz and to a new situation that had the makings of a good regular gig. It was these musicians who eventually formed the other wing of the 'blues boom' which majored on 'underground' musical virtuosity rather than R&B-based pop.

Alexis' upper-class connections to the likes of Gerald Lascelles helped secure for the band a couple of society gigs, the first of which, in July 1962, was given by the Marquis and Marchioness of Londonderry. Guest of honour on his way back from a tour of Russia was Benny Goodman. Dave Stevens was on piano, having taken over from Keith Scott in early summer. Ronnie Jones was the singer, and remembers: 'The band set up next to the main table and sitting at the head was a little white-haired man wearing glasses. As usual we were separated from the guests and given the customary bottle of spirits to consume with our food. I had already got through a quarter of my bottle of whisky and having a really good time when during a song a chap sauntered up to me and said, "Excuse me, Mr Jones, would you mind if Mr Goodman joins in with the band? He thinks a great deal of your singing and he likes the way Mr Korner plays." I told him I wasn't the band leader – I had no idea who "Mr Goodman" was at that time – so while we were in the middle of a song I referred the request to Alexis, who was sitting on the stool next to me. Dave Stevens whispered, "Yeah!!", I whispered into Alexis' ear and he said, "Of course." The chap went back to the table and I carried on singing. Then from under the table appeared a small black suitcase – I was by now half way through my bottle of whisky but none the wiser as to what was going on – and out from the case popped a clarinet. As the little white-haired man was putting the clarinet together, Alexis said to me, "Ronnie, don't you recognize Benny Goodman?" At that point I lost all touch with reality. I was dumbstruck, and I when I tried to sing the words they just wouldn't come out. During the instrumental part of a song Benny Goodman approached me, shook my hand and said, "You are a very great singer, what are you going to do next?" I replied, "Well, er . . . why don't you er umm why don't you ask Alexis?" Alexis just asked me to sing and the band would make up something to go with it. But I told him to do it without me because I was too gobsmacked to do anything.'

The following month it was the turn of Baron Rothschild to engage Britain's only professional blues band. Ronnie Jones trawls through the alcoholic haze surrounding the gig to recall what happened. 'The guest of honour was Prince Philip. The comedian Jimmy Edwards was there as the "court jester". He'd got his hands on a hunting horn and decided to entertain the guests. The next thing we knew he'd jumped up on the stage and decided he was going to join in with the band. We carried on, Alexis smiled and muttered, "Oh God, there's no way I can tell him to get off the stage." We tried to ignore him.

'Behind me Ginger was playing away and he leaned across his drum kit and said, "Ronnie, tell him to piss off." I turned to Ginger, shrugged my shoulders: what can I do? We'd almost got to the end of the song when, still playing in tempo, Ginger stood up and shouted, "Fuck off, bugger!" There was a huge hush, with only the band still trying to play because we were all laughing our heads off. I could no longer sing, and Alexis nearly swallowed his guitar. Dave Stevens was bent over his piano almost having a stroke, he was laughing so hard. Prince Philip was standing about twenty yards away turning two or three different colours. Dick had to turn and face Ginger while he was playing to stop himself laughing straight in the Prince's face. Jimmy Edwards just disappeared and didn't return to the bandstand at any point during the rest of the evening.'

Come the interval and the band were shuffled off to a side room where they were each given a bottle of spirits and something to eat. Cyril disappeared, while Ronnie Jones wandered back into the main

dining room. 'There were people standing around next to the piano.
I had no idea what was going on, so I politely edged myself across the
room and to my amazement, sitting in the middle of the floor with a
vase of flowers upside down on his head and water running down his
shirt and trousers, well drunk, playing the harmonica, was our Cyril.'

Many of the musicians were hard drinkers. Playing up to their 'outsider'
image, dealing with boredom on the road and the insecurity of the job all
contributed, as well as notions of drink and drug as aids to creativity. Cyril
had another reason. He'd had an attack of pleurisy which weakened his
heart and he'd been told by the doctors to ease up on his hard lifestyle
of panel-beating and playing. He could not stomach the notion that he
was 'weak' in any sense; not only did he ignore the advice, but took
to drinking even more heavily than usual to blot out his misery.

But coming back that night from the gig, says Ginger: 'Everybody was
out of their tree. We're all slugging from a big bottle of champagne and
got pulled over by the police. Alexis was absolutely wonderful – "Oh
good morning, officer" – and he just chatted us out of it. Everybody
was legless, but Alexis could appear stone-cold sober.'

By the end of August, Blues Incorporated had yet another new
keyboard player, Johnny Parker, completing what was probably Alexis'
finest band, with Jack, Ginger, Dick and Cyril and Ronnie Jones – a
'supergroup' if ever there was one. Johnny and Alexis' connection went
back to Ken Colyer's skiffle group in the early fifties. Johnny had gone on
to make his name with Humphrey Lyttelton and starred on the hit single
'Bad Penny Blues', but 'during the summer of 1962 I was with Monty
Sunshine's band and we'd just finished a big jazz festival. Afterwards
there were money problems which led to a flaming row. Monty was
behaving far too unreasonably for my liking, so when Alexis asked me
to join I had no hesitation in accepting.'

Although their fame was spreading and they had their début on *Saturday
Club* in early September, they weren't working all that often. They had
the Thursday-night gig at the Marquee and a few other odd jobs, but
the club scene was still in the grip of those who thought Alexis was
completely wasting his time. 'At one time I was given a serious lecture
by a record producer who said I was blighting my career with all this
R&B nonsense and suggested I play proper jazz instead.'

For Alexis, there was a positive side to being ignored. 'It meant we
were free to operate in a very innocent way for a long time. We were
shocked one day when Jet Harris wanted to have a blow with Blues Inc

at the Marquee. He came down with his axe, all ready, but before he got on stage, somebody from the management hauled him off. He was told it was not right for his image to be seen playing with an R&B band. This was the first time we'd ever come across anything like this.'

But Alexis had to look further afield for work. He took the band up to Manchester to the Twisted Wheel and the Bodega Club. In the audience one night at the Bodega was a commercial artist working for an advertising agency. His real love though was the jazz he heard from his father's record collection and the blues that was beginning to capture his attention. He had led a college band called the Powerhouse Four, but seeing Blues Inc sparked the revelation that playing the blues in Britain was possible. After the gig, John Mayall got talking with Alexis. He recalls: 'They went out for an Indian curry and I tagged along. I remember being very impressed with London musicians and the way they talked compared with days at the office. It seemed a very glamorous lifestyle to me.'

Blues Inc made so many trips to Manchester that it made economic sense for them to keep a flat there, which they did in the Cheetham Hill district of the city. The band were frequent visitors to John's house, where he lived with his wife, Pam, and their children. Pam remembers: 'I first met Alexis when he came with the band and he had Peggy Phango and the Velvettes as well doing back up. [The Velvettes were a black South African female singing group. Peggy later married Johnny Parker and they are still together.] None of them had any money and me and John had a small house with three small children running about. They stayed at the house one Saturday night. We played on the organ doing "Abide With Me" and "Will The Circle Be Unbroken" – Peggy and Alexis were in tears and everybody was weeping and howling.'

Encouraged by Alexis, John formed his own band, Blues Syndicate, with drummer Hughie Flint, and was further persuaded by Alexis to come to London. He arrived without the rest of the band, who never thought they could make it professionally. John kept the day job because it paid very well, while Alexis helped Pam and the family get established. 'He got John gigs, helped us find a house, got the kids into school. He was the real driving force behind getting the whole family to London.'

For John, Alexis was 'a very important friend who seemed to have massive experience of running bands and the trials and tribulations of musicians, vans breaking down and on all those matters I was in close contact with him. He was a great shoulder to lean on.' Alexis went on to introduce John to various musicians who formed the very fluid early line-ups of the Bluesbreakers (including Davy Graham). When John's first album came out in 1965, Alexis wrote the sleeve-notes.

In October 1962 the press carried a rumour that Alexis was planning to add to the line-up Graham Bond, Don Rendell's sax player who doubled on Hammond organ. This was the last straw for Cyril. A band meeting was called at Moscow Road. To Dick it was clear that Alexis and Cyril had thrashed it all out *in camera* because although the meeting was sombre, it was by no means acrimonious. There was no mention of the replacement for Cyril. As Dick said in his autobiography, Alexis seemed quite unperturbed by the split with Cyril. And when Dick asked who was coming in, ' "Graham Bond," said Alexis ecstatically, breathing out cigar smoke with the smug catlike smile of the bloke in the Panatella ad. He'd already thought the whole bloody thing through.'

Cyril, meanwhile, was planning his new band. He wanted John Baldry on vocals. John's reputation was growing across Europe and during 1962 he spent some time in Germany. Alexis also wanted John to rejoin when he came back, telling him once: 'I'd give my right arm to be able to sing like you.' John says he literally tossed a coin and it came down for Cyril, but though Cyril had 'won', he was very unhappy if John talked to Alexis even socially, which suggests that the split with Alexis was far from amicable. All of which was a bit rough on Alexis, who had paid for John Baldry's flight back from Germany.

Cyril turned to his recent partner, Geoff Bradford. Blues Inc had started other musicians thinking along similar lines. Geoff had got together with another Davies protégé, guitarist and singer Brian Knight (who also worked in Cyril's panel-beating yard) to form Blues by Six with Keith Scott and Charlie Waits (as one early gig poster put it). Geoff eventually joined Cyril, but at the time he preferred to carry on with Blues by Six. With no pool of blues players to call upon and jazz players out of the question, Cyril recruited a bunch of rock 'n' rollers: Screaming Lord Sutch's band the Savages, with pianist Nicky Hopkins, Bernie Watson on guitar and a rhythm section of drummer Carlo Little and Ricky Fensen. Together they became the Cyril Davies All Stars and released a single on Pye, 'Country Line Special'. The record had begun to get some serious airplay, and Cyril followed it up with an excellent version of Robert Johnson's 'Preachin' the Blues'. But it was then that his pleurisy-weakened heart eventually gave out and he died on 7 January 1964 aged only thirty-two.

117

Given what became commercial in the mid to late sixties with the 'British Blues Boom', Cyril was right to move away from jazz and stick tight to the Chicago blues sound. The Stones began their first UK tour the same month Cyril died and with increasing publicity for R&B, Cyril would have flourished. He still commands much affection in the hearts of those like John Baldry, Geoff Bradford and Brian Knight who knew him best. He was often surly and bad-tempered, and rarely known to praise the efforts of young musicians, although this spurred on the likes of Brian Knight. 'Cyril helped me enormously with my playing, but he told me, "You'll never be able to play", which did me good because I thought, sod him, I'll show him.' Cyril was also caught in a strange fantasy world of violence and paranoia where, for example, he once phoned Bobbie Korner at ten-minute intervals from different phone boxes for no apparent reason as if he was being followed.

But despite playing out the life of the hard-nosed, cynical bluesman, he was capable of great acts of individual kindness. One Christmas, when Geoff Bradford was particularly hard up, Cyril bought the biggest turkey he could find for Geoff and his family. He also bought Geoff a guitar, but not just any guitar. 'In the early sixties it was terribly hard to get decent instruments. You'd go down the Charing Cross Road and see an old Fender and there'd be a queue of people standing round it. We were walking past a shop one day and saw this brand-new Telecaster hanging in this shop. I just said what a great guitar it was and Cyril just walked into the shop and bought it for me.'

The album *R&B from the Marquee* was released in November 1962 to mixed reviews. The only reviewing outlet were the jazz publications, *New Musical Express* and *Melody Maker*, catering mainly for British pop tastes of the day and fans of American rock 'n' roll.

Jazz News & Review was enthusiastic. Noting the many personnel changes the band had gone through since the recording back in June, the reviewer thought the album 'practically a historic document' but observed that the band 'made exciting music, and the LP has captured much of the excitement'. *R&B from the Marquee* was a landmark album in the history of British rock. 'I think it is true to say that no sound like this has ever been made by any other British group.'

The reviewer also noted the success with which the album captured the band's raving live performances, 'but listen carefully and you will hear in among the solid beat and the relentless rhythmic drive, all sorts of modern jazz tricks and phrases, particularly from Dick Heckstall-Smith and Korner'. For readers of jazz magazines, to label any music as 'rock 'n' roll' was to condemn it out of existence, but fear not: 'people who accuse R&B of being rock 'n roll just haven't been listening'.

Jazz News & Review was relatively 'liberal' in its music taste, having started an R&B column 'until further notice' just a few weeks before it reviewed the album. The column mentioned Blues Inc at the Marquee, 'Mick Jagger and the Rollin' Stones' playing a residency at the Ealing Club and 'Keith Scott and the Blues Plus Six' (sic) drawing Sunday-afternoon crowds to the Ken Colyer Club in Great Newport Street. There was a wind of change blowing for the trad bands. As *Jazz News and Review's* new column pointed out, Dave Hunt's Rhythm & Blues Band, playing the Richmond Jazz club, 'drew a larger crowd than most visiting "trad" groups'.

Back in the jazz mainstream, *Jazz Journal* was predictably less enthusiastic about Blues Inc's first album. 'It is really very difficult to know what to write about this record,' began the review. 'Within its limitations it is quite interesting, but I fear that all those concerned are battling against impossible odds' – the 'odds' being that they weren't 'American negroes'. This theme dominated the rest of the review. It had never really come up before in the press, because no British band had ever recorded the music nor were there many electric blues records readily available with which to make comparisons. There had been a debate in folk circles about the singers sticking to their own culture, but for all except the most die-hard English folk purists, the songs of Leadbelly, for example, were annexed by every genre whether it was folk, blues or skiffle. Now in this *Jazz Journal* review, published in January 1963, were the beginnings of that tortuous and ultimately pointless debate which is still with us today: Can the white man sing the blues?

R&B was then in its early days; the Stones' first single and the live recording of the Yardbirds with Eric Clapton and Sonny Boy Williamson both came a year after the release of *R&B from the Marquee*, but already Alexis, in his inimitably perverse fashion, was steering the band away from the roots of their support. The gradual addition of modern jazz men and the split with Cyril was noted by *Jazz News* under the heading 'All Mod Cons': 'Notice how the wheel has turned full circle in the R&B world? Alexis Korner's mob Blues Incorporated more or less started life as a spot in Acker Bilk's programme just under a year ago at Ipswich. The musicians were all either ex-trad or direct from the earthy blues part of the jazz spectrum.

'The whole personnel has changed since then, and Alex now has with him none but modernists with the single exception of Johnny Parker. Alexis used to threaten to write a number called "What will the boys down Ronnie's think?" If he goes on acquiring modern players at his present rate, there won't be any of them left down there to think anything.'

The personnel changed and the music was beginning to change as well. The addition of Graham Bond on the Hammond organ brought in the influence of Ray Charles, while Jack Bruce and Dick Heckstall-Smith built on Alexis' already well-developed love affair with the music of Charles Mingus. The next change was one of venue. The press were reporting full houses for the Marquee residency, but then, without warning, Alexis pulled the band out and switched to the Flamingo.

The club started life in the late forties as a jazz spot called the Americana in the basement of the Mapleton Restaurant in Whitcomb Street. In the early fifties certain nights were designated as 'Jazz at the Flamingo' organized by Rik and John Gunnell, who eventually took the whole place over, named it the Flamingo and moved to new premises in Wardour Street.

There had always been a special atmosphere about the Flamingo. In contrast to the Marquee, it catered for a sophisticated older jazz audience, attracting, in particular, large numbers of black American servicemen fans of Ray Charles and Jimmy Smith. The dense clouds of reefer that hit you as you walked in didn't necessarily mellow out a clientele for whom fighting was all part of the evening's entertainment – especially when the 'all-nighters' were on.

As far as Harold Pendleton is concerned, Alexis switched to the Flamingo simply because he was offered more money by the Gunnells, and as a result an already strained relationship snapped. Alexis rationalized the move in musical terms: he wanted to play for the Flamingo audience, not the much younger Marquee crowd, who were on their way home by ten-thirty. Whatever the reason, the move from the Marquee set Alexis on a tangent away from the commercial R&B scene that was lurking around the corner.

8

MONEY HONEY

Alexis' all-embracing definition of blues meant the band could be playing three different styles in one night. When Cyril was there, they'd be doing Chicago blues. Once he'd left they drifted into Basie-type arrangements boosted by the vocals of Ronnie Jones while Graham added a free-form dimension in which Jack and Ginger revelled.

Blues Incorporated were working at peak performance around Christmas 1962 and into 1963; they were the most powerful band on the circuit with as much work as they wanted. Jack and Ginger were constantly trying to outplay each other, with Johnny Parker welding the rhythm together. Dick and Graham were blasting some of the most wailing blues sax anybody had ever heard, a raucous compliment to Ronnie's gutsy blues-soul vocals. Alexis positioned himself calmly as the focal point of the band, allowing people their musical freedom, giving everybody the space to play, an inspiring leader in every sense.

With fiery, intense jazz and blues, mercurial temperaments and heavy work schedules came chemical diversions. As Alexis later said: 'Blues Inc was a band of evil habits, but nobody's evil habit was the same as anybody else's.' Dick was a speed and booze man; he could easily see off a bottle of Teacher's on stage. Ginger was already building up a sizeable heroin habit and Graham was hovering on the edges. Everyone smoked grass, while amphetamines were almost part of the mess kit – and sometimes they had their uses.

It was Christmas 1962 and the band had a full date sheet, when Alexis went down with flu, the musician's nightmare. Sometimes he ducked out of gigs, calling up Geoff Bradford to dep for him while he went off to do a solo spot somewhere else. On more than one occasion Alexis Korner's Blues Incorporated went on stage without Alexis. But he still got paid as the band leader, plus whatever he earned doing another gig or perhaps a radio show. To be fair, it was always his stated intention that the line-up of the band should be totally fluid, which was precisely why he didn't want his name in the band's title.

But during that busy Christmas period there was no crying off. His doctor shot him full of penicillin and every evening Graham helped him to burn out the bug, keeping Alexis well topped up with bourbon and grass. 'Graham really looked after me. Nobody else was much concerned as long as I made the gig and we got paid. Dick was concerned, but didn't do anything. One night I fell flat on my face at the end of the second set. Ginger said, "'Ere, you all right, Alexis?" "Perfectly, Ginger." So he didn't bother any more.'

The biggest tragedy for this line-up is that they never recorded an album. What little they did record is largely buried or lost. Alexis secured a one-album contract for the *R&B from the Marquee* album running from June 1962 to June 1963. But Alexis hated working for Decca; they appeared to have little interest in what was then 'minority' music and did nothing to promote the first album. So in September 1962, although Alexis was still under contract to Decca, he took the band to EMI's Abbey Road studio for a demo session in search of a new deal. They recorded 'Dooji Wooji', 'Stormy Monday', 'Roberta', 'Sugar Man' and 'Kansas City'. Nothing was ever released and the tapes are long gone. This drove Alexis back to Decca; if he wanted a deal with a 'major', there were precious few options.

On Thursday 3 January 1963, after a Flamingo all-nighter, the band, plus around fifty fans, headed for Decca's studios in West Hampstead. Between one-fifteen a.m. and five a.m. they recorded several titles in the hope that Decca might find a single to release. Only two tracks ever surfaced: 'Night Time Is The Right Time', which Decca rejected because they thought Graham's alto-sax solo was too wayward, and 'Early In The Morning', based on an old Southern US work song. Both turned up on a 1964 compilation album called *Rhythm & Blues*. Among the other tracks they laid down that night were 'The Organiser', dedicated to Bobbie, 'Philboyd Sturge ('an imaginary breakfast food,' said Alexis), 'Everyday I Have The Blues' and 'Lonely Am I'. There were tapes of these and other tracks in limited circulation, so they almost certainly exist somewhere.

Johnny Parker recalls one gig in Bristol during January which encapsulated why the rise of R&B was the writing on the wall for trad jazz. 'We played the Chinese Jazz Club and shared the bill with Monty Sunshine. We went on first and did our set and when Monty went on afterwards it just sounded so puny and pathetic and the crowd just drifted away. We had the excitement and Monty was just doing the same as everybody else at the time. Trad jazz stuff with a banjo and no piano. There was no competition at all. We just carved them into little pieces.'

On 23 February they played the Wooden Bridge Hotel in Guildford, finishing at eleven p.m. Then they dashed back to London for the Flamingo all-nighter until seven a.m. That afternoon they boarded a coach for Exeter to play the University Rag Ball. After that it was back to London for the Flamingo, then Reading, followed by Windsor, Manchester, Coventry, Reading again and Swindon. The band weren't exactly idle, but they weren't all that well paid either, receiving just a few pounds per man.

Graham Bond was a big man who blew a huge, shouting alto sax, rent the air with soulful vocals and dominated the stage with his Hammond organ. Unfortunately, Alexis had been having trouble accommodating the organ in the line-up during the main sets, so he fell in with Graham's idea of having an interval spot to showcase the Hammond, backed by Jack and Ginger.

But like Alexis before him, Graham had ideas beyond playing interval sets for somebody else. He arranged a gig in Manchester just for the trio of him, Jack and Ginger. They earned £70 between them and says Jack: 'We thought we'd won the pools.' This was all Graham needed to strike out on his own.

Ginger, then a registered heroin addict, tells how the split happened. 'It was a rehearsal at the Flamingo. I'd just picked up my scripts and gone straight into the karzy and when I came out Jack had just arrived. Graham was talking to Alexis on the stage and then he came up to me and Jack and said, "We've left the band." I was astounded, I didn't feel in any way that I'd come to the end with Alexis. I was pretty stoned and Graham was the salesman all the time. Alexis came up and said, "It's really good you're doing this thing with Graham and I wish you the best of luck" and all that. It was a bit difficult to turn round and say, "Well, I don't really want to leave the band, you know."

'It was Alexis being a sweet guy that finished the band. If he'd turned round to Graham and said, "No fuckin' way are you taking my band away" it would have carried on and probably have been enormously successful, because it was going that way. Alexis was too nice, nothing ever fazed him and he was always incredibly pleasant.'

In fact, although he never showed it, Alexis was very cut up over the way the heart of his band just deserted him. He never took separation easily and it would be no exaggeration to say that he felt betrayed – especially by Jack Bruce. Despite being the father of two 'real' sons, he did feel that Jack too was his son, something of a protégé to whom he'd given 'the big break'. Also, Jack was an extremely talented musician and Alexis hated to lose that skill from the band. But it was the psychological aspect of the split that was more important to Alexis and their relationship was never the same again.

Jack had asked Dick if he wanted to join them as well. Dick declined, so Graham added a young guitarist from Georgie Fame's band, John McLaughlin. Whatever Alexis might have felt about losing the core of his band, he didn't seem to miss a beat in finding replacements. To play alongside Johnny Parker in the rhythm section, he recruited Phil Seamen, Ginger's mentor and arguably the best jazz drummer Britain ever produced. Parker found Phil 'a revelation. It was quite an eye-opener to play with a drummer of that standard. He was incredible and I learnt a lot about playing rhythmically. Sometimes, coming back from wherever we'd been, he'd give someone a box of matches to shake and someone else two coins to tap together and we'd get a bit of a rhythm going. Then he'd do something on top of it, the whole thing would blend together and we'd spend half an hour just doing that.'

On bass Alexis brought in Chris Thompson, described by Dick as 'magnificently talented . . . [his] intelligence shone everywhere'. Johnny Parker was less impressed: 'We never did find a decent replacement for Jack. After he had left we tried various bass players, but they were all really lightweight jazz types, none of them were used regularly and they certainly weren't up to Phil's standard. What we wanted was a bass player who could lay down a heavy blues bass line. Jack knew how to do it.'

The line-up had changed, but the 'evil habits' of Blues Inc continued unabated. Both Phil and Chris were heavyweight heroin addicts – and both are now dead. From being an occasional user, Phil had apparently made a conscious decision to become an addict in order to get through the punishing routines of life on the road. In the early sixties there were no motorways and no proper planning of gigs. Musicians chaotically criss-crossed the country, running out of petrol, spending money on vans fit only for scrap and ended the week with precious little cash to show for all the hassle.

It was Dick who recommended Art Themen, a medical student he knew from playing in Cambridge, to fill the sax spot vacated by Graham. Art's medical skills came in handy one night after a gig in Liverpool. Ronnie Jones tells the story: 'During the gig Phil Seamen fell off his stool, but continued to play his hi-hat, in tempo, while lying on the floor. I picked him up and put him back on his stool when I noticed he had a huge, pus-filled blister on his left wrist. Halfway along the motorway Phil started moaning and we saw that his hand was very swollen. The blister on his hand had burst, so Art Themen said we had to stop the van and do something to help him.

'Art took a clean shirt from my bag and tore it up in strips, then he took a razor from one of our shaving kits and burnt it with a cigarette lighter. He cut open the blister and used grass to clean it out – the chlorophyll acting as an antiseptic. Then he wrapped up the wound with strips of torn shirt. On top of the heroin, Phil had downed a bottle of Johnnie Walker, so he was oblivious to what was going on. Next morning Phil went to the doctor to get it checked out. The doctor asked him who had cleaned and dressed the wound because it had been done exceptionally well and the doctor was reluctant to re-dress it.'

Drugs caused problems because it meant musicians weren't reliable, especially if they were on heroin. Eventually Chris Thompson had to be replaced and Mike Scott came in on bass. He too, according to Art, was a heroin user. 'One day he just ran across the bandroom floor with his upright bass and spiked the door.' But somehow drug habits were accepted, nobody interfered and if somebody didn't turn up, Alexis just reached for the phone. Money was a different matter.

Reflecting on Alexis' career as a band leader, Bobbie says: 'We had terrible times with bands. Things just descended on us – like it turned out we had to pay people's [national] insurance stamps. We had no idea you had to do that. Phil Seamen would come round and complain that he hadn't been paid, because of course, he'd spent it all on drugs. They always complained, they were dreadful, really frightful. All they wanted was the gig money shared out – they didn't think of who was paying for the van. They just regarded it as Alexis' van and paying for it all was to come out of his share. There were all sorts of ways in which we lost money. I remember this student union social secretary deducting money because a key fell off Art Themen's saxophone, so the guy reckoned he couldn't have been playing at his best.'

Some musicians felt that Alexis played fair; certainly the system seemed to work for Keith Scott. 'Given what he had to handle, Alexis seemed to be reasonably well organized. In fact it's surprising it worked at all. He used to phone a variety of musicians at very short notice in order to put together a pick-up band for a gig, so I think it's fair to say that his method was fraught with all kinds of danger.

'The way it operated for the early gigs was that, generally speaking, the money was raised on the door and then shared out at the end of the evening. For concerts, Alexis carried out most of the wheeler-dealing with the agents and promoters, although for recording sessions there was a standard rate of MU fees which wasn't really up for negotiation. I don't recall personally ever having a problem with being paid. Alexis was fair to me in that respect.'

Another musician who first depped at short notice for Mike Scott at a Flamingo all-nighter and then replaced him in May 1963 was bassist Vernon Bown. Delivered in his West Country brogue, Vernon's catchphrase, 'He don't owe you any money, do 'ee?', was uttered to any current or ex-Korner sideman he happened to meet. But by Vernon's own account, 'I was lucky in that I never had any problems getting paid' even though 'Alexis was always broke and quite often had his electric or gas cut off. He tried to borrow money from all kinds of places, including his band members, so that he could pay his bills and get reconnected.'

Others remain bitter about what they viewed as Alexis' unwarranted slice of the payout and deeply resented the difficulties they say they endured in order to get paid. 'Alexis was a chiselling bastard,' was the opening comment of one musician interviewed for the book. 'There is no other side; you are either fair or you're a bastard. It wasn't an ordinary gig, it was quite magic – his view was that whatever you did, you were contributing. He was very good to work with in that respect, but I knew I was going to get screwed on the money. Inevitably this colours your judgement of the whole thing.'

A major row blew up over money in the summer of 1963, when Alexis took Blues Inc to Rome for a TV spot.

'When we arrived,' says Vernon Bown, 'the Italians made each of us sign separate contracts. The contracts stated we would be paid hundreds of thousands of lire, although we had no idea how much that was in sterling. After we finished the show, the TV people took us to a bank in the studio and paid us out wads of money. Then Art Themen worked out the sterling equivalent and told us that we'd been paid about three times what Alexis told us we were getting. Alexis came scurrying round trying to collect all the extra money back from us, but owed so much money to people like Art and Johnny Parker that they weren't at all happy to give it back.'

Alexis bought presents for the family, which incensed Johnny Parker, and they nearly came to blows on Victoria Station. 'I grabbed his lapels and said I wouldn't let go until he'd paid me some of what I was owed. Then Ronnie Jones came up and said that I was making a scene, but I asked him to stay out of it because the matter was between myself and Alexis. I told Alexis that his first duty was to pay his musicians rather than buying gifts for his family.'

Bobbie offers this explanation for the shenanigans in Rome: 'They didn't understand that when you get paid there, you had to give half to the promoter – a sort of backhander. All they saw was a big wodge of money suddenly reduced by half and there was a big fight. Ronnie Jones said he'd never go on the road with Phil Seamen again after that. Phil said, "Ooh, I don't like abroad, Alexis." '

One reason (if not the main reason) for Phil's dislike of leaving England was the near impossibility of obtaining heroin on the Continent. For all the criticism of Alexis over the money, he actually smuggled heroin into Italy for Phil so he wouldn't go short, an act both brave and foolhardy. Phil was also a regular on the floor of the Moscow Road flat. As Sappho Korner recalls, you woke him up at your peril and you certainly didn't share his breakfast. 'He was a miserable, bad-tempered bastard in the morning, you had to wake him up with a broom from around the door. He would get up, go in the kitchen and make Ready Brek, sprinkle a Cadbury's Flake on it and then chuck in a whole load of blues [amphetamines] and mix it up. That was his breakfast every morning.' To her horror, Bobbie came into the kitchen one day just as Phil was offering the children a spoonful.

Rows over money notwithstanding, because Phil was such a great drummer Alexis accommodated most of his idiosyncrasies. Not that this saved Alexis from the odd tongue-lashing. Phil was not used to playing with an electric band and often found Alexis a bit loud. At one gig Phil got so fed up with the volume of Alexis' guitar that halfway through a tune he leaned across his cymbals, poked the leader in the back with a drumstick and said: 'Turn that fucking thing down.'

Money problems seemed to dog Alexis at every turn; as Johnny Parker saw it: 'Alexis was always very pleasant, amusing and very charming – he had that voice and could talk the hind legs off a donkey. He had great ambition, but everything seemed to go wrong for various reasons. For example, I know he had a lot of trouble with Ivor Mairants. Alexis bought some guitars from him and didn't make the agreed payment. So the heavies went round to Alexis' place and said unless they got the money in so many days . . . so the band's money went to pay off Ivor Mairants. Alexis was always juggling one account to pay another and the band always seemed to be last in the queue. I don't think he was evil with it – it was just that character fault.'

Although the band were working quite regularly, Alexis still didn't have a record deal. He met up with a clarinet player turned jukebox impresario named Joe Marsala, who worked for the Seeburg Corporation in Chicago. They came to an arrangement whereby Alexis would provide tracks for possible distribution around America's jukebox empire. Alexis went into Dennis Preston's Lansdowne Studios in May 1963 to record these tracks, none of which had much of a future as songs that Americans would want to dance to. Marsala touted an acetate round Chicago; not unexpectedly, he failed to do any sort of deal for Alexis. Ironically, Seeburg's catalogue was eventually bought by Decca, who released the tracks as *Alexis Korner's Blues Incorporated* in June 1965. Two further tracks were picked up by King, a small British independent label, and also released that year.

The tracks they laid down were specially written for the session – mainly by Alexis staying up all night with Dick, who wrote out the arrangements so that they could rehearse them at the Flamingo. The album was instrumental, technically superb and has remained a firm favourite among Korner fans. There were many engaging performances: 'Blue Mink', Alexis' homage to Thelonious Monk and Charlie Mingus done as a country blues but built on some unconventional structures; the sax solos by Art and Dick on 'Yogi'; a fine solo from Alexis on 'Rainy Tuesday' and excellent piano throughout from Johnny Parker. But probably the best track was Alexis' reworking of 'Preachin' the Blues', very different from Cyril Davies's version, played on slide bouzouki using a door key picked up off the studio floor and complimented by sensitive drumming work from Phil: 'Mississippi blues gone Greek', as Alexis remarked. 'Chris Trundle's Habit', written by Johnny Parker, was inspired by toilet-wall graffiti claiming that Mr Trundle 'fucks pigs'. Only the band and Charles Fox ever knew the story behind the song.

What is important about the album is that it showed Alexis was able to take American blues and jazz beyond 'train-spotting' and slavish copying. The music had its own version of hipness for which Alexis was tailor-made. Once British musicians (and white blues players generally) got hold of the blues, they tended to straighten it out and reduce it largely to its simplest renditions. Alexis (and Graham Bond) put music back into the blues, mainly from jazz and were prepared to experiment rhythmically. This you can only do when you have good enough musicians, which Alexis always made sure he had. The best jazz musicians can take on challenging material, play around with time, set up internal cross rhythms and counter-rhythms, throw in funny harmonic nuances and so on. Invariably this makes the music more sophisticated; Alexis wanted Blues Inc to play in all manner of different grooves, so they took the music and did something with it.

Come August 1963 and it was all change yet again; Johnny Parker says he finally tired of all the money hassles and left. As a serving US airman, Ronnie Jones was coming under increasing pressure from his commanders not to involve himself with disreputable jazz and blues musicians; the Rome fiasco just about finished his interest in the band. For Dick it was different. He never got involved in fights and arguments; he just observed from the sidelines. But he was increasingly concerned that the band was drifting back towards the jazz he had joined Blues Inc to escape. A stark indication of where the band was headed came at the end of a festival where they were on the same bill as Dizzy Gillespie. He was so taken with the band that he announced he was joining and had to be hauled out of the band wagon by his manager.

Over at Graham's band, now called the Graham Bond Organisation, Ginger had sacked John McLaughlin, ostensibly for playing too fast, but also, he says, because he was fed up with John moaning about everything. Dick couldn't resist the temptation of playing once again with a hard-rocking outfit driven by England's best rhythm section. He quit Blues Inc, 'about three minutes before I got the sack, because "a little bird" told me that Alexis thought I was losing my fire'. It seems that Alexis had also run out of patience with Phil Seamen and gave him two weeks' notice.

It was another transitional period: nobody knew who was supposed to be in the band and, according to *Melody Maker*, Hughie Flint and Davy Graham were drafted in to keep it all going while Alexis sorted out more permanent replacements. The line-up settled down with Art Themen, Vernon Bown, who introduced drummer Ronnie Dunn, and a sax player, Dave Castle. Alexis now doubled on vocals, but because he had limited range, he was never comfortable as a singer. Interviewed for a radio programme, *Town and Country*, back in 1959, he'd admitted: 'quite honestly I think I'm an appalling singer'.

Alexis knew what you had to do to make a blues song work vocally. He knew that twisting and turning the vowel sounds in vernacular American made the song easier to sing. And for all his academic knowledge about .the music, he knew there was a certain 'uneducated' use of the language that puts it in the right place and you can't really clean it up. By the same token he had enough taste not to sit down and write an original song about pickin' cotton in the Delta.

But in a practical sense he didn't think of himself as a singer; he never planned out the right keys to sing in. He would work out 'How can I play this with the rest of the band?' rather than 'How can I sing this?' and he'd think about the singing later. This explains why his singing as a solo artist was far more controlled and less strained than when he was trying to sing with a band. Working with a full ensemble, he would need to sing up. And if the original notes of the tune were too low he would find himself having to shout the lyric because he didn't have sufficient range to go an octave higher and he wouldn't change the key of a song for the band situation. Often he would just make it up as he went along and settle for conveying the meaning of the words. This is why so much of his band-backed vocal work sounds so strained. By the end of the year he was looking round for another vocalist.

Zoot Money was playing a country club in the New Forest, guesting with a quartet that included Andy Somers and Roger Cook, later of Blue Mink. In the audience one night was one of Alexis' many agents, Peter Berman. 'Afterwards Peter Berman came up to me and asked if I would like to go to London because Alexis didn't have a regular singer.' Zoot showed interest and he got a telegram asking him to call Alexis at six p.m. the next day.

'Alexis was on the other end of the line. "I hear you could help me out. Would you consider just dropping everything? I realize . . ." "*When do want me there?*" "Tomorrow night, we've got a gig at the Six Bells in Chelsea . . ." "*No problem.*"

'I ran up the road to a mate of mine who had an old Buick and it was like "Goodbye, mother, I'm off to seek my fortune . . ." We got up to Moscow Road and then my mate Pete drove off. "What stuff do you want me to do?" "Oh, don't worry, you'll know it." Or he'd play me a record *once*. There was no taking it home or anything. But it was never a problem because I'd done so many different blues things.'

When he first arrived Zoot stayed with Alexis and Bobbie. 'I spent a month on the couch with my pac-a-mac and an A–Z and did the intervals solo for a few extra quid. I was always reluctant to call it a band. Alexis would talk about "the band" and I'd say, "Look, Alex, a band is where you have parts and you look smart." ' But Zoot soon cottoned on that musicians were coming in to 'dep' all the time; they had to pick up quickly on what was happening, so it couldn't be too formal or intricate.

Muddy Waters/Ray Charles and big-band-style R&B were still pretty much 'underground' in Britain when Zoot joined Blues Inc, but the audiences who came knew what they liked. 'We had this gig just outside Manchester. It was a pub at a crossroads, you'd look at the outside and think, no, no way. And then a half-hour or so before show time you'd get this incredibly well-informed raving crowd turning up who all knew what they were listening to. It wasn't as if what Alexis was doing was well-publicized – if people came it meant they knew what was going on.'

Audiences in the north of England were definitely more open about the music they were prepared to listen to and also very knowledgeable. Liverpool, for example, being a port, had black-American jazz and blues as an integral part of its music culture for much of the fifties. Encouraged by the rousing reception Blues Inc enjoyed when they played the 1963 Liverpool Beat Festival, Alexis loved working in the city and even arranged to have a Friday-night residency at Hope Hall, knowing that the band would have to be back in London for the weekend all-nighters. But one Saturday, instead of going back to London, Blues Inc stayed for the afternoon session at Hope Hall. Raphael Callaghan is now a regular on the British blues circuit. In 1964 he was an eager young blues fan.

'I'd seen the Beatles and I knew this band were big, so I thought I'd better get there early. I turned up at ten-thirty in the morning thinking there'd be a long queue. It was two-thirty when the band turned up and I was still a queue of one.

'The van drew up, this tall guy got out and there was a double bass under a tarpaulin strapped to the roof. I was really shy and nervous, but I asked if I could help with the instruments. As each member set up they started to play. It was like a jam session. Alexis arrived later, plugged in his guitar and wailed away on the stage. I was absolutely blown away by this thrilling music. I recognized it as jazz, but it was blues as well. I didn't know what to think. It moved me so much, I just sat there crying my eyes out.'

But the hot spot in Liverpool was the Cavern Club, which, like many venues up and down the country, had switched from jazz to R&B. The Decca album of 1962 had tried with only limited success to capture the sound of Blues Inc live. In February 1964 the band went one better and recorded a live album at the Cavern with a small independent label, Oriole, which had one of the first mobile recording units.

Inevitably, by the time the album was recorded the line-up had completely changed again. Like Johnny Parker, Art Themen had left over the money situation. In fact he says he was owed so much that he confiscated the band's PA until Alexis paid up. Zoot had begun using the Blues Inc intervals to showcase his own Big Roll Band. When Alexis drafted in another black-American serviceman vocalist, Herbie Goins, Zoot took the opportunity to leave and start his own career as a band leader.

Born in Florida and raised in New York, Herbie Goins went to Germany with the US Army and began singing around the bases. On the circuit he met band leader Eric Delaney, who later sent a telegram asking him to join his band in England. He got the chance to sing some Joe Williams material, but was also expected to croon 'Danny Boy'. He did his share of hanging around the London club scene and met Alexis early in 1964. Herbie had no hang-ups about 'the white man singing the blues', despite some criticism from home that he was involved with 'blue-eyed soul music': 'it was just great for me that there was interest in the music outside black America'.

On stage, Alexis was still carrying the show. The kaleidoscope of colours that formed the backdrop of the sixties did not actually fall into place until 1966–7. Up until then it was still the grey times. With an audience mostly wearing jackets, ties and short hair, Alexis still looked exotic and slightly dangerous – even in Liverpool.

Since Johnny Parker had left Blues Inc, the band had been without a pianist, so for the Cavern gig Herbie brought along Eric Delaney's organist, Malcolm Saul. It was all a blur for Herbie and the others. 'Before the gig, we'd gone to the pub and only then did we find out that Oriole were recording it. We'd been drinking Fine Selection, which was pretty strong ale. By the time we got to the stage [*laughs*] . . . the first thing I did when I got up on stage was to break the microphone.'

Alexis took the vocals for 'Whoa Babe', which was just within his range; 'Overdrive' was less so. Sensibly he then introduces 'someone who can really sing' and for the rest of a hard-driving album, Herbie's louche, city-slicker vocals, which won him an Apollo Theater talent contest, just about steal the show. The anaemic 'Hoochie Coochie Man' from *R&B from the Marquee* hardly compares with the storming version from *Live at the Cavern*. Taken together, this pair of recordings, presenting a stark contrast of styles, show Blues Inc at their best.

The Oriole deal began and ended with the one album. In less than a month Alexis had signed what he announced in *Melody Maker* was a 'four year contract' with Nathan Joseph and taken the band to Olympic to record his next studio album, *Red Hot From Alex*, with one of the new recruits, who stayed with Alexis on and off for over four years: bassist Danny Thompson.

Danny had played around with tenor sax, drums, and trumpet until somebody sold him a double bass for a fiver 'and I knew that was it immediately because it was such a physical instrument'. He went off into skiffle, New Orleans and Dixieland, most of which he hated because his main men were Charlie Mingus and Muddy Waters. After leaving the Army in 1963, he was driving lorries because he couldn't get a pro job playing bass. He picked up his jazz career in London and got back to playing in Tubby Hayes's student orchestra. Danny had heard about Blues Inc. 'People said it was a good blowing band. And when I heard Alexis, it was right up my street.'

Danny Thompson was very typical of the sort of musician who wanted to play with Alexis. He had to do his share of sessions, weddings and barmitzvahs; sometimes Blues Inc was working very frequently, other times dates might be more hard to come by. But Danny loved the blues, and wanted to jam and be part of a democratic band: 'it was really a musicians' playground'. Alexis surrounded himself with first-rate musicians like Danny, who says: 'While he was playing his blues augmented by a stellar brass section making up riffs on the night which then became the tune arrangements coming on the hoof, everybody made a contribution.'

For the new album organist Ron Edgeworth came from the John Barry

Seven, Barry Howton was the drummer and Dick Heckstall-Smith played on three tracks. 'Dooji Wooji' turns up yet again as 'Herbie's Tune'; more significant is Alexis' first try at a Mingus number, 'Haitian Fight Song'. In his sleeve-notes, Charles Fox observed that Blues Inc must have been one of the few bands to play both the Cavern and Ronnie Scott's and asks: 'can Blues Inc be both commercial and high minded?' Alexis had no trouble being commercial. 'I've no objection to making money, only bad music.' The music on this album, signalling a move towards to more free-form improvisations linked to a standard blues repertoire was by no means bad, but neither was it commercial.

From 1962 to 1964, whenever a new R&B club opened (often converting from mainstream or trad jazz), Blues Inc were the first band booked – at the time, they *were* rhythm and blues in this country. Alexis brought the blues to a number of London and Home Counties venues, including the Refectory at Golders Green, the Star and Garter Hotel in Windsor, the Six Bells in Chelsea, and the Discotheque in Wardour Street.

Even so, for Blues Inc a wind of change was blowing every bit as draughty as the one that had blown trad jazz to the sidelines. Alexis had written enthusiastically about harmonica bands, and now the likes of the Stones, Yardbirds, Pretty Things and Manfred Mann were beginning to deprive Blues Inc of work, especially around London and the South. For the young British blues fans of the mid sixties, while Alexis' music may have been sophisticated blues reframed, he had set his stall out as a small-venue jazz musician. And jazz did not sell.

So Alexis began to look overseas. His command of languages and cosmopolitan outlook made him think about taking the band abroad. He had one eye on Germany; Hamburg had already played host to a number of British bands, including the Beatles, and he could speak fluent German. There was talk of a residency in Wiesbaden and one in Paris; neither happened, but Blues Inc did undertake a twelve-date tour of Denmark in October 1964. However, Alexis' profile was not yet high enough for the European Grand Tour.

In November he recorded a single, 'I Need Your Loving', which music writer Ray Coleman predicted might be Alexis' first hit single. Alexis replied: 'I'll tell you one thing, if . . . we are successful with this disc and are called upon to make more singles, we shall try to make the next one as different as possible from this.' The single deserved at least minor-hit status, but as it transpired Alexis would have no need to worry about handling hit singles.

Many of the money problems that Alexis got into with his musicians stemmed from the fact that he had put himself in an almost impossible position. He was never going to compromise his musical taste simply to earn a living, so the take-home pay from travelling around the country in 1964 playing a combination of Muddy Waters and Charlie Mingus was pretty thin. Yet here was a thirty-six-year-old man with a wife and three young children and a penchant for the life of the *bon viveur*. He had to seek out other sources of income.

Alexis fancied himself as something of an entrepreneur and retained his propensity for associating with those of suspect integrity. He joined forces with Alex Herbidge, known to *Private Eye* readers as 'Fat Man'. Through lack of investment, Alexis had already failed with one project, the Mojo Club in Dean Street. Herbidge had money, but it was tied up in trust and he couldn't touch it. Instead the trust hired a lawyer who, according to Bobbie, spent much of the time showing Herbidge scams for getting hold of the inheritance while making sure he got a cut for himself. One scam was the Bank of Valetta, which went bust; another was the unsavoury occupation of buying debts from loan sharks and then putting pressure on for payment. He got Alexis to front Beat City, a short-lived venue in Oxford Street, where Alexis booked a number of acts, including the Stones and Tom Jones.

In Alexis' papers there is a reference to 'Alexis Blues Ltd' for this period, which nobody seems to know anything about. He would play solo gigs and give lectures on the blues, but a continuing albeit sporadic source of revenue was his radio work.

Devoting his time to Blues Inc meant that much of his radio journalism had tailed off; his radio appearances through 1963 and the early part of 1964 were mainly live sessions with different line-ups of Blues Inc – *Jazz Session* on Network Three, *Bandbeat* for the General Overseas Service and *Jazz Club*. Then he met a young radio producer called Jeff Griffin; they became the very best of friends and Jeff remained Alexis' producer for the next twenty years.

By the time they met, Jeff had already done a number of music programmes on domestic and overseas radio. 'The BBC were well up to speed on the UK blues boom and they wanted it to be represented on World Service. They knew of my interest and asked me to put together a fifteen-minute weekly blues programme, leaving me to sort out compère, format and so on.

'I wanted to find somebody who had the same authority as Humphrey Lyttelton had for jazz – and the obvious person was Alexis – I'd seen the band play at Ealing and once we met up my office, I thought, yes, and he was keen to do it.'

In those days programmes had to have titles and (unlike now) were rarely called by the name of the presenter. After a·lot of debate about the title, they settled simply for *Rhythm & Blues with Alexis Korner*. That was the first series they did together: not a record show, but live sessions featuring all the top British R&B acts, including Spencer Davis, the Yardbirds, John Mayall, the Stones, Georgie Fame and Zoot Money. The show could be heard three times a week: one origination and two repeats.

This was the beginning of Alexis having a BBC radio show, although he would have to wait until the mid seventies for a regular show of his own on the domestic airwaves. He was the ideal compère to promote the blues on radio; extremely knowledgeable, generous with his praise for the new bands, whose members he knew anyway, and, most importantly, always giving the writers credits on air, so that listeners could hear (many for the first time) who were the great black-American blues artists and writers.

Now that he was being heard regularly on GOS more work offers came in, making full use of his language skills: music and talk programmes for French Canada and the German service for which he was paid anything between eight and twelve guineas a time. He spoke in fluent German on the topic of race relations and, on 27 June 1965, on drug addiction. Managing a band with the likes of Phil Seamen, Chris Thompson, Graham Bond and Ginger Baker in its midst, he already knew a lot about the subject. Sadly, he was to become something of an expert. Alexis also appeared on early BBC2 music programmes like *Gadzooks, It's All Happening* and Rediffusion's *Heartsong*.

Out in the clubs, Blues Inc were still blasting away: a reasonable amount of work, ever-enthusiastic audiences, lots of playing fun for the musicians, but actually making little headway. At the back end of 1964 Alexis was interviewed by *Beat Instrumental*, whose correspondent rather unkindly, although with some justification, called the article 'The One They Left Behind'. Alexis betrayed no sense of bitterness. 'This type of thing often happens; the person who starts a thing rarely carries it through. Anyway,

I am still playing the music I love, am living comfortably and frankly from this "boom" will emerge some really fine young musicians.'

In the spring of 1965 Alexis conjured up another one-off record deal, this time with Spot Records, the label for the Ryemuse Studios, where the album was recorded. The line-up had been cut back to four: Alexis and Danny Thompson plus a new drummer, Terry Cox, and Duffy Power, a young vocalist on the run from rock 'n' roll.

Duffy had been spotted by the impresario Larry Parnes at a teenage dance competition and Parnes signed him up to his pop-star stable, which was headed by Billy Fury and Marty Wilde. But Duffy was always second-division in that set-up; none of his singles charted and Parnes lost interest. Duffy recalls: 'I was doing some tours in Scotland with Georgie Fame under the banner of the "Rock 'n' Trad Spectacular", promoted by a big time-Scottish farmer called Drunken Duncan and produced by Jack Good. I had a cathartic experience; I met a very bad woman with no morals whatsoever. There were fights, rows, she was shaggin' away when my back was turned, but she did turn me on to the blues. She also said I could do better out on my own away from Parnes.'

Duffy played with the original Graham Bond Trio doing the odd song on stage, but mainly gigs under his own name backed by Graham. After that he jumped back on the package-tour circuit plugging the five singles he released on EMI's Parlaphone label (backed on record either by Graham or the Paramounts with Gary Brooker and Robin Trower) and went on tour with the Fentones, 'but I was getting very wobbly, very paranoid, very disturbed and dropping the odd speed pill didn't help. They had enough and went back up North, but I learnt to sing with them and by the time it finished I was ten times the singer I was before.

'There was some minor scandal happened at EMI which I got caught up in and I wrote and recorded a song independent of EMI called "Love's Gonna Go" and I loved it. I met Graham in the street, we went back to my flat and I played him it and he said, "That's a new departure for you." And I thought, if he likes it . . . Big Jim Sullivan was on it and so was Jimmy Nichol, who'd stood in for Ringo. Decca were interested in it, but then said, "We don't want anything to do with jazz." It had nothing to do with jazz, it was bluesy, that's all. I was so fed up.

'I had a room in this rock 'n' roll house in Cleveland Square, Paddington, two houses joined together with a bar in the basement.

Parnes used to chuck all his artists in there; at one time Gene Vincent, Billy Fury and the rest stayed there. They had gone, but I was still there surrounded by dog-ends and broken glasses and by 1965 it had got a bit jazzy. Phil Kinorra lived there and he really liked what I was doing. At the time, Alexis lived round the corner at the Queensway flat [Alexis and Bobbie moved from the Moscow Road flat to 116a Queensway around May 1965] and I'd never met him.'

Phil Kinorra played 'Love's Gonna Go' to Alexis, who wanted to meet the composer. Duffy relates an odd tale of what happened next. 'Although I'd never met him, I looked upon Alexis as some godly father-figure who was blessed with everything, the upper-class education, everything better than me. Alexis spoke reams with a couple of chords. I loved it. Whenever he did blues you couldn't help going "yeah" because it sounded so natural, it was real, it was genuine, he was a genuine motherfucker and I say that with all respect – you have to have that element. I've been with Eric Clapton in a club and Alexis has got up and he's done his little three-chord trick with his plinks and plonks and little pull-offs and Eric's gone "yeah" and he's meant it. Alexis definitely had it and that's why we all make such a big fuss.

'So in my mind I foisted upon him certain rules that he shouldn't break. A couple of days after hearing the song he says, "Come round with your guitar" and I played him these tunes I'd been working on. He used to call me "Duff", which really irritated me, but I didn't say anything – I took it from him. This was on a Good Friday. He said come back on the Monday. When I turned up he said, "I've been away and I've made up this tune" – and it was the same tune I'd played him. I'd only met him twice and I thought, what is going on here? He's well above that. I was shocked.'

According to Damian Korner, Alexis thought he was doing Duffy a favour by giving him a few pounds for his songs and getting them published when he was down on his luck. Alexis also invited Duffy to do some sessions which became the Spot Records album *Sky High*.

Spot's studio, Ryemuse, was located above a chemist's shop in South Molton Street, off Oxford Street. The recording was made on a four-track Ampeg reel-to-reel using a home-built recording console. The album's title was unequivocally a reference to the state the band were in for the recording. John Timperley, who was the engineer, says: 'One particular session the guys in the band wouldn't play until they had the right kind of stuff to smoke. They sent out for some and it came back rolled up in newspaper. "This is no bloody good," they said, "we'll have to get the real thing." The session was held up for another hour until it arrived.'

The album was recorded late at night during the studio's 'down time', or rather 'up time', because the place was shrouded in a marijuana haze. Jack Winsley, the producer, recalls that the noise of the band brought in two policemen to investigate. They were seated in the fog for a chat and a cup of tea and their only comment on the proceedings as they left was: 'You're proper musicians, you lot, aren't you?' Out with the smoke came huge sighs of relief.

Duffy was not much impressed with the final result. 'It was very thin-sounding,' he says, and apparently some sound experiments were conducted which didn't quite come off. But on balance *Sky High* has much to commend it. Alexis retained Danny Thompson and added Terry Cox on drums, augmented by trombonist Chris Pyne and saxophonist Alan Skidmore. Listening to Duffy on tracks like Broonzy's 'Louise' and 'I'm So Glad', it is obvious that his was the voice of a 'blues shouter' rather than a pop star. It's a great shame that his personal problems got in the way of what should have been a successful career on the blues-rock scene. Aside from Duffy, Danny Thompson carried on the line of outstanding bassists to play with Alexis, especially on Mingus's 'Wednesday Night Prayer Meeting'. The contributions of Chris Pyne and Alan Skidmore ranked as some of their best on record up to that point.

But true to form, *Sky High* made no impact on the charts and there was now pressure on Blues Inc from another quarter. As the Stones and the other bands became more popular with regular chart hits, they left the club scene. In their place came the beginning of the second British 'blues boom', spearheaded by John Mayall, who now had Eric Clapton in his band. Guitar bands on the new 'underground' scene were in the ascendant. Financial salvation for Blues Inc came from a most unlikely source.

Alexis had been writing and broadcasting for children since the late fifties, mainly for radio. In September 1965 a new children's programme started on ITV twice a week called *Five O'Clock Funfair*. He appeared on the first show, demonstrating that you can get music from spoked wheels and hollowed-out logs as well as more conventional instruments such as the bouzouki.

Shortly afterwards the title was changed to *Five O'Clock Club*, and Blues Inc – the trio of Alexis, Danny Thompson and Terry Cox – was appointed as the house band. Alexis wasn't at all sure this was a good move either for his image or reputation, 'so I stipulated that we got to play one number of our choice on every show and the TV company Rediffusion never went back on that'. The credit for allowing an R&B band to play Charlie Mingus twice a week on national children's TV went to John Rhodes. Wally Whyton, who was the presenter, says: 'John was one of those guys who was absolutely wide open. With the BBC it was all these layers of people. At Rediffusion there was John as Head of Children's and the only other person involved was the guy who handled the money.'

But not only was Blues Inc the house band, Alexis was also the musical director, which caused Danny Thompson no end of amusement. 'He didn't know a crotchet from a hatchet and his bungling through *Five O'Clock Club* was sheer perfection. He played the blues. End of story. "Tea for Two", "Autumn in New York", forget it. Fine if it was a bluesy thing, but if you had a guest, say Cleo Laine, you had a problem. John Dankworth would come up and introduce himself, say hello and then, "Right, here are the charts." So Alexis, instead of saying, "I don't read music", he just bluffed away and got completely caught out. He'd put his whole hand over the frets and bang away. I don't know how he had the neck to do it. But he held down the job and I was getting £50 a show with a repeat. That was the first real-money job you could say, "Hang on, I can make a living playing music." Fantastic. *Five O'Clock Club* paid for my house in Wimbledon and Terry Cox's house in Hampstead. And later I sold that house to buy my manor house in Suffolk, which everybody assumed came from Pentangle. It all emanated from that work with Alexis, for which I will be eternally grateful. Terry Cox should go on his knees as well.'

Wally Whyton feels similarly grateful to the programme for much the same reason. 'People still say, "Didn't you feel a prick talking to Pussy Cat Willum?" "No, it bought me a house." ' Pussy Cat Willum was one of three puppets in the programme; the other two were Fred Barker and Ollie Beak.

The programme went out live, a process always fraught with danger. Duffy, who often sang with the trio, was caught smoking a huge joint, out of shot – so he thought – as the camera panned round. Another time Bert Weedon was the guest. The camera zoomed in for a close-up just as Wally Whyton and a friend were crouching out of shot to pull the hairs out of Bert's leg one by one as he was playing. There was also the singer who stroked a cat while he was singing and started sneezing the place down and another whose record came on at 78rpm. The sound man panicked and just knocked the speed back to 45rpm with the cameras still rolling.

In one sense the programme did Blues Inc no favours. Because they were on TV twice a week, all the bookers thought they would be too expensive and the gigs dropped away even more. Not that this mattered, until the gravy train ground to a halt. Wally Whyton remembers that 'Alexis was eventually replaced by a piano player who was a bit more commercial and could read the dots, especially as we had people like Roy Orbison singing live.'

During Alexis' time with *Five O'Clock Club*, he took Danny and Terry into the Philips Studio to record an album entitled *I Wonder Who* for Fontana, released in April 1967. The opening of *Beat Instrumental's* brief review spoke volumes: 'Good album this . . . if you're an Alexis Korner fan.' In other words, *I Wonder Who* was not likely to win over converts to Alexis' version of the blues, although it was undoubtedly his most straight-ahead blues album, more in tune with the British blues scene as it was developing – just a three-piece and no brass. Opinions differ over this album. Danny Thompson and many Korner fans cite it as their favourite Alexis album. Danny and Terry Cox were uniformly excellent; it boasted nice jazz-inflected blues guitar from Alexis, with Percy Mayfield's 'Rivers Invitation' and Jimmy Smith's 'Chicken Shack Back Home' the star tracks. But the album never really takes off and is let down by some erratic vocal pitching.

Why Alexis recorded an album like this is puzzling. The cynical view of the album's genesis would be to say that the band was on a good wage and any advance for the LP would have been tiny. Alexis wasn't that keen on studio work, there was no pressure to record an album and he already knew that the jazz-blues format wasn't working at the cash till. In his sleeve-notes, producer Terry Brown said 'everybody had a ball', and the whole thing was done in two sessions 'with time to spare', so really it was just play-time again for Alexis and the musicians he wanted around him.

But once the TV gig was over, it didn't take too long for money to be the big issue once more, to the point where Danny's wife took over the band's finances. Under these circumstances a break with Danny was almost inevitable. 'Our big bust-up came over money. I was depending on this money and he said the cheque hadn't cleared. He gave me a cheque and it bounced. So I phoned him and told him the cheque had bounced.

' "No it hasn't."

' "It has."

' "Phone your bank."

' "I have."

' "Well, your bank manager is lying."

' "Alexis, my bank manager is not going to lie. The money is not there."

' "There is some confusion."

'We were supposed to be working that night. I said, "Alexis, come over this afternoon with the cash." So he came over and he gave me the cash. I said, "Alexis, this is it." "What about the gig?" "Sorry, I can't do it." So he phoned up Cliff Barton. And that was me out. It meant me being out of work, but I couldn't handle that any more.'

In fact, the departure of Danny Thompson signalled the end of Blues Inc. Alexis recalled it like this: 'We got to the stage where we were a good working quartet [including a young Australian saxophonist, Ray Warleigh] with plenty of work coming in, but not the kind of work they wanted to do. We had an offer to do the 007 Room at the Hilton Hotel when it opened. The band came to see me about it and I said, "You must be joking. I'll do a helluva lot, man, but play the 007 Room? I'm afraid you'd better find yourselves another band leader. And that was the last of Blues Incorporated.'

As he had done in the 1950s, Alexis was becoming disillusioned with the music business. He was still very much the back-room priest of R&B, but now rather at a loose end with no real sense of direction in his career. Many of the people who guested or played in Blues Inc had become commercially successful. He wouldn't have been human if that didn't rankle somewhat and it came through in one interview in *Melody Maker* from March 1966, entitled 'Back To Square One With "R&B", in which Alexis observed: 'I sometimes wish I had percentages of all the people who got started with me.'

His remarks were considerably more pointed about the direction of the British blues when he responded to a *Melody Maker* article by Alan Walsh headlined 'The Plight of the Bluesman'. The article focused on John Mayall and the battle (first taken up by Alexis) to get the notion of white blues accepted. Alexis had always been a friend to Mayall and his family and although they were of very different temperaments, Alexis and John got on well enough. But Alexis was not one to let friendships get in the way of his strongly held views on music. He responded with

'Don't Judge A Book By Its Cover', a damning indictment of what passed for blues in the UK or, as he called it, 'a deliberately bastardised form of the country blues'. His point was that Robert Johnson and Blind Lemon Jefferson had brought the blues to the apotheosis of its sophistication; even Muddy Waters had only taken the 'Lowest Common Denominator' element of the music, i.e. the sensual, and amplified it for dramatic effect.

As far as Alexis was concerned, in terms of musical progression the natural heirs to the music of the great pre-war bluesmen were the modern free-form jazz players like Archie Shepp, Ornette Coleman, Charlie Mingus, Eric Dolphy and Roland Kirk. In the earlier *Melody Maker* interview mentioned above, Alexis expressed his regret that more young people had not found their way to jazz. Thus, in his view, moving Blues Inc towards modern jazz was an entirely logical, if totally uncommercial move.

But here was the killer: Alexis certainly admired the individual talents of an Eric Clapton or a Peter Green, yet this much-lauded 'Father of the British Blues' actually hated what the music he was revered for pioneering had become. In the article, he wasn't exactly fulsome in his praise, even of Muddy Waters; but he resolutely believed that John Mayall had contributed little of worth to the blues and while he chose not to name him, made the point in unnecessarily harsh terms. 'Alan Walsh's article was basically concerned with one man – no kin of mine in flesh or spirit – who "put in his thumb and pulled out a plum and said what a good boy am I". We blues players cannot expect plaudits just for following our chosen profession. Nobody lionizes bus conductors or even scientists unless they do something exceptional. A bluesman, let me remind you, is also judged by his performances, not his pretensions.'

Mayall, given a right of reply, was totally nonplussed by Alexis' comments, especially as Alexis had written the sleeve-notes to his début album. As Mayall had since gone on to score three Top Ten albums between July 1966 and September 1967 (this was Mayall's 'plight'?) he felt more than justified in dismissing Alexis' views as sour grapes.

Towards the end of 1965 Alexis went out as a solo artist and secured a residency doing the weekend all-nighter at Les Cousins in Greek Street, Soho, the club which became almost synonymous with the sixties folk scene. Cousins had the only all-night scene apart from the Flamingo; all the folk singers played there: Bert Jansch, John Renbourn, Ralph

McTell, John Martyn, Roy Harper, Donovan and Al Stewart. It was a perfect venue for Alexis; with his two-o'clock-in-the-morning voice roughed up by dope and the strongest cigarettes in the known universe, he could thump out earthy blues for a very mellow audience. As John Platt describes it in his book *London Rock Routes*: 'Cousins became an incredible meeting place – for seeing friends, indulging in a little hanky panky and buying grass. You could do what you liked as long as you didn't interfere with anybody else – and the music, of course, was usually superb.'

Alexis decided to come off the road, but was still interested in playing with other musicians. He went to see John Mayall's drummer, Hughie Flint. 'He came along to the very last gig I ever played with John. He was there in the dressing room when I came off and he asked me if I was interested in joining. He'd already contacted Cliff Barton and what he wanted was a trio rather than a big band – still play blues, but still carry on with the jazz influences.'

Alexis called the band Free At Last, and they played their first gig at Cousins in September 1966. But the conventional trio format didn't really work out. Hughie explains: 'A trio with Hendrix or Clapton was one thing, but Alexis wasn't a real lead guitarist as such, so he relied heavily on Cliff to play almost melody lines on bass. Alexis really bit off more than he could chew and we got mixed receptions.'

The format was changed and Alexis began performing a history of the blues. 'He would go on first without guitar and he'd sing work songs with us clapping. Then he'd get the guitar and do a Broonzy or a Robert Johnson-type number on his own. I might play tambourine along with him. He'd also narrate and include the audience in what he was doing. Finally we'd do the Chicago blues and more modern stuff. It seemed to work better than just going out on stage and playing this eclectic sort of mish-mash.'

Hughie Flint had played with John Mayall when they were both still living in Manchester. He contrasts the two band-leading styles of John Mayall and Alexis. 'Once John moved to London he became more of a band leader as he gained in confidence. So he was rather ambivalent when Eric joined because he was a great draw, a great foil, a great musician, just what John wanted. So John had to take a back seat and he wasn't quite as dominant as he'd been before. And we had Jack Bruce in the band for a while with Eric, which was quite electric. When Eric left, John became quite assertive. One of the reasons I left the Bluesbreakers was that it was quite clear John was paying me to play the drums and there wasn't much opportunity to contribute.

'With Alexis it more co-operative and he was a much more relaxed, warm, friendly man. John had this aloofness; Alexis I loved as a person the whole time I played with him. He was much easier to work with; if things didn't work, we'd sit down and talk about it, try something else.'

Cliff Barton was all for trying something else – heroin, speed, you name it. He had apparently come off heroin just before working with Alexis, but very soon he was back on. Hughie tells of a strange gig at the Twisted Wheel. 'Cliff was busted in the toilets. Alexis had to go to the police station and even had to phone through to Cliff's doctor to prove he was being prescribed purple hearts. Alexis came back to the club and we went on as a duo. It was the most bizarre gig I've ever done.

'There was a break then because we had to cancel some gigs, but the gigs weren't that prolific – quite often we'd go a whole week without one.' Nor were the record royalties exactly pouring in.

And then Alexis found a young black bass player, Binky McKenzie. Hughie remembers Binky as 'an amazing guy, very young and undisciplined. He slipped into the band quite easily and like Cliff had to learn all these melody bass lines.' In January 1967 Alexis recorded just one single with this trio, 'Rosie', which had been a hit for the Animals as 'Inside Looking Out'.

The band lasted in this format until the middle of 1967, when Hughie Flint accepted a job with Georgie Fame and shortly afterwards Binky left as well. It would be something of an understatement to say that Alexis had a run of bad luck with bass players; Jack Bruce and Danny Thompson left under a cloud; Chris Thompson, Mike Scott and Cliff Barton were all heroin addicts – Chris Thompson died of an overdose, Cliff died in a fire. And poor Binky McKenzie had some kind of breakdown and killed half his family.

Bobbie says they took the procession of lost musicians philosophically. 'It was like, "Oh dear, the drummer's gone, never mind I've always wanted to work without a drummer."' Undaunted, Alexis tried yet another line-up with drummer Gerry Conway, a young singer, Marsha Hunt, before she found fame in *Hair* and a multi-instrumentalist called Victor Brox. Alexis had known Victor from the days when Blues Inc made regular trips to Manchester. Victor had been a semi-professional keyboard player and singer on the blues circuit for many years, but actually gave up his teaching job to play with Alexis. He recalls: 'The band with Marsha lasted for about three weeks and then it was just me and Alexis as a duo. I did the music, Alexis did the charisma.' They played together around London for the next nine months, into the early part of 1968. Victor was either hitchhiking down from Manchester or sleeping on Alexis' floor. 'We had very similar voices; sometimes I would answer the phone and people would think it was Alexis. I used to get all sorts of "information" that I wasn't supposed to have.' Victor refuses to be specific on this point.

Victor says that he spent a lot of time in the studio with Alexis, although only three tracks have ever surfaced. Apparently there was one session to record a song written by Kenny Lynch which, according to Victor, Alexis was convinced was destined to be his first hit single. The story goes that Alexis went off with the tapes, which were subsequently wiped by accident when he sat on an Underground train seat mounted over a magnetic coil. The session was not repeated, so presumably the song wasn't that good.

Victor says that Alexis still harboured resentments over the defection of Graham Bond: his 'walking out on a moment's notice' and 'muscling in on my gigs'. And with Victor too, earning so little from playing with Alexis, the end came. He had a mortgage and family to support, but even so, when he accepted the offer to join Aynsley Dunbar's Retaliation (so called because Dunbar was fired by John Mayall), 'Alexis was furious and for a long time he never forgave me.'

If Alexis' career as a musician had temporarily run up a blind alley, stymied by lack of direction, defecting musicians and a declining audience, life at home was becoming no less of a worry.

9

NEW WORRIED BLUES

There was no doubt that Alexis was devoted to his wife and children. He desperately wanted to create around himself the kind of family life he felt he had been denied as a child. He also wanted to bind his family to him in a way calculated to forestall the yawning chasm that had opened up between himself and his relatives.

Bobbie was his rock, his safety-net amid the vicissitudes of trying to survive in the music business. She was the mother of his children, and given the importance accorded to family life that Alexis would have inherited from the Greek side of the family, that in itself was enough to earn his love and respect for her. But unusually for a music-business wife, Bobbie understood and loved the music. She helped Alexis learn guitar, was terrified when he turned professional — although she was determined for him to succeed — and throughout their life together was able to make informed comment and even directly influence the content of the music Alexis produced. Above all, they were very much in love.

Their best times as a family were when the children were younger, before Alexis was spending so much time on the road. Probably because of his time spent at Finchden when it was based near the English–Welsh border, Alexis had grown to love the area, and in 1961 they rented a Welsh longhouse. At one time condemned, the property had been roughly renovated and converted into two properties. At first they rented half of the building, but later took over the rest. Stone House was the scene of many happy holidays for Sappho and the boys. 'Those were the times when we were really together. Dad was really into all the country air and chopping wood and he loved going for long walks in the hills.'

Devoid of basic amenities such as electricity and running water, Stone House was nevertheless furnished with all the stuff that people in the sixties threw away – for example, brass bedsteads and genuine Victorian oil lamps. Located two fields away from the road, it was also a bolt-hole. 'It cost seven shillings and sixpence a week to rent,' says Bobbie. 'Even we could manage that and for the first time we could live within our means. We were sharing it with a friend, but he couldn't keep up the seven and six, so we had to find the whole fifteen shillings, but we did love it so much that we managed to scrape up the money for that. No telephone was brilliant. We owed so much money, people were always ringing asking when they were going to get paid.'

During the fifties and early sixties, when Alexis was scraping a living, there was never quite enough to eat, Sappho recalls. 'I always wanted to be one of those kids who came home from boarding school and their mum wouldn't stop feeding them. For years I thought my mum was really mean with food without knowing the reason why.' Sappho also hated 'having secondhand clothes and the ones mum made for me were dreadful. We didn't have any money, that's for sure.' But as far as they were able, Alexis and Bobbie shielded the children from the worst of the rows with musicians and other creditors and kept life as normal as possible.

Or as normal as possible in a house with a charismatic father trying to earn a living in the music business, who wore clothes that were totally outrageous for the time, took speed, smoked dope and made his home an open house for musicians with the full set of 'evil habits' and every kid on the block with aspirations to be a musician. Apart from the escapes to Wales, the family never had any privacy at the Moscow Road flat. Bobbie took to leaving the toilet window open so that the children, who had to be up next day for school, wouldn't be disturbed by musicians banging on the door at four in the morning in search of a floor to sleep on. Even the local prostitutes would pop in for a joint and a coffee if trade was slack. Sappho remains amazed at the way her mother coped. 'She must have been a saint, but we didn't know about living any other way and we found it exciting.'

Once Blues Incorporated got underway, 'we didn't expect to see dad unless there were other people there as well'. Alternatively, as Damian recalls: 'One of the ways you knew daddy was home was that Mum would go, "Sshh, daddy's trying to sleep." '

Part of the chaos came from trying to be a musician and raise a family at the same time. But most of it derived from Alexis' own personality and how his children responded to having **Alexis Korner** for a father. There were two defining aspects of his character which had developed over the years. One was the absolute certainty that what he was doing was right; he was a master at masking any insecurities. His supreme confidence, combined with his inordinate charm and intelligence, made him a force to be reckoned with both within the music business and in his own family.

In Alexis' younger days, under the reproachful glare of a father whom he could never please, he was riddled with self-doubt, which explained his urgent need to be liked. But he managed to carve a niche for himself well away from the milieu of his family. All his abundant personal qualities were in very short supply in others in the music business, and he hitched these qualities to an exquisite taste in music itself, earning himself deep admiration from all who came into contact with him. He became the 'patron saint of the blues', and he dealt with his own freely admitted limitations as a musician by becoming 'finder of all the talents' and having them in his band.

His second defining characteristic was a deep-seated belief in the principle of freedom. This was partly born of Finchden and partly a straightforward reaction against his upbringing and the attempt by the family, even when he was in his late teens, to take control of his life. He was determined that he would not impose repression on his own children. However, inescapably it seems, the sins of the father pass down the line. Emil had had high expectations of Alexis; he wanted his son to grow up quickly in order to take his place in the world and be a credit to the family. Alexis had similarly lofty hopes for his own children, not so that they could go and 'earn a good living', but because he wanted them as 'friends' rather than 'dependants', which meant, if they wanted to, partaking of the musician's life with all its risks. The expectations of Emil and Alexis might have been very different, but the pressures on the children were equally acute.

So Sappho, Nico and Damian had a supremely confident, single-minded father in the public eye, who dominated his family in the most benign way. He expected the earth from his children while the delinquent in him was prepared to tolerate, even encourage, outrageous behaviour which most parents (including Bobbie) would not countenance – so long as nobody expected him to clear up the mess afterwards. And to top it off, the normal family environment included young men, hanging on his every word, all of whom would have given their eye-teeth to be the son of Alexis Korner. As Damian succinctly puts it: 'You have to fuck up to get noticed, otherwise you just get ignored.'

Born of highly intelligent, articulate and well-read parents, the children were very bright, even precocious. As a young child, Sappho was often in the care of her grandmother, but Damian and Nico spent most of their time with Bobbie. Sappho was never close to Charles Fox, who lived with them. 'We never really sparked, to say the least. He never really liked women apart from mum and his one other lady friend.' There was a certain amount of jealousy because, like the boys, Charles might be more at home than Sappho was. She couldn't have articulated this resentment at the time, but she did subconsciously distance herself from the rest of the family.

Sappho wholeheartedly took to wearing the mantle of the delinquent Alexis. She was among the early intake of Holland Park Comprehensive, which became a model comprehensive school beloved of well-to-do radicals and celebrities. However, when Sappho first went there, the school took most of its pupils from local council estates, and during the era of *Five O'Clock Club*, when Alexis was seen on national television twice a week, she was mercilessly bullied. 'I hated that school, it was utter misery for me. I was bullied and taunted and my father's position made it ten times worse. Kids used to run around the playground singing the tune to the *Five O'Clock Club*. I just wanted my parents to be normal. It was a really bad time of my life.'

Like Alexis, she fell in with a 'bad lot' and, egged on by one of the gang, she threw a chair at a teacher. She became the first girl to be expelled from Holland Park and from then on it was downhill. She hung around with the scooter set, became pregnant and had an abortion, and by the time she got into drugs she was well beyond her parents' control. She was sent briefly to a boarding school at Box Hill, Surrey and then to a children's home in Earlsfield, south London. Finally, Alexis went to talk to George Lyward, the first time he had seen him in more than twenty years.

When Alexis went with the family to Finchden, by this time transferred to Kent, one of the boys in residence was singer Tom Robinson, who recalls: 'Chief was always mildly boasting about "old boys" who had done well. The excitement around the house was incredible. Alexis Korner was coming and he might play. We hardly knew what hit us when Damian and Nico were unleashed – wild, unruly, long-haired kids, you didn't see young kids with hair that long. Totally bohemian. They just wreaked havoc, screaming, shouting and running upstairs. Alexis had this Afro hairstyle and jeans. They just looked like a gypsy family with wild-eyed, ragged children.'

About three-quarters of the house crammed into Lyward's study. Alexis took his guitar and stood up to talk. Tom had a 'mind-blowing experience'. That's what I want to be, he thought. 'You saw lots of grown men at Finchden in various professions, teachers, doctors and so on. But to see a man stand up in front of a load of people and strap on a guitar with complete dignity and presence and charisma and open his mouth and sing – in a communicating, intense way was just . . . I'd never seen a professional performer up close – profoundly affecting.'

Tom was one of a group of Finchden boys (including guitarist Danny Kustow) who became friends with the Korner family and often went to see them in London. This caused problems for George Lyward. He was now quite elderly and the arrival of drugs at Finchden made it almost impossible for him to work with the boys. His technique, for want of a better word, demanded that boys could think through their problems, understand why they had come to Finchden and make conscious choices for themselves – very difficult if they were stoned out of their minds. So Alexis was doing Lyward no favours by inviting boys into the world of west London hippiedom, with all its distractions. In that environment the boys saw 'alternative acceptable ways of behaving', as Tom Robinson puts it. In fairness to Alexis, Tom says, 'You'd go there [to the flat] and they'd be passing a joint round, but he never offered any to us until quite late, about a year before I left. He smoked like a chimney, but didn't want to compromise his position of trust with Lyward.'

And Lyward did Alexis a favour – he accepted Sappho as one of the few girls ever to go to Finchden. Lyward found that he could not communicate with girls in the way he could with boys and so generally refused to take them. But he made an exception for Sappho and she loved it. 'I went there for a year and it was the best year of my life. I left there a totally different person, much happier with myself. Everybody there was in the same boat as me: couldn't cope with the outside, didn't know how to fit in. It was like the best part of boarding school, the pranks and the camaraderie without the shitty side. You didn't do bad things because you loved the guy who ran it and you didn't want to hurt him. And it was the first time that I experienced not doing things because I thought about someone else.' When Sappho left, her problems were by no means over, but at least she and the family had some positive respite.

So what of Damian and Nico? The boys also attended Holland Park Comprehensive and Steve Clyne, who taught them metalwork there, became a close friend of the family. 'It was a wonderful, loving, touching affectionate relationship between Alexis and the boys, to do with Alexis' European background and heritage.' This relationship was closer to male bonding than a true father–son relationship. It was very strong, passionate and physical. If the boys got into a 'play fight' with Alexis, no quarter was given. But Steve says he could never see Alexis kicking a ball around with them.

Like anybody bearing the Korner surname, the boys were free spirits. Damian tells a typical Nico story. 'When we were in Linden Gardens – Nico was about four or five – there was a rockery with a big drop on the other side. Nico rides his bike over the top and ends up in hospital. Shortly afterwards our grandparents came visiting. "How did you hurt your head, Nico?" says Grandad Melville. "I'll show you," says Nico, and promptly does it again.'

And for Damian's part: 'We used to have a Land Rover up at Stone House and between the house and the road there was a good half-mile of pasture-land. Dad wanted to teach me to drive – I must have been about eight or nine. What he forgot was that intersecting this land was a stream. I made a beeline straight for the stream.

'Me and my brother used to rebuild bikes – in other words he'd rebuild the bike and I'd sit and watch, get grease on my hand and do all the repainting. We had this restored Tiger Cub which we'd converted to a scrambler which had this really sloppy throttle cable – you could wind the whole thing right out. Nico had parked the bike about four foot from a six-foot-thick barbed wire fence. I ran downstairs one morning, jumped on the bike, revved it up and went straight through the fence. The thing I remember is my brother screaming, "What the fuck have you done to the bike? If you've damaged the bike I'll never let you ride it again" as I'm being dragged through with my hand wrapped around the throttle cable unable to stop it.'

Getting into scrapes was second nature for both of them, but Nico was doing fine at school until he got to Holland Park. By then, it had become a fashionable school. There was a rough hierarchy of kids at the school, described by Steve Clyne as 'white Anglo–Saxon professional, foreign professional, Shepherd's Bush poor white trash and Ladbroke Grove poor black'. Those at the top of the pecking order 'were more like little adults deprived of their childhood – more concerned to discuss the latest consignment of hash to hit the streets than anything else – and because of expectations, knowing they were going to do all right. If they were going to fail, they'd do it properly. And the staff didn't have a clue what was going on in the place – they really didn't.'

Steve points out that many of the top-drawer kids, the offspring of actors, architects, artists and so on, came from families who could afford to reject middle-class values. As a result, the children were caught up in very loose family structures and deprived of a stable family life, 'and in hindsight forced into adulthood and exposed to an adult "sixties" way of life that actually wasn't very adult'.

Alexis' approach to life put his own children in a similar position, but unlike many of their contemporaries they did have the stability of a strong marriage holding everything together. Even so, Steve can't understand Alexis' attitude to his children's education. 'Alexis was very well educated in the European sense, well rounded, but the artist in him encouraged his kids to walk away from that. He may well have had [his education] rammed down his throat, but it did stand him in very good stead.' Damian agrees: 'The way we were brought up was not normal, even by sixties standards. My mother was brought up in the generation whereby whatever the father said went. So regardless of what my mother thought, my father cried, "freedom, freedom, freedom". Our friends were very jealous, but there were times when the freedom became depressing because as long as they didn't have to pick up the pieces, you could do just about what you liked. But I really wanted somebody to tell me to do my homework because it got really boring telling myself. I was extremely lucky because I had almost a photographic memory and passed various exams.'

And there were other problems. Sappho's response to the family situation, as she saw it, was to kick out screaming. At the other extreme Nico found it impossible to emerge from Alexis' shadow and simply withdrew into himself. He was shaping up to be a very good guitarist, better than Alexis, but the powerful presence of his father defeated him. Steve Clyne recalls that 'Nico never existed – he always introduced himself as Alexis' son.' Nico also found Alexis' fame difficult to cope with; Bobbie tells the story of 'when Nico was on the train going to school saying to a boy, "It's really terrible having a famous father – my dad's Alexis Korner." To which the boy replied, "You think you've got problems – mine's Bob Monkhouse." '

Because of his long hair, Nico often used to get into fights at school and Damian would have to rescue him – a role he performed for his elder brother well into adulthood. Damian was a football hero who won a trial with Chelsea; he waded in when Nico was picked on, safe in the knowledge that nobody would touch him in case it put him out of action for the next match.

And, as with Sappho, drugs played a major part in Nico's life from an early age, to help him deal with all the pain in his life. But they weren't pestered by the dealer in big hat and dark glasses waiting at the school gates: drug use began at home – and for this Alexis must shoulder the blame. 'You accepted,' says Damian, 'from the age of nine or ten that drugs were cool. You accepted that you were going to get wrecked on alcohol and that it was totally cool so long as you wiped up your own mess. I sat up in a tree in Wales with half an ounce of Sun Valley and a packet of Rizlas and learnt to roll a joint.' Apparently, Alexis had never said anything about tobacco, so Bobbie banned the children from smoking at home. Consequently, Damian's big thrill was 'going to the bathroom, smoking a cigarette and blowing the smoke out of the window'.

Despite all the potential problems of young people drinking and taking illegal drugs, there might have been some justification for introducing the children to these at home in order to instil some element of responsibility about looking after yourself, knowing your limits and so on. But there was no 'structure' to what went on at home and so Nico often went to school still stoned from the night before.

Not surprisingly, it was the major bone of contention between Alexis and Bobbie, but there seemed little she could do about it. 'I tried to be protective of my children, but didn't succeed very well because he was so damned charismatic.' Bobbie would just get shouted down by everybody for being boring and old-fashioned. 'I would also get angry about the people who would come to the house – when the children were teenagers and the influence was bad. Earlier on the children had a wonderful time and he was a nice father. But all this was overshadowed in the later years when I became concerned at the influence on the children when they were at a vulnerable age.' Bobbie was all for freedom in the general sense, but having experienced the dubious 'freedoms' of Dora

Russell's school, she reacted against the kind of liberalism and *laissez-faire* approach that bred not so much freedom as anarchy.

And Alexis, being Alexis, couldn't just quietly do his drugs: he had to make public statements about it. He became a founder member of the Legalise Cannabis Campaign and spoke at a pro-cannabis rally in Hyde Park Rally on 16 July 1967.

By the mid sixties, 'pop stars' had become the new media aristocracy; arrogant, rich and supposedly posing a threat to the world order. Certain members of the Metropolitan Police were determined to humiliate them while at the same time gaining some media attention for themselves. In January 1966 Donovan was spotted smoking dope on a television documentary and was then subjected to constant police harassment. February 1967 saw the first major tabloid exposé of drug use in the music business, the same month that Keith Richard and Mick Jagger were arrested at Keith's home in probably the most famous drug bust of them all. Brian Jones, Eric Clapton and John Lennon were among many musicians under regular police surveillance. In some instances the press were given advance warning of a drug bust by the police so that the cameras would be in place.

For obvious reasons, few musicians would volunteer the information that they took drugs. Paul McCartney's owning up to trying LSD was one of the exceptions. But Alexis was a high-profile supporter of the campaign to change the laws on cannabis. He had been watched for some time; in August 1966 police raided the Queensway flat and he was fined £50 for being in possession of the drug. After the Hyde Park rally the situation worsened, not just for Alexis but for the whole family. Alexis had the courage to make public his controversial views on a subject that even today remains highly charged, but he didn't really understand what his overt stance on cannabis would do for his children, who then had to go and face the world the following day.

Sappho had to leave her boarding school when the Governors found out about the speech. Damian and Nico were often stopped by the police, as Damian explains: 'What they were looking for was dope, so they could get dad for corrupting minors. Also they would stop us *on the way* to school on the pretext that stationery had been stolen – like as if we'd be taking it back.

'They kept coming to the house to the point where mum did them for harassment. There was somebody at the station who didn't like what was going on and used to phone us up just before the police were coming round to bust us. If you were standing on the balcony at the right time you could have got yourself a mountain of draw because as soon as the phone call came it all went down the chute, out the door.

'We got a bit cocksure, which was a bit naughty because we were dealing with dad's freedom. We had this bar-football game and our dope stash was in one of the goals. They came round again and this time we'd had enough and we weren't going to throw our draw away yet again because it cost us £2 an ounce. The thing was that if you hit the ball into the right-hand side of the net, it would spring open, revealing the stash. These two policemen came up, all nice and friendly, asked us what was going on and said, "Let's have a game of football." Now Nico and I were demons at that game and we played stoned for hours. The cops took the goal with the dope in it. We scored forty goals in the left-hand side of the net – we swapped round and they never sussed that not once did we ever use the striker on the left.

'Another time they came round we had twenty-two cats and they bought the police dogs round. Three minutes later the dogs were haring down the balcony, one with two cats attached to its back.'

Clearly great fun at the time, but also a source of family tensions and worry. Not that the outside world (beyond a handful of intimates) would have been aware of problems in the Korner household. Alexis kept his family and his public life very separate. He has gone down in history as one of the great listeners; people would come to him with their worries, often about their struggles in the music business. He would give people his undivided attention, offer a few well-chosen words and they would leave feeling he had really understood their troubles. But there was an invisible wall which few were able to breach. He knew far more about his friends and associates than they ever knew about him. Very little information about his private life crept into the public domain. But as a musician, over the next few years the public would be hearing of him as never before.

10

A NEW GENERATION OF BLUES

lexis' lack of commercial success as a recording artist did nothing to diminish his stature within the music business as a mover and shaker. In fact, the more success accrued to the musicians he had helped along the way, the brighter his star shone. A guest at his fortieth birthday party at the Queensway flat in April 1968 would have met Mick Jagger and Marianne Faithfull, heard John Mayall playing organ on the balcony and Ginger Baker playing drums, seen Charlie Watts being nice to Alexis' children and noticed Ornette Coleman chewing the fat with another of the many celebrities who crowded into the flat.

But Alexis was more than just a guru for British rock stars. Through the 1960s he won the respect of American musicians like Charlie Mingus and Miles Davis. They joined him in front of his interviewer's microphone and at the dinner table rather than on stage or in the studio, but as musicians they found common ground. His knowledge and iconoclasm won over those whose attitude to white musicians, let alone white journalists, could be described as, at the very least, 'challenging'. Alexis also hit it off with another American musician, one who wrote the book on being taciturn with those outside his circle. Bob Dylan came to Britain in 1962 to record a dreadful film for the BBC and showed up alone at Troubadour Club.

Anthea Joseph was taking the money on the door that evening. 'The day before I'd been in Collet's and read this article by Bob Shelton about Bob Dylan. I listened to that first album in the shop. I didn't like it; none of us liked it – bits were OK, but you wouldn't buy it.

The following day I saw these feet coming down the stairs, cowboy boots and jeans, which was quite unusual, and I thought, Oh God, it's one of the Southend hillbillies, I can't bear it. Then he came down a bit further and I saw the face and thought, I know that face. He pushed some money at me and said, "Can I come in?" "Hang on, you are Bob Dylan?" "Yes, I am." "Right, if you play, you can come in for nothing." Half the audience loved it, the other half hated it.

'Alexis and Bob met in my house. It was fascinating; Alexis being the bluesman, Bob being a quasi-bluesman, Woody Guthrie, the two things crossing over. And they sat there on the floor with me delivering drinks, food, coffee, all of which was ignored because they were nose to nose. Alexis had this great capacity to get people to talk. Intellectually they gelled, it wasn't just music, but the conversation was obviously full of "Have you heard this riff?" "Do you know this song?" '

And then there was Jimi Hendrix. In the autumn of 1966 the 5th American Blues Festival came to town, to the Royal Albert Hall. After the show several artists on the bill, which included Little Brother Montgomery and Roosevelt Sykes, made a point of going to the all-nighter at Cousins in Greek Street to play with Alexis. Around the time of the blues tour, Chas Chandler had brought Jimi from New York and spent the next few months making sure he was seen and heard in all the right places. Jimi turned up at Cousins, paid his entrance money and quietly walked in. Later on he plugged in his Fender and went through the whole routine. Jaws dropped around the room. 'Isn't he fantastic?' said somebody to Alexis. He thought about this for a moment and nodded sagely, saying, 'Pretty good, yeah, pretty good.' About a year later Alexis managed to get Jimi on his R&B show for the BBC World Service.

By then the format had changed, as Jeff Griffin explains: 'I had this idea: instead of Alexis just doing the speech bits by themselves, it would be fun if he played his guitar behind the links and half-chanted the links, and he thought it would be quite fun as well and we gave it a try. So we always used to have him with his guitar in the studio. Now normally we didn't actually record the links as we recorded the bits of music. We recorded all of them and then once he knew what the keys of the numbers were then he would modulate from one to the other. But of course, the fact that he actually had the guitar in the studio, more often than not the band would say, "Hey do you want to sit in Alexis?"

'One of the best moments I can ever remember was when we did

Jimi Hendrix. We'd already got a couple of tracks down and then Jimi said, "Hey man, I want to do 'Hoochie Coochie Man' and it'd be great if we had slide guitar on it." '

Alexis sat in for the song. Playing and talking together, Alexis and Jimi were like fellow gypsies. Alexis was to narrate two films about Jimi: *See My Music Talking* (1968) and the 1973 Joe Boyd documentary simply called *A Film About Jimi Hendrix*. Unfortunately, Alexis and the BBC were later linked in litigation. That wonderfully impromptu collaboration, first broadcast on 13 November 1967, also turned up on the Jimi Hendrix Radio 1 album released in 1988. The BBC had failed to get permission of Alexis' estate and so the lawyers warmed up for battle. Eventually the matter was settled out of court for an undisclosed sum.

Back in a less litigious era of rock 'n' roll Alexis was still helping the young bloods and wannabes. Some of them did rather well.

In the spring of 1968 Robert Plant was in despair. By the age of fifteen he was a dedicated blues fan and much to his parents' disapproval began hanging out at local clubs, growing his hair long, wearing the 'wrong' clothes and all the other accoutrements of a rebel in the making. He joined long-forgotten Birmingham bands, left school at sixteen determined to succeed as a singer and after his relationship with his parents broke down completely – they wanted him to be a chartered accountant – he left his Kidderminster home as well. Other bands followed, including the Crawling King Snakes, where Robert first met John Bonham. Robert found home comforts with his Anglo-Indian girlfriend, Maureen, and her family packed into a house in Walsall. He first gained wider attention as a singer in the Band of Joy, the third version of which also included John Bonham. Together they backed 'progressive' bands like Ten Years After on the London club circuit. But the band were making no headway and in the spring of 1968, Bonham went to play with Tim Rose and Robert was left at a loose end. Born in August 1948, he'd given himself until the age of twenty to make it in the music business or quit. Time was running out.

Alexis had often played Birmingham clubs such as the Factory and met up with Robert, who was still looking for that magical combination that would propel him to success. Alexis warmed to him immediately; a young man with a deep love of the blues, a most powerful singer coming from a family who scorned his aspirations. They went out on the road together as a duo and Alexis often recounted warm memories of sharing brandy, wine and a few spliffs with 'Planty'. Alexis took Robert through his twentieth birthday in August 1968 and kept his faith in himself alive. 'Alexis absorbed me into his large family of musicians and friends in London . . . helped me build my confidence and aided my schooling for what was about to come, and is still coming.' Singer Terry Reid had mentioned Robert's name to Jimmy Page and Peter Grant, who were looking for a singer to be in a band calling themselves the New Yardbirds. Back in Walsall with a band called Hobbstweedle, Robert played a Birmingham college, watched by Page and Grant. A few days later Jimmy called Robert to his house in Pangbourne, Berkshire. Robert immediately called Alexis to ask his advice; the advice was 'go'.

Alexis, Robert and pianist Steve Miller did a session on Alexis' R&B show and the trio went into the De Lane Lea studios to lay down tracks for an album. They had got through just two songs, 'Operator' and 'Steal Away', when the sessions started for the first Led Zeppelin album and Robert was called away and gone for good. A snatch of 'Steal Away' can be heard on *Led Zeppelin* during 'How Many More Times'.

When Sappho left Finchden, she went off to Wales to live in a caravan with guitarist Danny Kustow. The relationship failed and she came back to London to attend Hammersmith Art College. There she met another musician, Andy Fraser. Like Sappho, he had been thrown out of school. They started seeing each other; Sappho introduced Fraser to Alexis and he was embraced into the Korner household. 'Alexis became a kind of father-figure to me because my own father split when I was very young, so I didn't really have a father relationship. For me, it was like an adopted family. Because Alexis was an older guy with a younger mind-set, it made him very attractive to me and I tried to pump as much information out of him as I could – not just music, but life in general.'

Since sacking John McVie, John Mayall had been having problems finding a permanent replacement. He called up Alexis for advice and although Andy was a guitarist, Alexis recommended him to Mayall, setting him on the path of a professional career as a bass player. The job lasted only two months, after which producer Mike Vernon put Andy on to a young guitarist named Paul Kossoff who had been rehearsing with a singer, Paul Rodgers, and a drummer, Simon Kirke, in a band called Brown Sugar. Simon had begun his playing career near the Korners' Welsh home. As Alexis later recalled: 'Simon used to play the dances in a place called Knighton which consisted of a record player and a speaker and a drummer who played along to the record.'

Alexis gave a lot of help and advice to this new band, to whom he gave the name Free. Andy Fraser acknowledges Alexis' assistance. 'He came down to the very first rehearsal and he flipped – he was very excited for us.' They had their first gig arranged for the 19 April 1968, at the Nag's Head pub in Battersea, the night of Alexis' fortieth birthday. Alexis planned to take Bobbie and by chance Anthea Joseph dropped in. 'Alexis said, "I'm glad you're here. I want to take you to see a band in Battersea. They're very young, but they are going to be huge." '

The next step was to get the band wider exposure, so Alexis took Andy and the others all round the country with him. Andy explains: 'He'd do a solo spot, we'd play with him and we'd do a spot by ourselves. This gave us the confidence we needed as a band and got us about until we started on our own.'

For a brief period Alexis was the band's co-manager with Bryan Morrison, but Morrison got into financial difficulties and needed some quick money. Relations between Morrison and the band quickly soured. Interviewed some years later by Chris Welch, Paul Rodgers claimed that Bryan Morrison threw a cheque and told them to make it last: 'it was if we were a charity or something. We threw it back and told him to get stuffed.' Alexis introduced Free to Chris Blackwell at Island Records, who bought the band on the cheap. Their first album, *Tons of Sobs*, was released to great acclaim in 1969, and so began a highly successful but very turbulent five-year career.

While he spent time helping others, Alexis was still very much engaged in helping himself. In fact 1968 was a very busy year for him. Through a contact of Danny Thompson, Alexis had put his voice to good use in the world of television commercials. With a vocal quality crafted for voice-overs, this new activity made a growing contribution to the family income and was to become a key element in his earnings for many years. Bobbie was very pleased. 'That was a day job, it was brilliant. It made money and he didn't have to do anything except turn up, which suited him perfectly. And it was all in the West End, where we lived. He loved doing commercials and he certainly wasn't ashamed of doing them. He wouldn't have advertised anything South African, but that was about all.' So you could hear Alexis Korner's dark-brown voice extolling the virtues of everything from Milky Way and shampoo to Max Factor eye shadow and Bird's Eye frozen foods.

The Blues Rolls On, a three-part series on the British blues, was broadcast in July and in August there was a new series of his World Service R&B

show featuring live sets by Free, Taste, the Aynsley Dunbar Retaliation, Jethro Tull, Duster Bennett, the Savoy Brown Blues Band, Chicken Shack and many others. Jeff Griffin was very pleased with audience feedback from the shows. 'We had quite a few cards from GIs serving in Vietnam. I found these very touching; in the middle of all that they'd been able to get round a radio and find something they liked for fifteen minutes to give them respite from the situation they were in.' Alexis played a number of anti-Vietnam, pro-CND and general anti-war benefits and signed a Folksingers for Freedom in Vietnam petition in March 1967 which called for an end to the bombing of the country and withdrawal of all foreign troops.

Alexis progressed further with his idea of presenting a live history of the blues to complement his ordinary gigs. Called *The Submerged Seven-Eighths Of The Blues*, the programme was presented over three sessions at the Hampstead Arts Centre. Alexis hosted the shows, which included contributions from Danny Thompson, Annie Ross, Jon Hendricks and Davy Graham. Alexis had his own spot and as ever his performance as a blues musician continued to extract diametrically opposite responses from music critics. One critic complained that Alexis wasn't given enough time to perform. 'He only played when everybody else had cleared off to recuperate, leaving him alone with his guitar enthralling the audience.' Another denied that Alexis was a true bluesman at all (because, of course, he wasn't black) and while acknowledging his role in promoting blues in the early sixties, opined that with so much of the 'real thing' now available on record and touring the country, Alexis as a blues performer was an irrelevance.

This was to miss the point. There was now a new breed of home-grown talent that Alexis was engaged in helping – even if the way the blues was now being interpreted did not always sit easy with him. He never regarded the blues as simply a fossilized ethnic form and quite clearly wanted the widest possible exposure for a music that many now realized had universal appeal.

Black and white blues came together over the weekend of 7–8 September 1968 with the first National Blues Convention, held at the Conway Hall in London. Alexis was one of the organizers and it was a testament to the success of his promotion of the music as a performer, broadcaster and journalist that the two-day event was a sell-out, with many hundreds turned away. On the first night Alexis shared the stage with Jo-Ann Kelly, Tony McPhee, Duster Bennett,

Champion Jack Dupree, Curtis Jones and Bobbie Parker. A number of activities were scheduled for the Sunday, including an Alexis Korner guitar workshop.

But in musical terms Alexis was a polymath, in demand across the range of music available on the airwaves. He was a featured artist on *Degrees of Folk*, a televised concert of international folk music from St Andrews University, and presented *Jazz at Night*, where he introduced a special on jazz in the cinema. He appeared with John Peel and Richard Neville on a new BBC2 arts programme, *How It Is*, produced by Tony Palmer, where he blasted a shot across the bows of the hallowed Promenade Concerts.

'As long as they know the work they'll applaud it,' he said. 'Given a certain minimum technical standard, it doesn't matter much about interpretation. And these same people have the nerve to accuse pop audiences of being undiscriminating. The choice of programme [for the Proms] would often be quite suitable for a London Palladium show. For me, most Prom concerts have a turgid malodorous atmosphere. If they are presented as a national service to music, then surely they must be honour bound to contribute more to the act of creation and less to the preservation of orchestral pieces so well known as to have lost much of their flavour. Only three of the fifty-three concerts were devoted to modern composers. In all there were some twenty-four modern compositions being performed – a total playing time of about eight hours. You can't tell me this is fair representation.'

Booking through Bryan Morrison's agency, Alexis had a pretty full date sheet both as a solo performer and as half of a (now occasional) duo with Victor Brox. They appeared together on the opening night of the Jazz Centre's Monday-evening sessions at the 100 Club with Sandy Brown's Quartet and pianist Chris McGregor. *Melody Maker* called Victor 'one of the most underrated people around' and hailed as a 'peak of excitement' the evening when Alexis and Victor were joined by Alexis' old friend, pianist Dave Stevens. The intensity and passion of the whole evening's entertainment was actually too much for the paper's critic, who said he would have preferred more light and shade to heighten the drama of the event.

Alexis also found a new duo partner, a seventeen-year-old bassist called Nick South. 'My father was a composer and my parents were pretty bohemian,' says Nick, 'so I wasn't coming from a strict, traditional family background. My parents were divorced when I was thirteen and

I moved to London. I took up the bass and dived into it. A friend of my younger brother was friends with Nico. By the time I met Alexis I'd been playing bass for about two years. Alexis had been playing once a week at a church in Ladbroke Grove over a few weekends. I went along to jam with him. Two weeks later we were on the road doing stuff like "Louisiana Blues", "Rosie", "Mary, Open the Door" and "Rock Me".'

As well as co-managing Free with Bryan Morrison and using him as his agent, Alexis signed a production deal with him for a new album on the Liberty label called *New Generation of Blues*. He persuaded his seasoned *Five O'Clock Club* trio of Danny Thompson and Terry Cox (both by now immersed in the folk group Pentangle, which also included Bert Jansch and John Renbourn) plus Ray Warleigh, back into the studio. The tracks were recorded over a number of sessions, so in a sense this was a compilation of tracks laid down over a three-month period. The stripped-down, stark production, with Ray Warleigh's flute adding a light, airy feel, gave the whole album a rather ethereal tone which sometimes tipped over into the insubstantial. The contrast was even more marked when compared with the sound of contemporary bands such as Fleetwood Mac, Cream and Free, a pantheon of rivals acknowledged by Alexis in the track 'What's That Sound I Hear': 'There's Clapton, Hendrix, Peter Green and John Mayall, too.' For Alexis, with this album, it was as usual the sound of one cash register ringing. But equally true to form, there were timeless songs full of blues passion, like 'Go Down Sunshine' and the achingly beautiful 'The Same For You'. Alexis' recording career is dotted with real gems such as these – often a perfect synthesis of man and his guitar – which taken together could perhaps yet make a creditable 'Alexis Unplugged' album.

Alexis had moved from a position in 1967 where his profile was fading to one of diverse activity. But there was a problem: his career was still shapeless, there was nobody guiding his activities, trying to make the best of his many talents. Tom Robinson sums it up well when he describes seeing Alexis play at Finchden. 'What we saw that night was riveting, marketable, saleable as a commodity. If somehow he could have presented that on his records, his publicity shots and the way he was perceived by the public, he would have been the star he deserved to be.' Alexis' career was like a jigsaw puzzle that nobody was bothering to put together. He needed something he had never had before: a proper manager.

ues Incorporated.

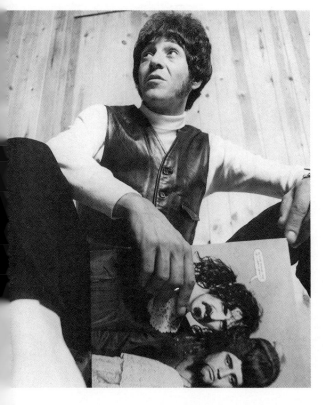

Alexis and Frank, 1967.

Just a man and his guitar at Stone House, 1970 ...

... Plus a few others called C.C.S.

...ape.

...n Alexis Korner, B. B. King and Steve Marriott London recording session.

Alexis with Guido Toffoletti, probably the last Korner protégé, 1976.

Alexis, Sappho and Colin Hodgkinson.

A rare look at Alexis on piano, 1978.

Alexis and Colin Hodgkinson.
(Credit: Hasse Ivarsson)

ike father, like sons and daughter . . .
Above) Nico, Sappho and Alexis.

Right) Alexis. *(Credit: Hans Harzheim)*

Below left) Nico and Alexis.
Credit: Helmut Roos)

Below right) Damian, Sappho and
obbie, 1996. *(Credit: Harry Shapiro)*

"BLUES FROM THE ROUNDHOUSE" VOL. I

ALEXIS KORNER

SKIFFLE GROUP

HE ROUNDHOUSE" VOL. 2

KORNER'S

BLUE
INCORPORATE

Featurin
CYRIL DAVI

I AIN'T GONNA
    WORRY NO MORE

COUNTY JAIL

KID MAN

EASY RIDER

SAIL ON

NATIONAL
    DEFENCE BLUE

GO DOWN
    SUNSHINE

DEATH LETTER

tempo EXA 76

tempo EXA 10

R&B from the MARQUEE

ALEXIS KORNER'S BLUES INCORPORATED

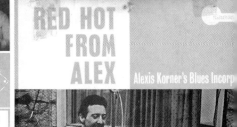

RED HOT FROM ALEX

Alexis Korner's Blues Incorp

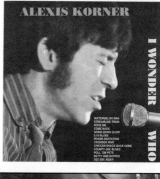

Alexis KORNER
MEMORIAL CONCER[T]

ALEXIS KORNER
THE FATHER OF BRITISH BLU[ES]

'He inspired us all'

PRODUCTION [CREDITS]

— FO[R]
ACTIVE MUSI[C]

NORMAN BEAKER: Art[istic]
HARRY LEE: Productio[n]
STEVE BAINBRIDGE:
BARRY HILLS: Marke[ting]

The Buxton Opera House b[ar]
open throughout the performance[s]
[sandwiches] and drinks are ava[ilable]

THE ROLLING STONES

BUXTON

Theatre manage[r]
Technical manag[er]
House manager[s]

Concert soun[d]
Phantom Po[wer]
Concert ligh[ting]

THE KORNER FAMILY

would like you to join them

in

"A Farewell to Alexis"

at
12.00 noon
on
Friday, 13th January 1984

at
Dingwalls
Camden Lock, Chalk Farm Road
London N W 1

Stephen Goddard & A[ssociates]
GRAPHIC DESIGN CO[MPANY]
PRODUCTION CO[MPANY]

We Feel Privileg[ed]
to have worked
with and for
Alexis Korner

A man who will
be sadly missed by All

For all at SG&A

[REA]D CAVERSHAM READING RG4 8DT
[07]34 · 471293

WE ARE PROUD TO HAVE BEEN ASSOCIATED WITH
AND A FRIEND OF ALEXIS KORNER

Chappell Music Ltd
129 Park Street
London
W1

Chappell & Co Gmb[H]
Heinrich-Barth-Stras[se]
2000 Hamburg [13]
West Germany

ALEXIS KOR[NER]

"I WAS A JUVENILE DELIN[QUENT]
JUST DELINQUISHING M[Y]
BUT MUSIC CAME AND GO[T ME]"

HIS INFECTIOUS ENTHUSIASM FOR MUS[IC]
AND SUPPORT OF TALENT TAUGHT ME
THAT THERE IS MORE TO OUR BUSINESS
THAN CONTRACTS AND LAWSUITS

Del Tay[lor]

I AM PROUD TO HAVE BEEN CHOSEN AS [A]
VITA VIVA ARTIST BY ALEXIS.

Daniel Webs[ter]

Since 1962 Alexis had been represented by a succession of agents: CANA Variety, Peter Berman, Eric Easton, International Artists Representation, Robert Stigwood, Roy Guest, Lyn Dutton and Bryan Morrison. Ronan O'Rahilly, who started pirate radio, had tried to manage Blues Inc at one time, getting them into suits and psychotherapy to improve their performance. There was the passing involvement of Giorgio Gomelsky and interest from Brian Epstein, but the Gunnell Brothers had it right: Alexis was unmanageable.

Most of those striving for success in sixties pop were hardly out of their teens, eager to sign anything put in front of them and more than happy (in the first instance at any rate, before the hits rolled in and while money didn't) to leave all business matters to the Svengalis of pop management. Alexis, Graham Bond and John Mayall were much older and far more independent. Of the three, John Mayall was easily the most businesslike; his musicians were often sacked at a moment's notice, but they did get a steady wage.

Graham and Alexis took a more short-term view. Graham simply ripped off agencies and promoters to feed his drug habit, leaving his musicians to cope as best they could. In their time, Ginger Baker and Jon Hiseman both took over the band finances because Graham could not be trusted. Alexis ran himself ragged booking gigs, signing record deals, arranging transport and so on, but he couldn't deal equitably with the money side, caught as he was between hungry musicians and a hungry family.

By 1968 Alexis had tired of doing it all himself and rather than simply hop from one agent to another trying to get gigs, he began to think about finding a manager who could take all the organizational responsibilities off his shoulders.

Phil Roberge, a high-flyer in the world of New York management consultancy, came to London on holiday in October 1968 on the last voyage of the QE1. On board he met an acquaintance of the PR firm Southcombe and West. They handled a big roster of pop and film stars, among them Judy Garland, Rock Hudson, Christopher Lee and Diana Dors. They also had Alexis on their books on an expenses-only basis, because he needed somebody to help with publicity and promotion.

Always looking for new business opportunities, Phil had various meetings at the office and one time when he came in, 'Alexis was sitting in a chair and just turns round and says, "So you want to be my manager?" I said, "No, no, I'm in management consulting." And he said, "Well, I want an American manager." It caught me completely off guard because I knew nothing about the music business. He took me to a university gig he had as a duo with Nick South and on the way he handed me a copy of the Rolling Stones' biography up to 1968.'

Reading it, Phil came to understand how important Alexis was. He went back to America at Christmas without having made up his mind what he was going to do. During the voyage, Phil befriended Lord and Lady Montagu of Beaulieu and on a return visit to London, Phil accompanied Edward Montagu to Mick Jagger's house in Chelsea. When Phil told Mick he was thinking of managing Alexis, Mick replied: 'You just think you're going to manage him. He's got a mind of his own, believe me.'

Phil took this thought back home with him and over the next three months Alexis would ring up once or twice a week. Alexis was serious, so Phil told his bosses that he was taking a year's leave of absence and returned to London on his birthday, 17 March 1969.

'At Southcombe and West they had a little kitchen they weren't using, so I brought in a carpenter and we put some plywood over the sink and I got a handsome red phone installed plus a chair and said, "Well now I'm a manager, what do I do?"'

Phil then set himself the task of learning the business and began to read all the trade papers. He had no idea who were the musicians to know about, so he'd go over to Alexis' flat, where he would hear about Robert Plant or Brian Jones, 'and I'd excuse myself to go to the bathroom, so I could make some notes and then come back for more. Soon I began to realize that as a real true talent-picker, his contribution was enormous.'

He also saw very quickly that while he might be able to help Alexis, simply being associated with the name of Alexis Korner was a novice manager's dream. 'His name was golden; it opened the door of every managing director of every record company, all the people who ran the business. All you had to say was that you were managing Alexis Korner.'

The first issue to address was Alexis' financial situation. It was clear from the start that without the voice-over income, Alexis would be in deep trouble. This was the delusion of his busy schedule; there was an awful lot going on in all sorts of areas, but it did not amount to much in the way of hard cash. Phil was a great administrator; his Shangri-La was to sit at a huge desk covered with papers, working out royalties.

From the point at which he took over as Alexis' manager, there was a voluminous correspondence with every record company Alexis had ever dealt with, in an effort to gain the ever-elusive information on sales and recoup any unpaid royalties. 'I was dumbfounded that an artist could be paid so little. Without the artist, the company has no product.'

Phil also managed to raise Alexis' fees for commercials and gigs, which helped fund the purchase of a derelict chapel close to their rented retreat, Stone House, deep in the Welsh countryside. Initially the restoration work was modest, but over the years, as income allowed and with the help of Nigel Stanger, an architect who had also played with Alexis, the Chapel was turned into a beautiful second home away from the helter-skelter of London life. Alexis kept it as private as possible and deliberately had only one bedroom installed to discourage visitors, who would instead be directed to a nearby guest house. As the children grew up, Bobbie and Alexis spent increasing amounts of time there. He so loved the Chapel, he would think nothing of doing the eight-hour round trip from London just for an overnight stop.

Phil even sorted out the mundane financial affairs such as insurance policies. Bobbie says Alexis took a philosophical view of insurance. 'He thought if things were going to happen, so be it. He never claimed on any insurance because he never believed that the company would pay up and anyway it would mean having to write a letter.' Meanwhile Alexis was turning his thoughts to forming a new band, and more importantly, to exactly where the performing base of this new band might be.

In a mid-sixties interview Alexis had commented that the Liverpool sound was basically guitar-led and that anything else was doomed to commercial failure. He used the example of Manfred Mann, who 'started his first band with string bass, piano, drums, piano, alto sax, tenor sax, trumpet. And he gave that up, you see, because it wasn't successful.' By about 1966 Alexis was in a similar position. As he had complained bitterly, in his view the blues had been stripped back to basics, narrowly focused on a particular time and place in its history. But as the album sales of John Mayall's Bluesbreakers showed, it also happened to be the most commercial way to present the music. And in encouraging the likes of Robert Plant and Free, Alexis had helped create a situation where a new generation of 'rock' bands would even further erode the audience for his own music. As a solo performer, he could always fill a pub or small club, but there was much less of a fan base for him at the larger concert venues. From 1968 onwards, therefore, he began to accept offers of work in Europe, where audiences were far more open to a range of music, especially jazz, and where, unlike in England, they tended not to sit back in their seats and say: 'Go on, impress me.'

With his family background, fluency in several languages and love of European culture and lifestyle, Alexis felt every bit as much at home in France, the Netherlands or Germany as he did in England. This put him in a unique position to re-create, for a European audience, the blues boom he had pioneered in England. Bringing his reputation, his knowledge of the music and his strong live performances to countries where interest in the blues was just beginning, Alexis made an impact in Europe similar to that of Big Bill Broonzy in England ten years earlier.

In 1968 he played the Jazz Jamboree in Warsaw and a Belgian music festival, as well as undertaking a ten-day tour of Czechoslovakia. But his real home from home was Germany; the Frankfurt Jazz Festival in March, the International Hot Jazz Meeting in Hamburg at the beginning of May and the International Essen Song Days in late September with Frank Zappa, Julie Driscoll and the Fugs.

Alexis held a special place in his heart for Hamburg. As a port city with easy access across the North Sea, Hamburg had always been the most 'English' of the German cities. In the late 1950s club owners in the Reeperbahn red-light district wanted to showcase the new rock 'n' roll, but couldn't afford to bring over American acts. One enterprising owner, Bruno Koschmider of the Kaiserkeller, on hearing about the 2Is coffee bar from visiting English sailors, went over to London to spy out the land and came back with Tony Sheridan and the Jets. Their immediate success generated a war between the clubs; Koschmider lost his band to a rival, then contacted a Merseyside agent, and in came a flood of Liverpool beat groups. Playing in sweaty, dangerous clubs, pilled up to the eyebrows for hours on end, they helped shape the sound of sixties pop in Britain and created a ready-made audience for British blues, jazz and rock bands in Germany.

From his broadcasting days with the British Forces Network, Alexis knew Hamburg well and came to play the Hot Jazz concerts on a regular basis. He made some close friends and important contacts. Klaus Welleshaus is a writer, producer and broadcaster for Nord-West Deutsche Rundfunk (NDR), a major German radio station reaching about a quarter of the German population. In 1968 Klaus had just come into popular music from a classical background. 'I had read how many famous people had described Alexis as a mentor, so it was quite exciting for me to meet him then because I was new to the business, especially as he could speak fluent German.' As well as learning about the 'business of pop', Klaus says he was also quite ignorant of the musical form itself. 'I had to learn what there was to hear behind the surface. Alexis told me about different angles, different ways to look at the emotional content, the idea that music is nothing if it isn't a trigger for thoughts and feelings. He told me about the certain feelings that made blues music without the formal structures being in place which I had to learn because I was a formally trained musician.'

A quiet, dignified, urbane and highly intelligent man, Klaus and his family were among that very select band of people to be invited to stay at the Chapel. The friendship between Alexis and Klaus was one based on intuition rather than knowledge; they spoke of 'quite personal matters', and Alexis indicated to Klaus that his family life was not the easiest, that he made 'unreasonable demands' on his family, how different he was at home and on the road, but how important each was to him and how he couldn't drop either. 'But he never really opened up in terms of "Look, this is Alexi in reality. This is the Alexi behind the leather hat and the guitar." ' Like many of Alexis' friends, Klaus says: 'I think he knew more about me than I knew about him.'

Klaus learnt from Alexis, 'a strange mixture of musical, professional and personal things about conducting your life. It was like talking to a father or a good uncle you could relate to, who had the experiences you were still looking for.'

He interviewed Alexis regularly on his radio show, presented in a loose format, with Alexis talking and playing live for up to an hour and a half – the kind of exposure he had never enjoyed in England.

The new band Alexis had been contemplating was slow in gestating and really began with Nick South. Among their very first dates was a trip to Düsseldorf and then Denmark. Alexis was just as keen on encouraging young European talent; at the Frankfurt Blues Festival he played with Harry Muskee's Cuby & the Blizzards and later penned the sleeve-notes to their début album. With Nick in Denmark, he fell in with a young band called the Beefeaters, led by singer–guitarist Peter Thorup, who joined the new band.

Alexis had in mind a band that would be another eclectic mix of styles, but this time including elements of gospel, which he had never explored before as a performing musician. Probably to that end, he named the band New Church. To Nick and Peter Thorup, he added

Ray Warleigh and, in another new and potentially fraught departure, he took his own daughter Sappho on the road as a singer.

Sappho's first gig with Alexis had been on 14 August 1968, just after her sixteenth birthday, at Rambling Jack's Blues Club in Bishop's Stortford, which was owned by Alexis' sometime pianist Steve Miller. Father and daughter sang together on 'Rock Me'; Sappho took the spotlight for 'Mean Old World' and 'I Can't Hold Out Much Longer'. She told a local reporter: 'I sang a bit rough, but if I get better I'll probably turn professional. I normally just sing to myself. It's the first time my father's heard me. I've never sung with other people around.'

While Alexis was helping fledgeling musicians like Nick South and his own daughter find their feet, another Korner protégé from an earlier time needed help of a different kind.

Intense rivalries had been building up within the Rolling Stones between Brian Jones on one side and Keith and Mick on the other. There was a battle over leadership of the band, the direction of the music, and women. All three had been busted for drugs in 1967 and were under constant pressure from the police. Keith and Mick took most of the hassles in their stride, but Brian was imploding with the strain of it all. Mentally and physically, he was in poor shape. Bobbie Korner recalls seeing Brian 'when they were in that period of dandification, dressing up in eighteenth-century clothes. We went to a concert and Brian came into a box above us and I looked at him and thought, my God, he's gone – that isn't somebody dressing up. It's somebody who has disappeared.'

The Stones turned to their mentor to help smooth Brian's transition to life outside the band. Mick and Keith separately phoned Alexis to say they were worried about Brian while Brian himself put through anxious calls to Alexis asking him what to do because he feared that the Stones were about to ditch him.

But when, in June 1969, Keith, Mick and (most reluctantly) Charlie paid Brian the inevitable visit, it came as a relief to Brian. Despite all his misgivings, he had clearly lost the will to carry on fighting. He had spent £32,000 buying A. A. Milne's Cotchford Farm, in Sussex. He loved the place, revelling in its extensive gardens and swimming pool, and with his new-found time, space and privacy he began to think about new directions. Brian was a very talented musician and his time spent with Morocco's Master Musicians of Jajouka demonstrated a vision well beyond that which the Stones could have countenanced; it was a foretaste of the West's love affair with 'world music'.

Brian wanted to share his visions of the future with the one group of people he could trust, who had shown him such kindness over the years and never abused his friendship for their own ends. He insisted that the Korner family come to stay at the farm. Whatever had happened to him, he remained, in Damian Korner's words, 'such a nice man, such a lovely man to be around. He was kind, considerate and thoughtful. He was a comforting person. If you don't have children, you have to be a nice person in order to comfort children. Staying at the house was a problem for me because it was haunted. But he had the capacity to make a young child who was feeling frightened, feel OK.'

Alexis later told the Stones' biographer Philip Norman that when he first went to see Brian after the break-up he was shocked by his friend's appearance, but sat patiently with him as he skipped from one idea to the next, such as a British version of his current favourite band, Creedence Clearwater Revival. Alexis organized rehearsals for the various musicians invited down to the farm, including the late Vincent Crane and Carl Palmer, then of Atomic Rooster, John Mayall, Mitch Mitchell and Jeff Beck's drummer, Micky Waller.

Meanwhile Sam Cutler from the Stones office called Phil Roberge, inviting Alexis to join the bill of a free Rolling Stones concert to be held in Hyde Park on Saturday 5 July. New Church interrupted their first European tour to come back for the gig, which was to be their London début, in front of an estimated audience of 250,000. Although Alexis and Phil had decided right from the start that New Church's future lay in Europe, this would be a marvellous showcase for the band. To announce the London début Phil issued a press release which contained details of their European tour and a reminder of Alexis' importance in British music history. It was, to coin a phrase, a small step, but Alexis had never had the benefit of even this most basic of PR exercises to raise his profile.

In the run-up to the concert New Church had been rehearsing with Brian at Cotchford Farm. At one time Brian had suggested becoming a full band member, but Alexis thought it was much better for him to be working on his own ideas in his own set-up. Then, because he was so eager to get back on the road, Brian suggested just joining the band as a guest when the tour resumed in Germany on 6 July. Alexis gently but firmly vetoed that idea too. As he told a biographer of Brian, he did not want the responsibility of looking after him on the road, especially in Germany, where 'for a long time it was Brian Jones and the Rolling Stones rather than Mick and the Rolling Stones. Brian was enormously popular in Germany and I was a bit worried. I felt we'd have to have security and I didn't think I could cope with that.' Then on 3 July came the news that Brian had been found dead in his swimming pool.

Numerous accounts have been published of what may have transpired at Cotchford Farm in the early hours of that morning and it is not the purpose of this book to go over the ground covered by other authors. Suffice to say, Nick South, who spent many hours at the farm with New Church in the days leading up to Brian's death, comments that 'even at the time we all thought it was very suspicious'.

Alexis was devastated and cancelled the rest of New Church's maiden European tour. However, the Hyde Park Concert went ahead as a memorial to Brian. Mick paid tribute to Brian, read a stanza from Shelley's 'Adonais' and released several hundred white butterflies into the warm July air. The general air of disquiet about Brian's last days with the band and the degree to which others had pushed him to the brink of insanity meant that much was read into the deaths of several butterflies who never made it into the skies, but died in the box.

The event went well for New Church, even though Nick South's amp exploded during the warm-up. Shortly after Hyde Park, Phil received an offer he couldn't refuse for New Church to play an extravagant party in Geneva hosted by the notorious international financier Bernie Cornfeld. Steve Clyne drove the band in a van well past its sell-by date which had been bought from Pink Floyd. 'The passenger door was welded shut and the back doors were held together by a wooden wedge.' Cornfeld's company, IOS, was celebrating huge successes for the year and the party was held on the banks of Lake Geneva with two hundred of the financier's insurance sales force, two hundred 'hostesses', the kitchen staff flown in from a West End hotel and the whole area laid out like a film set.

Back on planet earth, thoughts turned to recording the band, but not before New Church suffered a far more destructive explosion than the loss of one amp.

11

TAP TURNS ON THE WATER

Bobbie was not happy with Alexis taking Sappho out on the road. At sixteen her daughter was far too young, she thought, to be exposed to the rock 'n' roll lifestyle of a touring band. But, as ever, she was overruled. Sappho was very keen on becoming a singer, although she knew that as 'Alexis Korner's daughter' she would need to be damn good to succeed and she would have to do it on her own with little if any help from her father otherwise any success would be undermined.

For his part, Alexis wanted to help Sappho, but also saw an opportunity to get closer to the daughter whom he loved fiercely (as she did him) but who had distanced herself by her uncontrolled behaviour. Unfortunately, his way of getting closer was to try to make Sappho his friend and confidante, divulging some of the problems he claimed he was having – the ordinary cut and thrust of any marriage, but which nonetheless caught Sappho unprepared.

'I had no idea there were any problems, but because we were touring together he would start to talk to me. It was quite a shock to hear there were problems in his life – I thought he was God and then I discovered he wasn't God after all. Having been sheltered from this kind of thing, it was just the impact of realizing that everything wasn't perfect. I think it was grossly unfair. I often think that was a cop-out on his part of being a parent: to have your children as your best friends. One way or another, he made very high demands.'

Alexis was well aware of this; his main demand was that his children

173

learn to be independent, as he had been as a child. And if the children of a musician went out on the road they ought to know what to expect and deal with it. 'I felt extremely vulnerable on the road and I didn't feel he looked after me like he should have done. I was thrown in at the deep end and it was like, "Right 'Pho, you want to do this, OK, this is what it is all about, off you go." I wouldn't have missed it for the world, but going on the road didn't do me any good – I wasn't strong enough – and he was. You've got to be so tough and really believe you are it.' From Alexis' point of view, expecting this level of strength from his children marked him out as a strict parent.

But for Sappho, who wanted to make it as a singer, there were all the compensations of having a father who revelled in performance. 'He was such a wonderful person to play with, to sing with, just his absolutely overpowering, overwhelming love for it. That was something to see. I wish I had that drive, but it can be so destructive of everything else around it – it's all-consuming. The one thing you could never have done is say, "It's me or the music." With somebody like that down the line, you can only ever be second.'

Yet none of this was the cause of the showdown. Sappho and Nick South were still teenagers trying to operate in a grown-up world. Nick explains: 'It must have been terrible for Alexis to have me and Sappho in the band together because we were squabbling the whole time. He was very long-suffering about all that. It was probably jealousy of each other's position in relation to Alexis – just arrogant teenagers.'

And it was jealousy that Sappho claims brought matters to a head. 'I also saw Alexis Korner the major egoist – only later did I realize that you couldn't do what he did unless he was one. I really got into it, I loved being on stage and I was getting better and better. It became competitive and one day he wouldn't let me go on for an encore. I said, "They want ME" and then I said things children shouldn't say to parents like, "I am what you made me" and "Why are you so jealous?" ' He had to react and a major row ensued. Sappho left the band in the autumn of 1969 and says she didn't speak to Alexis for over a year.

Fortunately they were to enjoy good times playing together, away from the public gaze. 'My greatest pleasures with daddy were not on stage, but at home jamming, not performing . . . sitting around and he might say, "Hey 'Pho, that was great" . . . No bullshit, just family, door shut, window locked . . . That's why I went out on the road, to try and recreate that thing, but it never worked like that because he was so competitive.'

Nick South followed Sappho out of New Church shortly afterwards, just before they went into the studio to record the band's only studio album, *Both Sides*, which wasn't so much 'released' as emerged snail-like from under a rock of indecision.

Alexis and Phil approached Jeff Griffin to produce the album. Jeff agreed and Alexis and Nick South (then still in the band) went to Jeff's house to discuss the album. Jeff recalls: 'He wanted some big band arrangements done and he got John Surman to do a couple and I got some done by a good arranger I knew. The rest was going to be stuff that Alexis was playing at the time.'

All-night sessions were booked at Olympic for 23–25 September. Alexis turned up and the first thing he did was to announce to Jeff that he had sacked Nick. 'Here we are just about to record a brand-new album, studio time booked and no bass player. I said, "What are you going to do?" "I'm going to give Andy Fraser a call." Andy came down and did all the bass parts. Sacking Nick South in that way was a very Alexis thing to do. It wouldn't matter if there was a tour coming up or whatever. If something didn't feel right, that was it.'

The album was recorded. Victor Brox's wife, Annette, replaced Sappho and the rest of the musicians included a brass section of Lol Coxhill, Harry Beckett, Chris Pyne and Ray Warleigh, drummer John Marshall and Peter Thorup, with Free's Paul Rodgers as backing vocalist. They mixed it the following week and everybody seemed reasonably happy.

And then it all went very quiet. Jeff heard nothing about the album for ages, 'then Alexis told me that Bobbie didn't like the brass arrangements', although Bobbie says: 'I could only influence what he had already decided would be changed.'

Eventually four tracks, including 'Louisiana Blues' and 'Will The Circle Be Unbroken' were replaced with live material from a New Church concert recorded at the Auditorium Maximum in Hamburg on 9 December 1969. Andy Fraser was committed to Free, so Colin Hodgkinson became the latest New Church recruit and played bass on the live recordings.

Colin was a major find for Alexis; a world-class bass player, he was arguably the most talented musician ever to play with him on a long-term basis. They formed a working partnership that survived on and off from 1969 right through to the end of Alexis' career.

Colin Hodgkinson had turned professional in 1966 with a jazz–blues trio and then spent a year with a showband whose line-up included

Ron Asprey. Ray Warleigh and Ron were friends and Ray passed on the information that Alexis was looking for a new bass player. Alexis asked Colin if he had a tape. Colin and Ron had been working together on an idea for a band that eventually became Back Door.

Colin explains: 'I had a tape of the first songs that Back Door had written, so I sent him that and he thought it was great and asked me over to talk about things. He said the band had a gig the following week in Vienna. I said, "When do we rehearse?" He said, "Oh, I'll sort it out." This was a big gig, two or three thousand people, and it's getting nearer and nearer and I wanted to run through the tunes and was getting a bit nervous about it. He said, "You'll be all right, don't worry about it." The upshot was that we went on stage in Vienna, we had no rehearsals, I had no idea what we were going to play. It was one of the drummerless groups we had: Peter, Alexis, Ray Warleigh, me, and I think Annette Brox was singing. Halfway through he said, "Do a bass solo." I said, "I don't know anything." Well in actual fact I'd started playing some Robert Johnson songs like "32-20 Blues". He said, "Just do a bass solo" and he went off the stage. I was just left standing there, I was freaked out enough as it was. Anyway, I did this solo, it went down tremendously well and that's what really got me started off playing the solo legs. I don't know how much of that was calculated or just him being incredibly loose, but that was my introduction to Alexis.'

For Alexis to be leading a band headlining in front of three thousand people would have been hard enough to imagine in England in 1969. For fans to be rioting to get in was inconceivable, but this is exactly what happened in Germany in the winter of 1969 when New Church resumed their abandoned European tour.

The trouble began when they played a big rock festival in Essen at the Gruge Halle. The agent who booked the bands for the festival was Del Taylor, who later worked for Phil Roberge and became Alexis' manager, but was then just finding his feet in the music business. Among the acts scheduled to play were Pink Floyd, Free, Blind Faith, Spooky Tooth and New Church. Del recollects that the festival itself 'was a fiasco. There were a load of forged tickets and lots of people with real tickets couldn't get in because it was a sell-out – so there was a riot outside. I remember somebody driving a VW through the plate-glass window at the front of the hall. It was getting very, very dodgy; there was thick fog, Pink Floyd's gear hadn't arrived. Blind Faith didn't show up. Three days of total mayhem.'

Then in the midst of what was clearly a very dangerous and escalating situation – a full house of eleven thousand inside, with two thousand outside, tear-gas and stones flying, injured people lying in heaps around the building – Alexis and Rory Gallagher went out into the hall foyer and played an impromptu concert for all those fans who couldn't get in. Alexis then went back into the main hall to compère the show. This wasn't the last time that Alexis calmed a raging rock audience. It became something of a feature of major rock festivals in Germany during the early seventies for riots to break out on the back of a belief that music should be free. Both as compère speaking immaculate German and as a performer, Alexis saved more than one venue from being razed to the ground.

The German tour proper started in Frankfurt on 1 December and then moved on to Lüdenscheid the next day. A TV appearance and word of mouth about the first two concerts built up a head of publicity so that the concerts at Bremen's Freizeitheim Altamund Hall and the Berlin Philharmonic Hall were both completely sold out. By the time they reached Hamburg on 9 December (where the *Both Sides* live material was recorded) the hall was besieged by fans desperate for tickets. On the night, disappointed fans rushed the doors and many got in to see the concert without paying. They all sat in a circle surrounding Alexis and the band – so many that the stewards were powerless to remove them. The gatecrashers stayed and the evening was a tremendous success. Immediately, top German promoter Karsten Jahnke, who went on to handle many of Alexis' German gigs, was frantically trying to book concert-hall space in Berlin and Hamburg to run extra shows.

Back in England, Alexis' fans had no idea of just how successful New Church was in Europe and there was precious little chance of the band playing here. The *Bedfordshire Recorder* revealed all: 'The reason why British people don't get a chance to hear them is simple. Peter Thorup is Danish and various authorities, including those fearless champions of middle-aged second trombonists, the Musicians' Union, will not let him live and work in Britain.' Describing a New Church performance on Alexis' World Service programme, the paper went on: 'The standard of all them, vocal and instrumental work, was way above the above-average British bands and the arrangements were certainly more original than most. I do hope they get round the red-tape and other problems and are allowed to play in this country soon. I don't see why the Continent should have all the good things because of British bureaucrats.'

In between excursions to Europe, Alexis carried on with his many
other activities, only this time Phil Roberge made sure that the press were
kept constantly updated with all the new developments and presented
with a publicity biography.

In September 1969 Alexis had begun a fifth series of his R&B show on
the World Service, only the title had been changed to *Blues Is Where You
Hear It*. The blues bubble had pretty much burst; many musicians such as
Eric Clapton, Fleetwood Mac, Led Zeppelin and Free had moved away
from the clubs to become part of the campus, concert, festival and arena
rock-band scene. The name change signified an attempt by Alexis and
Jeff to include soul, gospel and other forms by broadening the definition
of the blues, although it was irksome to both of them that the blues spot
on Radio 1, which had come onstream in the wake of the demise of
pirate radio, had gone to Mike Raven rather than Alexis.

It is possible that Alexis had his share of enemies at the BBC,
those whom he had antagonized through his notorious lack of tact
and diplomacy or perhaps his lack of conformity even during an era
when Auntie was trying to get 'hip' and 'in the groove'. There are one
or two internal BBC memos from that period which indicate certain
antipathies towards 'The Father of the Blues'. The young boy who was
so eager to please had become the man who spoke his mind.

Alexis once again helped organize the National Blues Convention. At
the Sunday-morning workshop session he introduced two young blues
musicians, Jim James and die-hard Blues Inc fan Raphael Callaghan.
Eager to attend the workshop, they had travelled down to London
overnight. 'We'd slept in Jim's car and wandered bleary-eyed into this
seminar. Alexis said, "Here are two friends of mine from Liverpool who
are going to do a half-hour set for us." We were very tired and we did this
very laid-back set of Jim's songs. Because he was so tired, Jim had never
sung like that before – it was magical, very quiet and soulful blues. It
went down really well and Alexis was very impressed.'

They had already been recommended to Liberty Records by Jo-Ann
Kelly and laid down some tracks for a compilation album called *Gasoline*.
Now they wanted to do a whole album of Jim's songs. It had just
been announced in the trade press that Alexis and Phil had formed a
production company called Perception Productions. The first fruit of
this was an album by the Austrian singer Jack Grunsky for Amadeo
Records, produced by Alexis, with Mick Taylor on guitar. Liberty had
offered Jim and Raphael a contract, but Alexis persuaded them not to

sign it. He had been unhappy with Liberty over the choice of studio for *New Generation of Blues* and in any case was anxious to help young artists make records. Instead they signed with Alexis' company, encouraged by a guarantee from Alexis that within a year they would have their own album out.

They recorded twelve tracks at De Lane Lea, but Alexis was then unable to keep his promise because Perception couldn't find a record company to whom they could lease the tapes. Alexis was probably sincere in his belief that he could do a deal, but it was very typical of his undying optimism that he should make a promise in advance of delivery.

Phil Roberge wrote to Doug Dobell, who replied: "Fraid I would not be interested in putting out the Jim James and Raphael Callaghan material as my policy is to myself record all the material I issue other than that by American artists I am unable to record personally. Anyway best of luck, I'm sure the album must be first class with Alexis producing. Maybe Transatlantic would be interested?' They weren't.

In the latter part of 1969 Alexis continued to make occasional solo appearances, often on the increasingly lucrative campus circuit, where he combined music with lectures on the blues. He was also announced as the musical director of a Greenwich Theatre production on the life of Martin Luther King. But probably the biggest publicity coup of the year was the 24 October edition of *LIFE* magazine, which ran a major feature on Blind Faith. At the end of a lengthy piece was drawn 'The Genealogy of a Supergroup' and smack in the middle was the band from which all radiated: Alexis Korner's Blues Inc.

Nineteen-seventy came and New Church were milking the German market for all it was worth. Colin Hodgkinson dropped out to concentrate on Back Door, his place being taken by Peter Fensome and then a young Danish bassist, Per Frost. *Both Sides* was released in May after Phil Roberge struck a deal with the German label Intercord. In July the *Darmstadter Tagblatt*, reviewing a New Church concert watched by a 'fascinated audience', gushed: 'This is a unity, a single long blues which will echo long after the concert is finished'; a Heidelberg paper called the concert there 'blues at its best'.

Alexis had made some solo appearances in England during the year, most notably on the same Lyceum bill as Eric Clapton in his new incarnation as Derek & the Dominoes in aid of Dr Spock's Civil Liberties Legal Defence Fund. The guru of parenting had been arrested on a pro-peace demo in the USA. But it wasn't until September that New Church finally came to Britain for a UK tour.

Just before Alexis left Germany for this tour, he was invited to compère a rock festival on an island off the German coast, due to be held on 6 September. Trouble seemed to follow Alexis around. Already that year he'd been involved in another concert riot in Hamburg. The Isle of Fehmarn gig was blighted by the weather, complete lack of organization and some very nasty German hell's angels employed as 'security'.

Torrential rain prevented many of the bands playing for fear of electrocution. Those who did manage to get on played very short sets because of the cold. All through the proceedings, Alexis had been patiently explaining the problems to the crowd. There were supposed to be two compères, but the other one fled in terror of the bikers. Alexis stood his ground and when top-of-the-bill Jimi Hendrix was hours late arriving on stage, he temporarily soothed the savage beast with an acoustic set. Eventually Hendrix played, but the whole 'Love and Peace' concert (as it was billed) had collapsed into chaos. The bikers went berserk, smashed everything in sight, battered Jimi's road manager, Gerry Stickells, and shot one of the stagehands. Jimi's band just managed to get through the set and then fled. It was the last concert Jimi Hendrix ever played.

New Church toured the UK through September and October, but Alexis was beginning to tire of the concept and wanted a break from touring, although he still wanted to carry on as a duo with Peter Thorup. New Church had kept Alexis away from home longer than at any other time since he had turned professional. In November the Chapel was finally ready for occupation and, as he told the German paper *Bild*: 'I like to play in front of a German audience, but every few weeks I've got to show my face at home otherwise Roberta gets cross with me.'

With Alexis back in Britain for really the first time that year, there were more publicity opportunities. *New Musical Express* ran a whole-page feature on Alexis in which he roundly and at some length condemned the Musicians' Union for the trouble New Church had experienced over Peter Thorup. *Melody Maker* chose him to be a 'Blind Date' guest (where he mistook the Strawbs for Emerson Lake and Palmer) and he was interviewed by *Penthouse*. Even Nico and Damian, then fourteen and thirteen years old, got in on the act.

In an article headlined 'The Generation Gap Is A Beautiful Excuse' the fashion magazine for the fashionable, *Harper's Bazaar*, heard from the boys about life as a member of the Korner family. Given the amount of freedom they enjoyed, it was hardly surprising that they almost dismissed the idea of a Generation Gap entirely. While Damian now wishes in retrospect that there had been more of a brake on them, in 1970 they were having a whale of a time. They explained life as members of the Korner family with a calm sophistication that totally belied some of the struggles behind the scenes.

'The generation gap obviously does exist ' said Nico, 'but between different kinds of people rather than between people of different ages. I don't feel it at all. But then we have a quite exceptional family, exceptional parents. It would be stupid to say we didn't. There's a good family relationship. Of course, there are some differences like mum doesn't like me having a motor bike, but in the end she bought me one. Now we let the subject pass. She asks me to wear a crash helmet and I respect that.'

'I don't feel any gap in our family at all,' explained Damian, 'but I know a lot of people at school who do. But I think if people of different generations tried to get on, it would work better. You hear a lot of people saying "I'm 17 and my parents don't understand me", but you've got to remember they don't understand their parents either . . . Children will always go on rebelling about something, but I hope in the next generation there'll be more families like us.'

What with the Hyde Park concert, the success of New Church in Europe, the *LIFE* feature and the other media coverage, not to mention all his past achievements and connections, public awareness of Alexis was growing at a steady if not spectacular pace. But what happened next could not have been predicted even by Alexis at his most hopeful.

In 1970 Mickie Most was one of the hottest independent producers around. During the sixties he was hardly out of the charts, producing hits for the Animals, Herman's Hermits, the Nashville Teens, Lulu and Donovan. In 1969 he had set up his own RAK label, named after his early days in the music business as a 'rack-jobber' trying to convince the likes of Boots and W H Smith to sell records. Mickie has always been interested in what he calls 'a challenge . . . I've had success with singers who can't sing, which is a challenge, isn't it?' A close collaborator on a number of projects was arranger and conductor John Cameron. 'John and I had been working a lot on other people's arrangements. Now we were thinking of doing something a bit off the wall using a big band jazz sound like Don Ellis.'

A Cambridge graduate, John Cameron was also a singer and pianist who starred in the Footlights cabaret with Eric Idle. He later had his own gig at the Take One Club, where the resident band was the Ronnie Ross Quartet. 'I was a classically trained pianist with my feet very much in the blues and hard-bop camp. I'd been working in the folk world with Joni Mitchell, Randy Newman and Bobbie Gentry, but I hankered to get back to something more hard-nosed. I saw the Don Ellis band at Ronnie Scott's and thought I'd love to put together an album with a band that big, but perhaps not quite so esoteric, a bit more commercial, but with the double rhythm section, the impossible brass licks and strange time signatures.

'It was one of those chance conversations. I'd been doing six songs for Eurovision with Mary Hopkin for Mickie. We reached the end of that and Mickie said, "What's new?" "Well, I want to do this ridiculous band with big brass sections." I'd taken the idea to Decca who I'd just done a jazz album for and they turned it down.'

Meanwhile Mickie had been talking to Phil Roberge about the possibility of signing Alexis and Peter Thorup to RAK. Alexis, too, was keen on the idea of a big band. 'I'd always wanted to work with a big palais band. When I was a kid in wartime, I used to go to the Hammersmith Palais because all the bands had boogie-woogie players.'

Mickie invited everybody to his yacht in the south of France. He had a piano shipped out there and they started talking and writing, 'as well as drinking the whole of my wine cellar dry, but it kinda started to work'. John Cameron says: 'Although we were coming from different areas, we had a lot in common in the way we viewed music as not being stuck in pigeon-holes and that musicians from all fields could work together.'

This collective view of music which they all shared led to a meandering conversation on Jung's theories about a society underpinned by a collective consciousness at which point Mickie announced: 'Right, that's the name: Collective Consciousness Society – CCS.'

Although Mickie was quite happy to construct a sound based on off-the-wall arrangements founded on blues and jazz, nevertheless he was highly focused on the commercial angle. He told John Cameron that 'he wanted to root it in "upfront", "in your face" riffs'. Mickie thought that for this to stand any chance commercially they had to avoid comparisons with Glen Miller or Tommy Dorsey by placing a heavy emphasis on projecting the sound of a modern rhythm section.

Then they began to work on the presentation. Alexis was the key; he had the credibility, the arresting character and now the public profile to carry it off as a front man. Peter Thorup had the pyrotechnic vocals, but it was Alexis who would capture the attention. Thoughts moved on to the musicians they might involve. There was no problem here: between them, Alexis, Mickie and John were on first-name terms with every hot session player in London. Eventually they pulled together Blue Mink's rhythm section and the cream of British jazz musicians, including Henry Lowther, Ronnie Ross, Tony Coe, Harold McNair and Pete King.

In the studio it was left to Alexis and Peter to give the feel of the songs to the session musicians because there was no opportunity for everybody to sit down and have meetings in advance. To some extent the recording of CCS was akin to the old Blues Inc idea of a musicians' playground. As John Cameron explains: 'You can't get guys to blow their socks off just by giving them money.' All the musicians brought into the recording sessions were there to have a good time. Of course, they were disciplined musicians, but the sessions were arranged so that, 'you came in, blew hard, went down the pub, drank too much and came back and blew the arse off the next lot of charts. I shouted at people something awful – it was the only way to get the band going. A lot of heat and adrenalin; it existed as a high-energy band. All live with no overdubs.'

Because all the musicians were engaged elsewhere on their regular gigs and sessions, nobody depended on CCS for a living, which lessened the chance of acrimony. And it was perfect for Alexis; all he had to do was turn up, with nothing to arrange, nobody waiting to be paid. Instead all the energy went into the music, which actually required great physical effort: the drummers were working flat out against a huge brass section, and pianos were left in bits.

The plan for the album was to have original material like Peter Thorup's 'Waiting Song' and John Cameron's 'Dos Cantos' together with the traditional jazz approach of reworking familiar material, in this case Jethro Tull's 'Living In The Past' and 'Satisfaction'.

But in a display of breathtaking audacity, Mickie Most decided that the band's first single would be Led Zeppelin's 'Whole Lotta Love', which had been in the charts in 1969 and was from the band's second album. Zeppelin were signed to the management company co-owned by Mickie and Zeppelin manager Peter Grant, and the two men worked out of the same office, so there was no problem using the track. 'Whole Lotta Love' by CCS entered the singles chart on 31 October 1970, went to number thirteen, stayed in the chart for thirteen weeks and for several years after was the theme tune to the BBC's *Top Of The Pops*. The next two singles did even better. 'Walkin' got to number seven in February 1971 and 'Tap Turns On The Water', a song written by Alexis about growing up, reached number five the following September. If it hadn't been for 'Maggie May' hogging the number one spot that month, 'Tap' could easily have gone all the way. Not that Damian was too pleased with a lyric that went 'Have you ever seen your sister in the raw?' 'All the kids were running round singing it and asking me and Nico what Sappho looked like. It was murder.'

The début album received ecstatic praise from critics and fans alike; *Disc and Music Echo* gave it the maximum four stars, saying 'this cannot be recommended too highly'; Noel Edmonds predicted that the album would be 'the rage of the seventies'. In fact the album didn't do well chart-wise, but even so, readers of *Record Mirror* voted CCS the 'World's Best Instrumental Group' ahead of Chicago and Blood, Sweat and Tears.

And Alexis Korner, a musician for nearly a quarter of a century, found himself an overnight sensation. Phil Roberge couldn't believe what had happened. 'To see him on the front cover of every pop magazine and newspaper when we were usually only ever ten pages in and never on the cover was just incredible.' Alexis' lived-in face was everywhere, eyes hidden by shades, big Afro hairstyle stuffed under a black leather hat, and he was written about in articles headlined 'The Master', 'A Highly Respected Man', 'How Alexis Korner Became Conscious of Being Revered' and so on.

Typically though, Alexis had his feet firmly on the ground. He was earning more money than at any time in his career, but he knew, for two reasons, that the band would shortly run its course. First, because it would be far too expensive to take out on the road. In fact they played only two gigs. They played at Ronnie Scott's, where they blew all the fuses in the place performing a benefit for the family of flautist Harold McNair, who, tragically, had just died. Their only other gig was at the Royal Albert Hall. Secondly, he knew better than anyone else that he would never be content to stay in the same groove for too long. As he made clear in all the interviews he gave at the time, he was quite determined that he was not going to use CCS to further his career; you would never catch Alexis miming on TV to a CCS song or including any of their songs in his set. For Alexis, CCS, however successful, was simply a diversion.

The band recorded two further albums on RAK, with the second making the Top Thirty in 1972, until the enterprise was wound up in 1973 with 'The Best Band In The Land'. Amazingly CCS retains a fan base in Europe, particularly in Scandinavia, where Peter Thorup plays with a CCS tribute band.

Exactly why CCS was so successful is impossible to fathom; it was simply a sound that struck a chord, using a heavy rhythm section to stay just about on the right side of music for shopping malls. Obviously pop fans were buying it, but possibly older people as well, for it harked back to an earlier era when the big-band sound *was* the hit music of its day.

There is an irreverent and deeply cynical view of the success of CCS which goes something like this:

Mickie Most receives a call from his accountant, who is clearly agitated.

'Mickie, Mickie, ya gotta find a way to lose some money immediately. The Inland Revenue are on your tail and they'll eat you alive if you don't do something quick'.

'OK, OK, I'll give it some thought.'

'Mickie, ya gotta do better than that. I'll call you in the morning.'

Mickie goes home to bed. At four a.m. he sits bolt upright in a sweat and lunges for the phone.

'Max, Max, I got it, I got it.'

'What, what Mickie, whaddya got?'

'A money-losing scheme, can't fail.'

'Tell me, tell me.'

'Right. We do a big band, loads of musicians to pay, mega money to set up. Best studios, the works.'

'Nice, Mickie, a big band in 1970, thirty years outta date, nice. Go on . . .'

'OK, we get in a load of BRITISH jazz musicians.'

[*gales of laughter down the phone*]

'I'm liking the sound of this. More, more . . .'

'Right, now we get in a DANISH blues guitarist.'

[*Max on the verge of hysteria*]

'You still there, Max?'

'STOP, STOP, YOU'LL GIMME A CORONARY!'

'Hang on, Max, this is the best bit. Guess who the lead singer is?
'WHO? WHO?'
'ALEXIS KORNER!!'
[*sound of phone being dropped*]

In 1971 Alexis formally disbanded New Church, preferring instead to tour as a duo with Peter Thorup. But in the light of the current publicity he did want to have one last crack at getting some album success in the UK under his own name. Phil negotiated a one-off solo album deal with RAK. The album, simply called *Alexis Korner*, was recorded in Bermuda by Jean-Paul Salvatori, a Frenchman from Corsica who was, according to Mickie Most, 'a bit of a mystery man who was said to be worth millions. He kept mumbling on about Trust Funds.' With his wealth – which actually belonged to the woman he lived with – Salvatori apparently bought time in all the major recording studio around the world, learning about recording techniques.

An American guitarist and drummer were flown in, Chris McGregor played piano and Colin Hodgkinson was on bass. Colin says: 'That was bizarre – it was done in the basement of a radio station. We had a couple of weeks out there, swimming in the morning and working in the afternoon. A strange album for me, not really a blues album at all.'

Salvatori was, in Phil's words 'an Alexis Korner fan in a fierce way' and was very keen to produce an album by his hero. As Alexis told Roy Carr of *NME*, once in the studio, he felt that Jean Paul 'has done a lot for my limited technical abilities . . . he hears things in a different way from how I hear them. It's got to the point where Jean-Paul has got me doing things that I haven't done before.' What he helped produce for Alexis was easily the worst album of his career, rightly slammed by the critics. With the single exception of Broonzy's 'Stump Blues', the record was a dog.

In April, Alexis took a holiday in Morocco while Phil carried on seeking out publicity opportunities. He booked Alexis to appear on Italian television to debate the issue of 'Youth In the Sixties' with the notorious American senator Eugene McCarthy, while in July Alexis was the subject of a major feature in *Rolling Stone* entitled 'Alexis Korner: father of us all'.

Musically it was back to Germany; a look at his schedule for November–December 1971 reveals that in Germany at least, Alexis was, in the vernacular of the day, a 'superstar':

27 Nov – Lindau
28 Nov – Freiburg
30 Nov – Nürnberg
 1 Dec – Tübingen
 3 Dec – Aalen
 5 Dec – Karlsruhe
 6 Dec – Würzburg

All concert-hall venues and every one sold out in advance.

Alexis was on TV in Bremen, did some recording for a film about the German political underground and was seen several times on repeat showings of his blues series for German TV, *Sympathy For The Devil*.

He flew back to Britain for CCS's Albert Hall concert on 9 December and took part in rehearsals for a Tribute to Alexis concert to be held in Hamburg on 15 December to mark his twenty-fifth anniversary in the music business. The band included Zoot Money, Dick Heckstall-Smith, drummer John Marshall, Hendrix bassist Billy Cox, Peter Thorup and Ray Warleigh. In the run-up to the concert, the Hamburg paper *Abendblatt* distributed thousands of posters depicting Alexis' life story. He was interviewed by *Bild* and called in by Philips Records to assist in the preparation of the Chess catalogue blues series. In addition he brought together Alexis Korner and Friends to play a televised concert in Cologne and fitted in three concerts as a duo with Peter Thorup. It was all over by Christmas; he went back to the UK for an appearance on *The Old Grey Whistle Test* and then to the Chapel for a well-earned break through to the New Year.

But Phil persisted with the idea of trying to break Alexis not only in the UK, but also in America – the land of serious money. He took the view that if the record-buying public wouldn't swallow contemporary Alexis whole, he at least wanted to remind them just how many great musicians had started out with Alexis.

So they came up with the idea that emerged after five months of hard work and negotiating rights as *Bootleg Him*, so named because the album contained many previously unreleased tracks with those who had since become famous. Gems (and some turkeys) from the past were mixed with modern recordings of New Church and the Korner–Thorup duo. The double album, released in 1972, came with extensive sleeve-notes and a twelve-page, album-size booklet containing the whole of the *Rolling Stone* article, the sleeve-notes to Alexis' early recordings on

Tempo and a number of historical and contemporary photos. It was an impressive package apart from the singularly inappropriate 'fantasy' cover by Roger Dean.

One of the photos for *Bootleg Him* was shot in June 1971 at Olympic Studios during the recording of the *B. B. King in London* album; it shows B. B. King, Alexis and Steve Marriott in acoustic mood on the track Alexis wrote, 'Alexis Boogie'. King was in London for a week and drew star musicians like a magnet: Ringo Starr, Ian Stewart, Peter Green, Stevie Winwood, Jim Keltner and Gary Wright, with Dave Mason and Jim Capaldi just hanging out watching the action. The set with Alexis and Steve Marriott marked the first time that King played acoustic on record.

Marriott's own band, Humble Pie, was in a period of transition. Originally a vehicle for Peter Frampton, they were set up to be a big-league US arena rock band. However, with Frampton's light touch dominating, the first two albums had done only moderately well. Fed up with being a front man, Marriott had joined only on condition that he could stay in the background. A number of bands had broken up in the late sixties because the 'lead face' had become tired of the constant pressure and attention; Cream and the Jimi Hendrix Experience were two examples, the Small Faces another.

But Humble Pie's new American manager, Dee Anthony, had other ideas. He surmised that for the band to fulfil its potential in the States, they would have to become much heavier. Steve Marriott could supply that hard–driving blues–rock feel. Peter Frampton could not and he left.

On the back of substantial album sales of *Rock On* and *Smokin'* (with Alexis on vocals) Humble Pie were booked for a major US tour and Steve persuaded Dee Anthony to have Alexis and Peter Thorup as the support act. Alexis had always resisted the idea of playing blues in America on the principle of 'coals to Newcastle', but this was a chance too good to miss. Once he got there, Alexis was pleasantly surprised at the warm reception he received from other musicians. Everyone had read the *Rolling Stone* and *LIFE* pieces and showed him much respect. When the Bermuda solo album was being finished in London, the James Gang were in town. Joe Walsh came to the studio as a favour for Alexis and sang his heart out all night long as backing vocalist on 'You Can Make It Like You Want It To Be'. The *Bootleg Him* album was out in the USA on Warner Brothers at the same time, giving Alexis not only more publicity but also some very appreciative reviews.

During 1972 Alexis had a monthly column in *Disc*. The first one, in May, described how he and Peter went to America as a duo and came back as a band. After playing well-received gigs in New York, Boston and other northern cities, the tour moved south, where Alexis anticipated that, as they were closing in on the source of the blues, the audience response would get even better.

'And it was true. The first concert, at Roanoke, Virginia, had a bright sparkling feel which had not been there before. There were three of us on: Humble Pie, King Crimson and us two. Ian Wallace, Crimson's drummer, sat in with us. Stevie suddenly appeared in our "Rock Me", blowing that fine harp and on "Gospel Ship" we had a full chorus from the "Pie Sisters" [Steve, Greg Ridley and Dave Clempson] plus incidental tambourine from Jerry [Shirley] and Robert Fripp, and Mel [Collins] and Boz [Burrell] also got involved.'

They played two more gigs in Virginia and Atlanta. Meanwhile King Crimson went off to Birmingham, Alabama for what was their last gig as a band, on April Fool's Day 1972, before breaking up. Life in Crimson had not been easy of late, with the band staging a palace revolution against Robert Fripp, who then had the last word by disbanding altogether. Immediately, Ian Wallace flew to Tampa, Florida to rejoin Alexis and Peter on the Humble Pie tour. Alexis wrote: 'Humble Pie's crew very kindly took Ian's drums along and so we were THREE. St Petersburg, Florida turned out to be one of the best gigs of the tour. What an audience! Fort Lauderdale next and then to New Orleans.

'We played a storm at the Warehouse and had the next day off. Mel and Boz (also at a loose end after the break-up of Crimson) had been living there for a week and after blowing with us at The Warehouse, thought they would like to move on with us. Now we were FIVE.'

Eventually they moved back up north to Chicago and across to the West Coast to Santa Monica, California. By this time they had played nine gigs together and realized that they had what is known in common parlance as 'a band'. They went into a studio in San Francisco to do some demos and brought the results back to Island Studios in London. The British music press were full of expectations about the new band, but also rather confused, initially thinking Alexis was going to join King Crimson.

Choosing a name proved difficult. It started out as 'Alexis Korner and Friends', then 'Alexis' and finally Snape – Something Nasty 'Appens Practically Every day. The name came from a dare game played by bands on the road since the early sixties. Dares were issued, each one more nasty than its predecessor, until the whole thing got completely out of control. Never was a band better named. Perhaps they learnt the art of excess from Humble Pie, whose tours were the stuff of rock legends. With hefty record-label support, Humble Pie, led by the voracious Steve Marriott, would roll into town, every town, and find $5000 waiting for them in cash for drugs, women and afternoon tea. Or perhaps it was being let off the leash from King Crimson. Or simply that whenever you were in a band with Alexis Korner, it was play time. Whatever its genesis, Zoot Money says: 'I'd have wanted an armed escort to go out with that band.'

Snape made their debut at the rain-sodden Great Western Festival in May 1972, but were soon off to Germany and the ill-fated Munich Olympics, where the band played out their allotted time just before Israeli athletes were murdered by terrorists. Since the success of CCS, Phil Roberge had received several requests to manage artists. He took on Duster Bennett, Colin Hodgkinson and Back Door, Principal Edward's Magic Theatre, Claire Hammill and Ronnie Montrose. He also became Dee Anthony's European representative for Humble Pie, Gary Wright and Spooky Tooth, Alvin Lee and Peter Frampton. But he had no experience of managing a band on the road. He knew Del Taylor both as an agent and manager and suggested he come and look after Alexis and Snape.

'I walked straight into a Snape tour, which (once it got going) was something like twenty-eight shows in thirty days, starting with two shows in Hamburg and then a week off. We took over the second floor of some unsuspecting hotel in Hamburg which nobody else would go to after we'd been there for three days. It was an incredible tour; they were an amazing live band, so successful that I remember the band paying US dollars at the end of the tour for all the damage they had caused as they wreaked havoc across Germany.'

Drummer Ian Wallace admits: 'Snape was pretty wild at the time. There was a lot of drinking, drug taking and womanizing going on. We were all living the rock 'n' roll myth. Alexis enjoyed it all. He joined in – and in no small way. I think Alexis was the worst of us.'

Snape brought out in Alexis the juvenile delinquent, always bubbling under the surface of his character. Like many musicians on the road who have family at home, Alexis made very clear distinctions, at least in his own mind, between life on the road and life at home. Except that on this occasion he took with him his fifteen-year-old son Damian, who says: 'They were ravaging tours. Snape was a bad, bad band to go on tour with. It was excess in a mindless fashion. It was "Where can we abuse ourselves next; how can we do it?" It was amusing to be around. Going on the road with a band like Snape teaches you when to say, "No, thank you." You can't be a purist about it, but at the same time you have to be damn careful that you don't live the life. And Snape were living the life.

'I went on a Swiss tour as Mel Collins's sax roadie; I was so small, there wasn't anything else I could do. Brotherhood of Breath were also on the show. Chris McGregor tried to teach me piano when I was about eight and gave up when I asked him which note was the centre forward and which was the inside right – a bit disheartening for a free-form jazz pianist from South Africa who calls it "soccer".

'We were sitting in this pub after the gig in Zurich and there's this long table with Snape and Brotherhood of Breath. Everybody is drinking and I'm sitting having a conversation with Tony Ashton of Ashton, Gardner and Dyke. I'm in mid conversation and I just barfed all over him – didn't stop talking, just carried on. And he didn't move. Daddy hauled me out and we're both dying with laughter. Then he does the worst thing you can do to anybody who has just been sick: he starts whacking me on the back, at which point I throw up again and then *he* throws up. He always accused me after that of making him sick: "If you hadn't puked out there" etc etc. I said to him, "Leave it out, you were fit to go."

'Three a.m.: a call comes through to our room in Geneva. One of the band is up in his room with a female reporter. He's in the middle of "doing it" and he's got water on the knee and he cannot fucking move. My dad's idea of a joke was to take me up there to haul him off.'

And so on to some more Snape-shots of life on the road with a band which was, says Del Taylor, 'complete lunacy'. 'It was quite a nice hotel. They had asked the owner if the sauna and pool would be open when they got back. Normally the answer would be no, but the manager rather reluctantly agreed – a decision he later came to regret. It was about two a.m. by the time they got back and with a plane to catch at six a.m. it wasn't worth going to bed. They decided to use the sauna and swimming pool – all the band plus the entourage and others. Everybody was drinking. The owner turned up to find all hell breaking loose; broken bottles, bodies lying everywhere – and he was a little upset. Alexis waded through the debris, confronted the boss with a completely straight face and tried to explain to him how very normal all this was and moreover, it was completely outrageous that he should adopt this attitude. The guy just turned round and left.'

In another hotel, a new wing had been added since their last visit. A wedding reception was underway and one of the band decided that Snape should be invited. The wedding party did not agree that these lunatics should join the throng. Snape repaired to one of their own rooms. The wedding was in full swing while the party coming from Snape's room was even more raucous as they took it apart piece by piece. Alexis' contribution was to pretend he was swimming across the room with a waste-paper basket on his head. The waiters were so fascinated by what was happening that they kept bringing up unrequested food and drink just to see what was going on. Snape took keyboardist Tim Hinkley on the tour – by all accounts another demon of the road. He found a fire extinguisher, got somebody to hold him by his legs out of the window and let off the extinguisher through the skylight of the extension, all over the wedding guests. In normal circumstances this would have upset a lot of people, but Tim ended up in the party playing the organ.

In the morning Del Taylor was left to face to the music. 'When I checked out I got a bill that read, like, twenty-three fire extinguishers, two wardrobes and three sets of bed linen.'

They were in yet another hotel. The bar was downstairs from reception and reached by a staircase which swept around in an elegant parabola like a Hollywood film set. With the public library shut, the band ended up in the bar, where a Mexican bartender mixed a multitude of cocktails. The bar was packed. Suddenly the whole room went quiet. At the top of the stairs was Mel Collins with his trousers rolled up, dressed in a skirt with a Durex on the end of his nose and a woman on each arm. They made a grand entrance, sat down at a table and ordered a drink as if this was completely normal – while everyone else looked on in complete disbelief.

So that was Snape, not forgetting the time they had half the Gross National Product of Colombia in the car when they were stopped by the German police. Or the time when Alexis tried to pay a suitcase load of money into a bank and was questioned intensively about where it had all come from. Or the time when Alexis actually jumped out of a first-floor hotel window to remonstrate with some German youths who were hurling insults at the band. Their road-hardened American tour manager walked out half way through because he couldn't take it any more.

And the music? On the basis of their stage show, which could be sampled on the live album released in Germany, they had the potential to become a fairly major touring band. Unfortunately, the album *Accidentally Born in New Orleans*, released in December 1972, had all the guts produced out of it in an era where engineers wore white gloves in pursuit of perfection. The clinical aura of the studio also revealed a central weakness in the choice of material, generally dull and undemanding blues, although in the opinion of those present some of the best music did not reach the album. Even so when they came back off tour, on the strength of some tremendous live performances and the enthusiastic audience response, there was significant interest from America. Del and Phil were raring to go, and it was a chance to break Alexis on the America stadium circuit, but, as Del relates, they hadn't reckoned with Alexis' view of the situation.

'I remember spending twenty-four hours in a room with Phil and Alexis trying to convince him that we should take this amazing offer both record and support-wise. He didn't want to do it because it would have meant being over there for a year – and he had his other commitments: his radio, voice-overs. Snape started by accident, built itself up to something perceived by the rest of the business as being able to make large amounts of money and everybody was interested and *that* was the point where Alexis became uninterested, wanted to do something else and find another band. If something looked like it had the remotest chance of becoming successful he stopped doing it.'

Why did Alexis feel like this? He had always been very clear in public statements that he was not envious of those he had brought along who then went on to become rich and famous. Yet he clearly revelled in the attention and financial security brought about by CCS. Some people have suggested that Alexis might have been frightened by the thought of success or conversely the risk of meeting headlining public failure trying to compete with the biggest and the best in America. Then again he might simply have been canny enough to realize that in Europe he was a big fish – success there was self-evidently attainable.

What is clear, however, is that Alexis did not want to be drawn into the grinding cycle of album, tour, album – nor did he want to be spending months away from home. To break Snape in America would have taken at least a year. The rock 'n' roll juggernaut beckoned, but Alexis walked away.

12

YOU CAN MAKE IT
LIKE YOU WANT IT TO BE

If Alexis was not prepared to slog around the States, Phil Roberge wanted to have another crack at producing the album that could serve as a platform to launch him into another league – or at least rack up some decent sales. *Bootleg Him* did the job of raising Alexis' general profile, but it needed strong original material for his recording career to really take off. There was another more pressing rationale for doing album deals. Since Alexis had received nationwide publicity as a member of CCS, the Inland Revenue was in hot pursuit of unpaid tax. Do a deal, get some money in advance and fend off the wolf for another day. In truth, much of the impetus for Alexis' recording history from here on was driven as much by the arrival of those little brown envelopes on the doormat as any great desire to record an album.

Alexis signed a two-album deal with Polydor in Germany. Although Polydor knew that he was not bankable as a recording artist, even in Germany, this was still the era when accountants did not run the business, so, as then label boss Willi Schlosser says: 'We wanted Alexis because it was a good image for the company.' The first album, simply called *Alexis Korner*, was recorded at CBS in London through June and July 1973 and produced by Peter Thorup. Essentially it was Snape with guests, among them Colin Hodgkinson and Zoot Money. A very dry, separated sound spoilt was what in fact a rather good album combining some strong original songs like 'Wild Women and Desperate Men' and 'Captain America' and well-chosen covers like 'Geneva' and J. J. Cale's 'Lies', a perfect choice for Alexis' vocal range.

The second album, *Get Off My Cloud*, recorded eighteen months later, was the one that Phil pinned his hopes on. 'I was calling all these people up and everybody said they would do it. I just couldn't believe it.' The same studio, December 1974, and standing side by side are Keith Richard, Steve Marriott and Peter Frampton. Behind the desk, producer George Caldwell and a young engineer, Damian Korner. Damian had been destined for football glory. But once he discovered that the gentle arts of ankle tapping and shin scraping were part of the training schedule, he turned his back on the opportunity. 'I didn't really know what to do, so I asked Dad about what being in a studio was all about. He told me and I said, "OK, I'll try that." '

Without Alexis' help he got himself a job; *Get Off My Cloud* was the first of several albums on which Damian would work with Alexis. But by his own admission, 'working with Dad was very hard. In one respect it was easy because we were such good friends by this time. But when we were doing that first album together, you know, you're a kid of eighteen and you are easily embarrassed by your dad. We're doing this vocal on a certain track. And his version of doing this is to lie down on the floor against the bass cab singing.

' "Get up Dad, for fuck's sake." '

' "I'm going to do this vocal this way. It's the only way it's going to work." '

' "That's because you're legless." '

'He would have to get out of it to get relaxed enough to enjoy the performance, which is why he spent most of his time in the studio wrecked. He never liked the studio, he liked live music. I understood and appreciated that. We got on well in the studio because I could get sounds. To listen to what he said and not be prejudiced, not making him do what he obviously didn't want to do.

'The problem my father had with studios was that everything was sterile and clinical. A snare-drum mike had to be so close that it just sounded like "dock" and "pliff", but in the studio a snare drum is vibrant. He was choked by studios because he had to do the vocal as an overdub; the spit into the microphone would not make it "permissible" to record the vocal at the same time and he might "pop" on the microphone. He was never allowed to get the sound quickly, to allow the performance to come through, because engineers were pedantically slow, to make sure they were technically correct.

'If you asked him to do a drop-in on acoustic guitar, it was mayhem because he never played the same thing twice. As an engineer it taught me that you are there to get their expression down and not yours.'

Damian feels that *Get Off My Cloud* was a 'nice idea that got out of hand' because of the involvement of big-time American management. Mick Taylor had just left the Stones, so Steve Marriott spent much of the time trying to prove to Keith just what a great Rolling Stone he would make. Because Keith had come to play with Alexis, there were some pretty unlikely rumours that Alexis was in line for the job, something that today Mick Jagger firmly rules out.

Like the previous album, there were some good moments, in particular a crisply sardonic version of the Doors' 'WASP', poignant self-penned tributes to Robert Johnson and Jimi Hendrix, and a storming opener, 'I Gotcha Number'. As we have seen, Alexis' recording history was decidedly patchy, strong early material giving way to much that was unmemorable. However, like the notion of 'Alexis Unplugged', a sympathetic compilation taken from these two mid-seventies albums would be worth listening to.

But at the time, despite the all-star cast and some of Alexis' best-ever reviews, *Get Off My Cloud* made little impression. As Del Taylor saw it, the lack of co-ordinated promotion in the States hadn't helped. 'The idea was that the album would be released to tie in with the Stones' tour. Alexis would go to the States and interview the Stones in different towns and cities and the record would be available. CBS managed to screw up every single town on the tour bar one, where they got the record into the shops. The Stones arrived and they sold around 25,000 copies.'

In fact it was Alexis who found himself the subject of a *Rolling Stone* interview to promote the highly praised Radio 1 Rolling Stones documentary that he narrated and which was produced by Jeff Griffin and syndicated across seventy-five US radio stations. None of this did much for album sales, however. When the CBS deal was signed, Alexis went to meet Maurice Oberstein, who said: 'Tell me, Alexis, how does it feel to be with CBS?' 'Obe,' Alexis replied, 'it's a bit like one tug trying to pull the *Queen Mary* up the Thames.'

This mid-seventies period saw Alexis, as a performing artist, give up on Britain altogether. As he told Karl Dallas for *Melody Maker*, being ignored in Britain dented his pride considerably, but 'I got used to it and the result is that now I don't really mind all that much. I've got used to not having an audience here. I've also got used to the fact that, I'm sorry, but I'm right and they're wrong. I am good and I do know what I'm doing and I can get other musicians to play their arses off and so people here are missing something . . . The situation in Germany, for instance, is that I can go over and have a 45 minute TV show and actually have control of who is on the show. Here, I can't get on a television show. So I'm not unhappy.'

It was a transitional period for British rock. The blues boom had died, several bands had broken up and those that survived the sixties were now predominantly locked into the international stadium circuit. Back home, while disco ruled, the pub-rock scene was underway in the run-up to punk. Whichever way you looked at it, Alexis was not simply playing outside the mainstream – he was old hat. Germany and northern Europe were now, even more than ever, his stamping ground.

The general plan was to take out duos, trios and other small line-ups whenever he felt like touring, when there might be an album to promote (although, with no record-company tour support, the album was rarely in the shops at the right time) or whenever the Chapel might need redecorating.

But not all the German tour concerts during this time were successful; Alexis possibly played Germany too often, and didn't always take out or invite up the musicians best suited to his style. One tour band from late 1975 included ex-Fleetwood Mac guitarist Bob Weston, a German–Indian keyboard player called Pete 'Wyoming' Bender and Kokomo drummer Terry Stannard. A review in the *Frankenpost Hof* called the band 'rock in first gear' and the concert review in *Alb-Bote Münsingen* gave Alexis possibly one of his worst-ever write-ups. The headline 'the name on its own is no guarantee; Alexis' third appearance in Münsingen was not convincing' set the tone. The choice of musicians seems to have been the main problem. Bob Weston 'gave the impression of being completely indifferent to the proceedings as if he had nothing to do with the gig'. Pete Bender sang 'Light My Fire', which 'couldn't fit in with the other songs', while the reviewer also claimed that Terry Stannard was 'not up to the job'. Alexis, too, was out of sorts: 'Korner himself seemed unwell and remote in places; it was not otherwise explainable why he didn't realize that the PA system had outstretched itself and was hopelessly distorted.'

Alexis had a view of touring, especially in Germany. He saw no reason why he should live any less well on the road than he did at home. So the schedule was routed to take in a favourite town with a particular restaurant or a certain vineyard. He stayed in good hotels, but always wanted the road crew to have the best of everything as·well. Thus it was most uncharacteristic of Alexis to get annoyed with the roadie at this particular concert simply for failing to set the mike high enough for him to sing while seated at the piano when, as the reviewer sternly noted, 'he could easily have done it for himself. Expressions like "Fuck it" do not really support his pre-concert statement that "nowhere do I have as much fun as playing in Münsingen".'

Concerts such as these are memorable for their rarity. Sometimes it was the audience rather than the musicians that wasn't quite right. Colin Hodgkinson recalls the end of one concert in Germany which was packed, 'but the audience was very indifferent. Then we got to the last tune and when we said that they started to react. When we came off, the guy running it said, "You do an encore?" So Alexis went out to the microphone and said, "It's our privilege to play you an encore. But you have to earn it. You haven't. Good night." '

Only when playing with musicians like Colin, Peter Thorup and Zoot Money could Alexis feel truly at ease. Like Alexis in the late sixties, Zoot had just come through a period of being a solo artist. He had tired of running bands and doing all the organizing.

It was, says Zoot, 'a quartet to remember – all quite strong characters, musically together, which was quite remarkable considering how much we were drinking. You could have four voices at any one time, three of which were lead vocals.

'Alexis knew Germany inside out, all the places to play. We might do one part of Germany on one tour and another part next time round. It was well paid, not many people were doing a concert blues tour. Alexis was sure it would work just doing his normal repertoire – and he was right: they absolutely loved it. The German audience tuned in to every nuance and twist and turn of what we were doing because there were no drums cluttering up the sound. I wasn't sure it would go without a drummer, but Alexis said it would be OK. And without a drummer it really happened.

'It was great just doing the trio; you could hear all the things Alexis was doing – he would throw part of a lyric away, but if you were that close to the microphone you could hear that it wasn't completely thrown away, it would actually go down to a note somewhere, but it didn't always carry to the microphone and out to the audience. There was a knowledgeable aficionado appreciative crowd in Germany who knew the difference between this blues and that blues.'

Alexis was prepared to go some distance to preach the blues – even to Australia and New Zealand, where Alexis and Duster Bennett had been signed to Mushroom Records. For once there was at least the semblance of synergy between touring and record releases as Alexis and Duster played the National Blues/Rock Festival sponsored by Levi with albums (in Alexis' case the 1974 solo album retitled *Mr Blues*) in the shops. However, perhaps the most memorable aspect of the tour was the sight of Alexis throwing up over journalists waiting to greet him at the airport.

Aside from regular touring line-ups, Alexis took out a band with Stevie Marriott, Ian Wallace and Nick South for a live TV appearance in *Musik Laden*, Berlin's version of *The Old Grey Whistle Test*. With an unprecedented three hours' rehearsal to play four songs, they launched into a typical Snape thirst-quencher, 'One Scotch, One Bourbon, One Beer'. Alexis rasped out the vocal, with Steve Marriott's superbly ravaged voice floating over the top for the chorus. Ian Wallace, grinning through a mountainous hangover, thundered along the set, bringing Nick South in his wake as they steamed through 'Slow Down' and 'Get Off My Cloud'. The rhythm section then sat back for an almighty a cappella version of the gospel song 'Diamonds In The Rough', which had Alexis and Steve collapsed in laughter at the end and the audience on its feet giving them both a standing ovation. Alexis was the ultimate gentleman, very together and composed but with a fast stream of naughtiness running through his veins. Steve was a master musician with advanced qualifications in lout. Together they could make great music and of all Alexis' musical associations, this one (but for the fact that Steve's drug use was getting more and more out of control) could have stood a little more exploration.

They stopped over in Hamburg and played at the top after-hours club, Uncle Pohl's. This was at the tail end of Alexis' time with Polydor. Jochen Albrecht, then Polydor's promotions man, says that Alexis' celebrity status in Hamburg was such that for Jochen, who was picking up the tabs of Alexis' hospitality, 'if I wasn't careful we could have forty people around us in a bar or restaurant'. Alexis' close friends like Karsten Jahnke who tended to eschew the rock 'n' roll circus found all this attention problematic. 'There were so many people around, more and more people, men and women admirers, following him everywhere. I didn't like the scene that was gathering around him.' Karsten had the distinct impression that Alexis was none too happy with this situation either.

In fact, Jochen feels that this desire for more privacy and less lunacy was the fallout from the Snape experience, which he thinks changed Alexis. Wherever possible after gigs, the two of them would often just slip away together for a quiet meal or a drink. Alexis visited many friends (outside the music scene) when he was in Hamburg, including one recently divorced woman who had met him at a vulnerable time and become, in the words of one of his German connections, 'addicted to Alexis'. There is no doubt that Alexis viewed his marriage as the complete foundation of his life and that his love for Bobbie was absolute and unconditional. Anybody who befriended Alexis, male or female, needed to understand from day one that Alexis had all his relationships pigeon-holed and none would be allowed to damage his marriage. But he was also a musician on the road and in that role was typical of the breed.

Yet the realities of family life were never far away. Alexis took both Sappho and Nico out on the road again during the seventies. However, this well-meaning act spelt disaster for Nico. Although Nico was a very good musician, Damian believes that, 'this finished him off entirely because he wasn't strong enough to cope with it and dad took the view that if you're out there then you have to cope with it or you go home'.

In her own quiet way Bobbie was, and remains, deeply anguished about what happened to her son, especially his drug use. 'I'm not going to name names, but there was one – I don't suppose he'd recognize himself – who used to say to Nico, "Here try these" and give him a handful of pills. At the gigs, they'd think it funny if Nico fell over. "Never mind, he's young yet." '

The Korners were a tower of strength for many casualties of rock 'n' roll. They were particularly supportive of Jenny Marriott when Steve's cocaine use made him totally impossible to live with: 'their capacity for kindness, care and compassion was unlimited'. In the endlessly chauvinistic world of rock, the last thing a man wants is to be seen to be 'understanding' of a woman's point of view, especially the wife of a fellow musician. Even less are they likely to intervene in a situation. 'Alexis was unique on both points, this was the feminine side of his nature, plus he'd seen it all before and knew all the pressures.' Alexis had tried his best to help out Paul Kossoff, who, like Nico, was spiralling downwards in a jetstream of self-destructive drug use. Unfortunately, Paul died in March 1976.

But their help was never related to 'position' in the business. They were both friends of a young unknown blues musician, Tony Vines (founder of the Mean Red Spiders) and his wife, who lived in a town close by the Chapel. 'Alexis was really a part of the community, not like some, who just had houses there when it was fashionable for musicians to have a place in Wales. He would get involved with any local issues that came up.' At different times both Tony and his wife suffered personal problems and found Alexis and Bobbie unstinting in their help and support.

Sadly, however, when it came to helping Nico, they were clearly not acting in concert. Nico's problems cut through Alexis like a knife; daily he beat himself up with guilt. Yet while he was at his wits' end with worry and frantically wanted Nico to become his own person, Alexis still didn't seem to acknowledge that his approach to his son could have been part of the problem. Or if he did then he seemed powerless to change. Steve Clyne, the Holland Park Comprehensive teacher, says of Nico that 'every time Nico nearly got things together he fell apart. The biggest risk to Nico's sanity would have been for him to succeed.' And of Bobbie he observed: 'She got so desperate at one point she rehearsed saying that Nico was dead.' Tragically, the dread vision became reality. After a number of failed suicide attempts, Nico was to hang himself on his sister's birthday in July 1989.

Nineteen seventy-six was something of a watershed for Alexis. His manager, Phil Roberge, was becoming increasingly unhappy in England. Phil's mother died in 1975, one of his artists, Duster Bennett, was killed in a road crash in 1976 and 'when John Lydon beat up Bob Harris at the Marquee, I knew it was time to go back to the States'. Before he went home to manage guitarist Al DiMeola, he sat down together with Del Taylor and between them they worked out one of those rare music-business beasts, 'the perfectly amicable agreement', whereby, with Alexis' full consent, Del would take over as manager. Already Del and Alexis had been working together for four years, so it was a natural step once Phil dropped out of the picture.

Alexis had a good deal of respect for Del which was crucial for him even to listen to what Del had to say about his affairs. Whether he

actually agreed with any proposal was another matter. Having already
experienced Alexis' unshakeable attitude to the future of Snape, Del
was fully aware what he was getting into.

'We certainly didn't agree all the time and we had quite violent
arguments, but they were verbal games. You had to play head games
or you weren't going to survive, so there was an element of that as
well. A lot of people have said to me that he must have been difficult
to manage, but I never saw it that way – if there was something that I
really thought he should do and he didn't want to do it, it wasn't, "I'm
not going to do it", like in a big huff. We would sit down, sometimes
all night, and I would put the argument as forcefully as I could with
every conceivable angle I could possibly dream up to try and convince
him. Sometimes I would get my point across and he would agree to
do it. But if he didn't want to do something, there was always a logical
reason – it wasn't just for the sake of being difficult. We would always
listen to each other's point of view.'

There were perennial sticking points with Alexis – like recording
albums.

'When Alexis first started making records it was an extension of a live
gig – you turned up with the band, recorded the album and then went off
and did the gig at the Flamingo or wherever. So you were basically playing
live. As recording became more sophisticated, it never sat comfortably
with him, he never really enjoyed it. His thing was playing live with
the spontaneity and the reaction and excitement of the audience. He
really wasn't interested in the clinical business of making a record. He'd
write some songs, play them live and then later he might fancy recording
them. Then you'd go through the purgatory of the next album – trying
to get to the point where you can start it and then for the first three or
four days he'd be Mr Enthusiasm. By day five he'd got fed up with it.
So the finishing of it became more difficult.'

Nor was Alexis very interested in playing to promote a record because
once he'd made it he was writing songs or getting into the next thing.
He could never understand why people would go to a show just to
hear the album – his view was that you could sit at home, get stoned
with a pair of cans on and that was far more enjoyable. He would play
what he considered to be the material for a good show that would get
an audience reaction – not what happened to be on a record.

Del adds: 'Also, given that Alexis would do everything from acoustic,
jazz, blues, gospel and rock, he was pretty impossible to market. This

was further complicated by the deals that record companies would want to strike. They wouldn't just do a one-off album; they'd be committed to two, perhaps three, albums when you could just about get Alexis to do one.'

But for Del any difficulties were more than outweighed by Alexis' infectious enthusiasm for everything he did. 'If he could turn one person on to what he considered to be a good musician or a type of music that was at the root of what he was doing – everything else, like the money involved, was secondary.'

Alexis' radio career had been in the doldrums. His general beef at the time was that he got on air only when a blues man died and the BBC wanted an obituary. He was deeply unhappy about this because he loved broadcasting: 'Radio is marvellous. Television is too much of a block medium because it presents you with a flat picture which is a dead end to your imagination. Whereas radio gives you all that space in your head, which is absolutely limitless, to make up all the pictures you like in all the dimensions you can imagine and all the sounds and all the colours. It's an unending imaginary trip that you can get out of hearing music if you don't have these pictures in front of you on a flat screen.'

Alexis made some progress in 1975 when he again teamed up with Jeff Griffin for a series of R&B shows on the British Forces Broadcasting Service. This was an important prelude to the big breakthrough in 1976: his own show on the domestic airwaves. On 11 August 1976 Alexis and Jeff recorded two pilot shows, one for Radio 1 and the other for Radio 2. At five-thirty p.m. on Saturday 1 January 1977 Radio 1 broadcast the first *Alexis Korner's Blues and Soul Show*. Initial reactions were varied; the magazine *Black Music* felt that the mix of old and new black music that Alexis presented was more suited to a three-hour slot in the early hours of the morning. 'When a national station allows a certain type of music a mere specialist hour per week then each moment should be used to emphasize the potency of its newest music.' Readers disagreed; one wrote: 'I found the content and presentation of Alexis' shows both admirable.' And of one columnist's gripe about the lack of chart records in the show, the same reader opined: 'surely the entire point of a review programme is to expose new product (i.e. newly released rather than necessarily newly produced) since chart discs are adequately aired elsewhere. With respect to reissue material, are there not people who might have interest kindled in Robert Johnson via Korner's programme in preference to another earful of Boney M? Maybe Korner's clever segues of African tribal rhythms into apparently nouveau soul/disco arrangements hit too close to the truth for some people's liking!'

Mr Clive Richardson of Chislehurst in Kent had got right to the meat of what Alexis was trying to do. Once again Alexis was coming at music from left field and taking stick for his troubles. 'Jeff and I pursued a belief. When we started playing African records, people said, "What so you think you are doing playing African ethnic music to *the kids* . . . *the kids* don't want that sort of stuff, *the kids* like to bop . . . *The kids* etc etc . . ." "Well, have you tried them with it?" "No, they don't want to know." "Well, we *know* they want to know. They really do." It's turning people on to things they might not have heard – and there's no greater buzz than turning people on to things.'

As Jeff saw it, 'there were so many things he wanted to do with the programme; Alexis was particularly keen to show how the music we listen to today had been "arrived at" and once we'd actually got the series going, Alexis would introduce other types of music – almost well away from the blues – but actually really relevant to the origins of the blues. But without any question the record we always got the greatest listener response to was an album on the French label Ocora called *Musique du Burundi* and sometimes you could jump a whole generation. We demonstrated this in the pilot programme – we used a track from the album of whisper chant and that went straight into a track by Al Jarreau and you can see the link immediately.'

And it was the manner of Alexis' enthusiasm for doing this that kept fans tuning in, series after series, right up to his death. In the sixties you either listened to pop or 'underground'. For the 'hippies', there were very clear distinctions: pop was crass while the underground was hip, élitist, a great secret. CBS tried to cash in on this with their ridiculous slogan 'The Man Can't Bust Our Music' as if the fans didn't realize that there is no bigger 'Man' than a multinational record company. Particularly after the sinking of pirate radio, the BBC was undoubtedly seen as one of *them* rather than one of *us*.

What Alexis achieved a decade after 1967's Summer of Love, through a combination of his voice, his taste and his personally scripted presentation, was to lull you into a sense that one of *us* had crept in under cover of darkness. One of *us* had taken over a transmitter and was beaming out all the music that under normal circumstances *they* wouldn't let *us* hear. Alexis became your best mate, who comes running round to your house with a new record, saying: 'Hey, hey, drop what you're doing and listen to this – it's great.'

Alexis made music important; he gave it meaning, substance and context. His total and absolute devotion to the subject and the way he wanted to present it had undoubtedly caused him both professional and personal problems. But he communicated that sense of wonder and delight that no other DJ has really accomplished, although Andy Kershaw and Bob Harris certainly carried on some fine traditions. For a time Bob and Alexis shared the same manager in Phil Roberge, which gave Bob a hot line to a share of the Korner sympathetic magic.

'It was great to be able to talk to somebody who had experienced some of the problems I was beginning to run into. He had a genuine understanding, had been there himself, and so could offer advice that really meant something. This was particularly so with *Whistle Test* as I was trying to see through the sycophants. It's not something you think would happen. But when you've been on TV for forty-two weeks a year for over seven years, everybody's seen you, everybody has a view, and you were fielding stuff that was either complimentary or wasn't. This got more and more difficult for me; my radar system went somewhat awry and one of the very important points of contact to help me focus on things was Alexis. He genuinely had time for people; you got eye contact, complete concentration on what you were saying and a terrific amount of wisdom and care in what he was saying to you.'

And as a broadcaster with twenty years' experience, Alexis had much to pass on: 'his advice on programming, microphone techniques and general knowledge on how to broadcast, I found absolutely fascinating'.

Alexis clearly had an exceptional broadcast voice, but Bob maintains that Alexis 'didn't use it', in other words, play up to it. 'Alexis used to present his programmes in the most natural way and when he got enthusiastic, he got carried away, his voice would go up. He never wanted to be completely in control of it and he wasn't. So you had this liquid-chocolate voice that Alexis just let go. He wasn't microphone-conscious and I found that liberating.'

But, despite Alexis' skill as a broadcaster, Jeff insisted that every show should be scripted: 'not for BBC reasons in case anything untoward slipped out, but because we tried recording a couple once or twice when he hadn't scripted because there wasn't enough time and trying to do it off the top of his head didn't sound as professional as I wanted them, and I told him this and he was great about it because he was a professional. I often asked him to go over things again, especially if he was narrating and there was never any problem.'

Listening to old tapes of the shows, it is hard to believe that every word was scripted. 'He had that relatively rare gift of being able to take the written word off the page and make it sound spontaneous,' says Jeff. And Alexis was highly conscientious about the scripts; working hard at polishing them was actually the only way to make a script sound natural. 'He would work on scripts all night, drinking copious amounts of coffee and God knows what else to keep him awake, drive to London, light a joint to get him in the mood to do the shows at ten a.m. I let him get away with smoking because it got him in the right mood, but there were areas where I wouldn't let him and he respected that, like in my office or walking about the place.

'I had to rap him over the knuckles a few times when he put bits into the scripts. But he got away with things because of his inestimable charm and after you'd spoken to him about something you'd wonder why you brought the subject up in the first place.'

But even when everything was scripted, Alexis was not to be denied. The last track he played on one show was 'I Was Too Nice' by Wilson Pickett from the album *Pickett In The Pocket*, which had a front-cover shot of the singer leaning over playing pool. 'Bright-green baize and all those coloured balls on the table,' said Alexis. He caught sight of Jeff's face and followed up with: 'Definitely time to say "goodbye" from our producer, "Gorgeous" Jeff Griffin. Oh come on, Jeff, you're still taking me to see Millie Jackson, aren't you?' Afterwards Alexis assured Jeff that 'we'll get away with it'. 'You'll get away with it,' Jeff replied, 'but if there are any letters afterwards they're coming straight to you.'

But when Jeff went away to Jamaica with Linton Kwesi Johnson, Alexis almost went too far. 'There just wasn't enough time for me to pre-record the shows, so another producer was going to do them. I said to Alexis, a bit tongue in cheek, "Don't do anything naughty while I'm away." "No, no, Jeff, of course not." I got back and found out there had been a bit of a contretemps. One of the records he'd chosen during the two weeks I was away had the word "fuck" in it. Now Alexis knew jolly well that I would never have let him get away with that. But because the producer was a bit nervous of Alexis and his reputation, rather than say, "You can't play that", he did what you are supposed to do at the BBC and refer upwards.

'The normal person would have been Teddy Warwick and he almost certainly would have said no – but he was away, so it went to Doreen Davis and she had an aversion to words like "belly" let alone "fuck". So the record was taken up to her but she let him get away with it because she said you couldn't hear it very well and anyway we're all adults and so on . . . I couldn't believe it, and I gave him a right telling-off for putting somebody in that position. He denied that he knew it was in there, but I'm not a hundred percent sure about that.'

Alexis found other ways to disarm Jeff which weren't calculated – they were just Alexis. 'I was in the studio and he was a bit late and he came bustling in with loads of bags as usual, shoulder bag, box of records. And he also had this Tesco carrier bag with him.

' "Er Jeff, keep an eye on this for me, will you? Look after it while I'm doing the programme."

' "Yeah, OK."

' "Be a bit careful with it."

' "Oh, right, what have you just bought?"

' "I've haven't bought anything, it's just getting on a bit now."

' "What is it, then?"

' "Well, it's a painting actually."

' "Can I have a look at it?"

'And when I pulled it out the bag I couldn't believe my eyes. It was a Magritte.

' "What are you doing with this?"

' "Belongs to my father-in-law. He wants it valued. I didn't have time to call in the flat so I brought it with me."

' "What are you doing with it in a carrier bag?"

' "Well, it was the safest way to carry it." '

The summer of 1977 saw some career twists that were bizarre even by Alexis' standards.

For reasons which are still unclear he was offered a large sum of money to play Gessler in a Swiss musical on the life of William Tell. Del Taylor say the plan was 'to put this on in Switzerland, warm it up and if it went successfully, they were going to tour it everywhere, bring it to London and all the rest of it. The whole point of this show was to send up William Tell – so you didn't have to be Einstein to work out that it was unlikely to be a resounding success in Switzerland. Alexis was asked if he would like to play the part of Gessler. It was a musical and he decided he would do it. The reason he did it was that he had never done a musical. Everything about this was "you shouldn't really do this" and it was just a complete flip of the career kind of thing. And because it was sending up Tell in Switzerland, he just couldn't say no.' It was no surprise when the whole enterprise flopped badly. Alexis was rumoured to have been the only one who got paid.

The era of the concept album had sadly not passed; one of its last gasps was a fantasy saga *The King of Elfland's Daughter*, conceived by Bob Johnson with Peter Knight, who were on the English folk scene with the likes of Steeleye Span, the Albion Band and Ashley Hutchings. Alexis played a troll and, with Christopher Lee, provided narration, while the strong vocal line-up included Frankie Miller, Chris Farlowe and P P Arnold.

And then there was another saga: the recording for the album which has gone down in the chronicles of Korner discography as *The Lost Album*. Alexis had a two-album deal with a production company called Sunshine owned by Michael Lang, who was one of the organizers of 1969's Woodstock festival and later Joe Cocker's manager. The first album delivered was *Get Off My Cloud* and the pressure was on to do the second.

They went to a studio in Wales to record the backing tracks, with Snape's tour manager Pete Walmsley producing, as he had done on the band's live album. At the time Del Taylor was managing Bandit, led by singer Jim Diamond, and most of the band were brought in to back Alexis, along with Colin Hodgkinson and Sappho.

The sessions were beset with problems, largely because the sound equipment kept picking up local taxis' radio messages. There was a big row, everybody left and they returned to London, to Advision, to continue. More delays ensued, Pete Walmsley moved on and meanwhile the company were agitating for the album. Jean-Paul Salvatori took over production, first at Pebble Beach in Worthing and then at Island. Eventually the album was released in Germany only on the Intercord Label under the title *Just Easy*, a loose collection of soul- and gospel-influenced material.

Years after Alexis died, an album came out in Germany called *The Lost Album*. This turned out to be the basic tapes from the Welsh studio drowned with echo to fill in the holes. The studio boss claimed Alexis had signed a production deal with him. In the sixties Alexis would have done that, but now, with a proper management, it is most unlikely he would have done side deals. Alexis would listen to any proposal and then pass it over to Del. Then the studio claimed that they were owed money for the time spent there. A further attempt was made to release this album in the UK as recently as 1995.

Alexis never lost any opportunity to play, however far flung and however unlikely the possibility of finding a blues audience. When Snape were touring Germany, Alexis met Tomaz Domicelj (pronounced 'Domicell'), a young student, budding musician and freelance journalist born in what is now the independent republic of Slovenia, formerly part of Yugoslavia. On trips to London Tomaz became friendly with Jeff Griffin, who describes him as 'a very genuine guy, great musician, raconteur, journalist and all sorts of other things. I think Alexis sensed a fellow being, a fellow rebel as well.'

In March 1978, on his thirtieth birthday, Tomaz arranged a gig at the Tivoli Hall in Ljubljana with Alexis as guest artist and bands from Belgrade, Macedonia and Croatia. Jeff had been to the country before to visit the Ljubljana Song Festival. 'I was dead keen to go over and be unpaid roadie.'

After the Tivoli Hall gig, there was a 'return match' in Pula, home of the Croatian band Atomic Shelter, local heavy-metal heroes. The idea was for Jeff, Alexis and Tomaz to have lunch with Tomaz' parents on the way to the gig. Tomaz' father was a hard-line communist who had travelled on business all over Eastern Europe, Germany, Greece, Turkey and North Africa, much as Alexis' own father had done. 'Alexis and my father were talking away in fluent German about politics and history, looking at old pictures and books, and we were all drinking wine and brandy and the cigars came out. It was four p.m., time was getting on, and I thought we ought to be going because Pula was over the mountains. And then it began to snow. And if it snows in Ljubljana, you know it's going to be bad on the mountain roads. Lorries were hitting each other, police everywhere. But Alexis was very cool. He lit a double joint and had the lot himself.'

Jeff was less cool. 'The police tried to stop us and send us back. Tomaz insisted on going on and they all said, "You're mad, Domicelj" because most of them knew him. I remember looking behind me as we went up this hill and there were cars all over the place, but Alexis was going, "Yeah, let's do it" – he had nerves of steel and I never ever recall him being afraid of any situation. Alexis told Tomaz that he'd take over the driving if Tomaz got tired. Now Tomaz has only got ten percent vision in one eye and that was bad enough, but if Alexis had taken over . . . I kept my eyes closed at the back most of the time.'

Rock musicians are the same the world over. When they got to the gig there was a big row over who was going on first. The band from Belgrade refused, Atomic Shelter said no because it was their home town and they wanted to go on last. Tomaz was a guest artist and he didn't want to do it, but, he recalls, Alexis then said: "What a big fuss, I'll go on first." He went on, brought the house down and made it twice as hard for everybody else.'

Alexis paid a subsequent trip to Yugoslavia, again accompanied by Jeff. *En route* to a gig, they stopped on the motorway. Alexis was wearing a silver bomber jacket, tight trousers and boots. 'Alexis and I went in the toilet and there was a guy in there, I think he was a Russian lorry driver. Alexis was dressed the way he always was, which to this guy looked a bit like a gypsy. The guy made some disparaging remark about him in Russian – and Alexis not only understood what the guy said but said something back to him and the guy was absolutely dumbfounded.'

Tomaz had also tried to fix Alexis up with a gig in Sarajevo, 'but he didn't play because of a load of local wankers. I offered these guys to put Alexis on the bill, but they said no.' Tomaz was also due to play because he was big news in the country. Alexis was sitting in the audience and having refused to pay him, the promoters announced that Alexis was going to play. Cue another row and Tomaz, in his ebullient, forceful manner, put a stop to it. Interviewed in Ljubljana, Alexis took a sideswipe at the city that wouldn't pay him to play. Asked by the interviewer to name his favourite city he said: 'Sarajevo.' 'Why Sarajevo?' 'Because I've always wanted to see the city where my father's king was shot.' This was relayed to listeners as 'because it's such a famous historical city'.

In between the two trips to Yugoslavia, Alexis celebrated a milestone. He was the first high-profile musician of the sixties rock explosion to hit fifty.

13

'IF YOU DON'T WANT THE PRIZE, DON'T JOIN THE COMPETITION'

I f it had been left to Alexis and Bobbie, celebrations for Alexis' fiftieth birthday may well have been confined to another gathering of the great and the good, packed into 116a Queensway. Willie Lang of WDR in Germany had other ideas, or rather one big idea. He wanted to film an all-star birthday concert for German television. Jeff Griffin became involved and wanted to do a BBC TV–Radio 1 'simulcast', an idea which had started back in 1974 with Van Morrison at the Rainbow. But British television turned down the chance to televise a celebrity concert in honour of the most influential person in the history of British blues and rock and so it was left to Jeff to record the event for Radio 1 and leave the pictures to German TV.

When the proposal was put to Bobbie, her first reaction was: 'Why do you have to do a gig for your birthday?' For a while Alexis was caught between the logic of what she was saying and the chance to play with some old mates – even if it was for his birthday. But this was not going to be some seedy lig in a hot, sweaty club. WDR proposed hiring, at their expense, no less than the Gatsby Room at Pinewood Studios, with free food and booze. Alexis would be playing with those he admired and respected as friends and musicians, it would be recorded and filmed and he wouldn't have to go into a studio to do it. The deal was done.

Alexis began the customary phone round. The basic band for this night would be his classic touring trio with Colin and Zoot plus a man mountain of a drummer, Stu Speer, who played with Max Merritt and the Meteors, an Australian band, protégés of Alexis. An impressive brass section came together comprising Dick Heckstall-Smith, Art Themen, John Surman, Dick Morrissey, Mike Zwerin and Mel Collins. They all met for two days' rehearsals or, as Zoot light-heartedly puts it: ' "There's not much money, but come to this room and you'll have a lot of laughs." Yeah, OK, Alex, I've heard that one before . . .' Some, like Charlie Watts, couldn't make it. Many brought their guitars on the night in the hope of having a blow.

The invitation depicted Alexis as a baby naked on a rug. It was an inspired choice, a metaphor for Alexis as the eternal Peter Pan character, not so much Father but Child of the Blues, respectful of the roots but retaining a youthful enthusiasm for all the possibilities in honest, unpretentious popular music.

Musicians started rolling up in the late afternoon, eyes out on stalks at the spread before them, tables heaving with food, an endless free bar. All you had to do was negotiate miles of recording and TV cables to get at it. Norman Beaker, leader of No Mystery, in 1978 probably the only blues band in Britain who could get a gig, recalls: 'I must admit, I made a total pillock of myself. I went into the place, you know, liking a drink, and I said to Dick Heckstall-Smith, "I'm just off to get a pint." He had a mouthful of sandwich, tried to grab me to tell me something, but I was off to the bar. I said, "I'll have a pint of bitter, please." "Sorry sir, champagne or wine only." "Oh right, well, I'll have a pint of champagne then." The atmosphere was fantastic, the odd ego floating about, you know, people deliberately not wanting to know you, but all these people came, just for Alexis.' Dave Lunt, No Mystery's bassist, was also there. 'Musically it was excellent, the sound was superb. It was all very cleverly orchestrated, there was a sea of Faces, but a very happy, joyous feeling about the whole thing.'

The small group with Alexis, Colin and Zoot worked extremely well doing songs like 'Lining Track' and 'Mess of Blues', propelled along by Stu Speer, who had the knack of driving the band along without appearing to make any effort whatsoever. Then the brass section kicked in, switching through the Ellington, Bechet and Mingus-style arrangements with equal facility.

During 'Spoonful', Del's wife, Yolande, wheeled in an enormous cake in the shape of a guitar for Alexis, resplendent in his new suit and peach shirt bought for the occasion, to blow out fifty candles at the end of the song.

Around midnight other guests came up on stage, including Chris Farlowe and Duffy Power, and, to most people's surprise, Eric Clapton. Obviously all eyes turned to him, but he was determined to keep as low a profile as possible. This caused a few problems for Jeff, who was trying to record the show. 'We had microphones all the way up the stage and we'd been told to cover this one particular amp. We could hear the guitar on the cans and see it on the scanner, but we couldn't see Eric. "Where the hell is he?" In fact he was sitting off stage playing with a very long guitar lead.' Eventually he made his way cautiously to the stage, smiling nervously, looking rather pale and fragile, for much of the time playing his Black Beauty Stratocaster perched on the end of Zoot's organ bench. Alexis came over between songs for a few words, giving him a reassuring pat on the cheek. By the time Eric had begun to relax, on stage was Paul Jones, who says: 'I remember I had this very boyish hair cut which I wasn't at all sure about and this short grey jacket which you might almost have worn as a kid. Alexis called me up and Eric was already on stage. He just looked at me, burst out laughing and said, "Go back to school." '

Musicians met up who hadn't seen or spoken to each other for years, apart from a passing grunt as they staggered bleary-eyed through a motorway service station or airport lounge. There were also new alliances forged. According to Paul Jones, 'it was that night that Ian Stewart had the idea for Rocket 88.' The pianist had been the 'sixth' Rolling Stone since the band was formed. Ousted by Andrew Oldham for his lack of pop-star looks, Ian had nevertheless toured and played with the band for many years, but never led his own outfit. Jones recalls: 'He said, "What I want is to get together an R&B big band like the Ellington or Basie 'small' group and I don't want any guitarists unless they can play like Freddie Green," which meant just about the only guitarist who could be in it was Alexis. I said, "Would there be any room for a harmonica player in all this?" and his eyes sort of glazed over.'

The idea seemed to marry with the thoughts of another blues pianist, Bob Hall. 'Rocket 88 was originally formed to play a farewell concert for me when I was living and working in Swindon and planning to move back to London. They had a nice little theatre and I suggested to Ian we might do a concert. Stu said, "I know a drummer who's quite good" – and that was Charlie Watts. We got a local bass player and a brass section of Colin Smith, John Pickard and Al Gay. We never practised at all, just went up on stage and did this show.'

Bob had a similar aversion to 'guitar heroes'. 'In fact Eric Clapton was a friend of Stu's and was very anxious to join the band and it got to the point where Eric would ask Stu where the band was playing and Stu wouldn't tell him.' They were both right to think that if Eric played, all the focus would be on him. But as he had already shown with Delaney and Bonnie, the early plans for Derek & the Dominoes, his years of self-imposed exile and Alexis's party, he was more than happy to take a back seat. However, as Paul Jones says, the only guitarist who really fitted their bill was Alexis.

Before the band played again, Bob met Alexis at a Professor Longhair concert. 'I said do you fancy coming along and playing with our band? He was very enthusiastic and we organized another concert in Swindon.' They went on to do a gig at Dingwalls celebrating fifty years of boogie-woogie. That night Jack Bruce joined Alexis and Charlie; the crowd stretched around the block, and hundreds were turned away. Bob and Ian were clearly on to something, but the band was still called the Bob Hall Band. 'It was put to me by Stu that as I was the least known of anyone in the band it might be better if we had a more neutral name. Stu suggested Rocket 88.'

With the promise of star names in the line-up, they secured a recording contract with Atlantic and began a series of *ad hoc* concerts around Europe. Bob called each gig 'an event of one sort or another'. They backed Jimmy Witherspoon, Chris Farlowe and Country Joe Pleasance and toured with the Woodstock Tenth Anniversary Revival, where Alexis performed one of his legendary 'get the promoter off the hook' routines. Joe Cocker's manager, Michael Lang, declared the headliner unfit to play. The man in the hot spot was Alexis' old friend, promoter Karsten Jahnke, who said to Michael Lang: 'I will kill you if this guy can't play because no promoter in the world can go on stage at nine o'clock in the evening after seven hours of music and say, "Ladies and gentleman, I'm very sorry Joe Cocker can't play." ' Enter Alexis and large quantities of peppermint tea, Joe drinks, up comes whatever was preventing him performing and Alexis helps propel Joe Cocker him on to the stage with the mike set at a angle so that he can grab it as he teeters past.

Bob Hall was under no illusions about why people came to see Rocket 88. 'It was Charlie's call. If he said he could do it we'd get major shows. It was Charlie's name that made the difference.' But for Charlie it was like old times, just doing some fun gigs with old mates in fairly chaotic circumstances, away from the pressures and scheduling precisions of being a Rolling Stone. 'It was just great, I never knew really what was going or anything, we just had a great time doing it.'

For Jack Bruce, 'musically it wasn't challenging or anything, it was like a holiday, the chance to hang out as much as anything. There was some very good playing within improvising blues patterns.' But by his own admission, 'my whole life had come to a grinding halt in many ways. I'd split up with my wife, I was living in Germany most of the time.' His most recent attempt at a potentially very exciting band, with Mick Taylor and Carla Bley, had collapsed in a general drug morass. This was partly the reason why Bob Hall says that the Rocket 88 live album was recorded in Germany and was completed under 'trying circumstances'.

'The idea was to record the album at a gig we were doing in Hamburg. It was one of those occasions where there was a lot of hanging about before the show started. At that time I didn't drink. Alexis could always play no matter how much he had to drink or what strange substances he'd consumed. He was always there. To be honest, the same couldn't be said of others. We were all waiting to go on at the side of the stage. Jack was standing behind the curtain, just on the edge. Some guy was out front babbling away in German and the crowd's going "Yeah" and "Right" – and then Jack lost it. There was this slow-motion movement of Jack and his upright bass falling on to the stage from behind the curtain. He just flipped through ninety degrees. There was this shocked silence. He got up and then he and Charlie [who had also had a few] proceeded to play – separately – for the entire evening.'

The recording was a washout and they moved on to the next gig in Hanover, where the venue was more suited to warehousing than recording music. The acoustics were terrible, the pianos worse and the mikes kept falling off. Mick McKenna, in charge of the Rolling Stones Mobile, managed to patch something together, but in Bob's opinion, 'it was nothing like the band at its best'.

Yet it was a band the musicians put themselves out for; Alexis was on tour in Switzerland and flew to the UK for one gig and back again at his own expense. Stu drove Charlie from a Stones recording session in Paris for a Rocket 88 spot at the North Sea Jazz Festival in the Netherlands, then turned round and brought him all the way back to France. Apparently Mick McKenna taped every single gig; assuming the tapes still exist, there is possibly a great Rocket 88 live compilation album waiting to be done.

There was one possible chance for Alexis to do himself some justice in the studio and that was to perform live without having any overdubs. On 1 and 2 July 1979 he went to the Tonstudio Bauer in Ludwigsburg to record a direct-cut album called *Me*, on which, unusually, he plays piano on some tracks. On doing the session as one long take Alexis said on the sleeve-notes: 'I think that's the way it should be. I am going to try and play only titles that I have never practised before. I want to try and create the true blues feeling that you only get from improvisation.' He also said: 'I love listening to this album.'

The record company didn't. Intercord rejected the album and a very strange deal was struck with another company whereby it was available only in 'non-record outlets' such as hi-fi shops and limited to a run of 12,000 copies. The album sold out in Germany, more copies were pressed and then the company went bust. The liquidators dumped some of the stock in ordinary record shops, the inevitable litigation ensued and yet more deals were struck, this time to release the album in vinyl and CD through two different companies. Not until 1987 was the album, now retitled *Hammer and Nails*, released in the UK.

Bobbie sided with Intercord. 'I disliked that album intensely. Alexis often forgot the words to songs and that's bound to be the day when you do an album like that and you don't get it together. He wouldn't have made half the records he made if I'd had anything to do with it. He just wasn't very good in the studio. I've heard lots of tapes of live shows and much of it was absolutely superb, but rarely in the studio. He just didn't work that way. It all dried up; he was communicating with nobody in the studio and he needed an audience with the response.'

Since 1962 Alexis had been encouraging young musicians to follow their instincts about music, not to be discouraged by the kind of cynicism and hostility that he had faced and overcome first from his family and then the London jazz mafia. Brian Jones, Andy Fraser, Robert Plant and Paul Kossoff had all been helped in this way; attentive ears and comforting words were apparently available for Alison Moyet and Paul Young, too, as they struggled early on in their careers. When guitarist Mick Abrahams walked away from Jethro Tull when they were on their way to becoming a major international rock band, 'Alexis said I'd done the right thing, but not just to stop me feeling bad: he thought I had something else to offer. He was never trite or patronizing to get you off his back. He was one of the very few people who made me feel valid as a person in the music business. If I ever wanted an ear, he was always there.'

And he was there for the total unknowns and complete strangers as well. Italy is by and large a country of 'little villages', a conservative society unlikely to look favourably on a twenty-five-year-old vagabond, beatnik musician 'with the longest hair in Venice'. Living in an totally blues-free zone drove guitarist Guido Toffoletti to London in December 1975 with a one-way ticket. Christmas saw him at the Golden Lion pub in Fulham for a Long John Baldry gig. They got talking and John gave Guido Phil Roberge's number. Alexis and Guido met, talked at length about making it in the music business and then moved on to more personal areas. 'When I first came to London my father had been dead for two or three years, I didn't really know how to "arrange" my life,' Guido says. But on the strength of one meeting with Alexis, he went straight back home to form a band named Blues Society, to the same scorn and vilification that Alexis had received all those years ago. Guido took his cue from Alexis, combining playing with promoting and creating for himself an alternative way of being a musician in the business while avoiding the tour-album-tour syndrome. In 1979 Alexis played in Venice at a festival promoted by Guido. For the sleeve-notes of Guido's first album with Alexis and singer Herbie Goins (by then himself living in Italy) Alexis wrote: 'And to you Guido, what can I say? Just another Blues Situation? Without the persistence of Guido none of this would have happened. He is a blues fanatic . . . and he is right! Keep on playing and believing Guido. It is your only defence against all the prancing bitches and pudding-heavy downers of the business. They may try and fuck you up . . . the music never will . . . Spread the word, open the scene; that's all this is about. Success sometimes comes easy but the GOOD THINGS usually require a bit of sweat. So, sweat! You're bound to win . . . we always do!' Consider the 'blues boom' of the nineties and this is a point hard to argue.

During the seventies Alexis had taken his music to almost every country in Europe, America and halfway across the world to Australia and New Zealand. But what of his adopted homeland? Once the first flush of punk was over and the major record companies had snapped everybody up, the music scene was left in a vacuum. This left some small openings for the likes of Alexis, but it took time to develop. A poorly attended concert with No Mystery in 1977, a better one early in 1978, then storming Rocket 88 pub gigs in 1979. The turning point came with Colin Hodgkinson's agreement to partner Alexis in a permanent duo rather than the *ad hoc* association they had enjoyed up until then.

Colin had made a international name for himself in the seventies with Back Door, a jazz-fusion band with real warmth and heart, greatly loved and promoted by Alexis at every opportunity, in print, on his radio shows and as a tour support. From there, Colin went to New York and the world of Jan Hammer and Neil Schon, before playing with Alexis at the Edinburgh Festival in 1979. It was here that they agreed to form the duo.

They drew large, appreciative crowds, and off stage enjoyed good food, wine and other joys of the chemical carousel because the relatively small touring expenses allowed them their indulgences. Playing together brought mutual benefits; Alexis had helped promote Colin's career; his virtuosity made Alexis look good on stage. Colin later went on to play in Whitesnake, where the contrast couldn't have been more marked: same set night after night, played in exactly the same way, no deviations. But, Colin says, 'if you've got total freedom, you've got ultimate responsibility. For me it was great, it's actually difficult playing in a duo in lots of ways. Alexis himself said, "I wouldn't have anybody in the band who couldn't play ten times better than me." There was a lot for me to do, it was a challenge and much more fun than playing in Whitesnake on and off the stage. It was such a nice atmosphere when we played together.

'We'd do this thing called "Lining Track", which was a Leadbelly song. I'd sing and play the bass and he'd play two tambourines. So he announces it and says, "Oh, I've left the tambourines in the car. I'll just go and get them. Tell some jokes or something." I said, "What do you mean tell some jokes?" Off he went. You'd hear the theatre doors closing and then you'd hear the tambourines coming back.'

With Colin, Alexis even managed to have fun in the studio. Together they recorded *Bedtime Gories*, an EP of railway songs with Pete Sayers on dobro and banjo. Damian was producing. 'This is the cult album that everybody wants. We did it under the names Schtick and Futz. It was so tongue in cheek – and it never got released.' Two of the songs, 'Wreck Of The Old '97' and 'Casey Jones', did appear on a posthumous compilation album; others, like 'Blood on the Saddle', where Alexis hit the lowest notes possible, are due for release.

Just how well Colin and Alexis meshed could be seen on the Channel 4 programme *Individual Voices*, which filmed a duo concert at the Roundhouse in Chalk Farm, north London in 1981 – one of the very few times that Alexis ever appeared on British television after *Five O'Clock Club*. He was now fifty-three and as he said on the programme, coming to that age when bluesmen often give of their best work in a genre 'not crippled by the youth-cult thing which says if you haven't made it by the time you're twenty-three you're finished'. He was obviously pleased at the chance to play in England, but was under no illusion that if the scene closed down again he would be off back to Europe. He said he was never willing to play the game of trying to get records into the charts simply to get a gig 'and if you don't want the prize, don't join the competition'.

Standing on stage in the spotlight grasping his trademark gold-coloured Gibson, he delivered a self-penned song which encapsulated all the difficulties he had faced to achieve his career in music.

'When I was a kid in the War, the exciting things all started with B: blitz, bombs, boogie-woogie . . . [which] wasn't approved of in my family, wanting to play boogie-woogie. Wanting to be the world's greatest boogie piano player was not considered an ambition. Piano was locked, key taken away and I became a juvenile delinquent. And that what's this song is called:

I was a juvenile delinquent
Just delinquishing my time
I was a juvenile delinquent
Just delinquishing my time
But then the music came and got me
Now they pay me just to sing my songs in rhyme.

Three times seven now that was heaven, 21
Sweet 16 was no schoolboy dream, life had not begun
School was zero, but then most of my heroes played the blues
And that old boogie-woogie sort of got caught up in my wartime news
Then my brain exploded
Overloaded with the kicks you get from flying

Time was cool
For some brand new rules
Time to change it all
We spat right in the eyes of the guys
Who said blues was off the wall

Big Bill Broonzy was the first big Face in town
And that was back in the '50s before the Beatles and the
  Stones came around
We were not deranged
But simply rearranged
A changing world of sound

I was a juvenile delinquent
I had anti-social ways
(I did nasty things in the park in the dark)
I was a juvenile delinquent
My folks all said I'd never play
They laughed until they cried, they almost died
But now they pay to see my face
Hear my song, see my face
And hear me sing in rhyme.

Because of the age difference between Alexis and most of the very young talent he brought along, he had always seemed like an 'elder statesman' of the music scene even when he was still in his thirties. In 1983 and now in his mid fifties, Alexis decided he wanted to rein in the touring and refocus his activities, though his enthusiasm for playing in the right circumstances remained undiminished. He pulled together another all-star band to play two nights at the Marquee to celebrate the club's twenty-fifth anniversary. Even though Alexis had played at the club's tenth-anniversary celebrations in 1968, the acrimony between Alexis and Harold Pendleton had never been fully repaired. According to Harold, it was Alexis who made the first conciliatory moves by apologizing over the Broonzy benefit gig, an event by then a quarter of a century into history. Del Taylor maintains that Harold's wife rang to try to book Alexis for the whole week. Alexis refused, saying he would only do two days and only then as long as he could hand-pick the musicians. And pick them he did, including Charlie Watts and Bill Wyman, singer Geno Washington and another young artist actively promoted by Alexis, singer Ruby Turner. Like so many of these events that Alexis instigated, it was a great success – premier musical talent driven, coaxed and encouraged by the man in the eye of the storm.

But these one-offs aside, Alexis was looking for some shelter. His radio show was going from strength to strength and he had finally got a strong foothold in domestic radio. Writing in the *Guardian* on 'how Radio 1 finally became wonderful', Mick Brown commented: 'Alexis Korner's Sunday evening show . . . is probably the only place on British radio where you will hear black gospel music and certainly the only place you will hear it alongside Rickie Lee Jones, Jerry Lee Lewis and lot of other artists with three names. Korner is a true fan with singular passions – Little Willie Littlefield for example, a blues singer so obscure, one is tempted to think Korner may have invented him. His programme is always hugely enjoyable . . .' Brown could have picked an even better example of Alexis' love of the obscure, possibly the greatest-sounding name in the history of popular music: blues singer Arizona Dranes.

Producer Stuart Grundy engaged Alexis' voice to narrate the radio series *Guitar Greats*. Alexis was not enamoured of the concept, which involved fresh interviews, so that only living guitarists could be included, but his work brought this review from the *Sheffield Morning Telegraph*: 'Mr Korner managed throughout to avoid the pitfalls which come with taking rock and roll seriously as music. Not that it shouldn't be, but in doing so too many commentators end up sounding both pompous and patronising at the same time. Alexis Korner's relaxed approach would have convinced the most prejudiced of listeners that here was something worth listening to.'

In a sense Alexis was entering the Third Age of his career from struggling nonentity, through well-established performance artist and now into a period where he wanted to diversify into film and television alongside his radio and voice-over work, which remained a lucrative source of income.

Alexis and Del formed a group of companies around the name Vita Viva, and had various documentary projects at the planning stage. One was called *Jody Grinder*, a film tracing the derivation of American Army marching songs back to Africa; it was, says Del, 'a project very close to his heart'.

Another project was *Dream Cars*, based on an idea that current Grand Prix drivers would be filmed driving classic cars during the season. Alexis and Del were both speed freaks and often went to Formula One races (with Jeff Griffin) or thrashed cars around Goodwood. 'We vowed never to race against each other,' says Del, 'because we knew that if we arrived at the same point at the same time, neither one of us was going to give way.' Alexis' passion was his TVR sports car, which, Damian says, 'he used to drive around the country lanes at seventy-five mph. If anything had been coming the other way that would have been it. He didn't really appreciate that it's not what you are doing, it's what the bozo front and back is doing. His idea was: I'm driving safely so everything is going to be all right.' His insistence on driving whatever state he was in, and however tired, put the fear of God into many of his musicians, some of whom actually threatened him physically as one near miss followed another.

Damian recalls the closest Alexis came to tragedy. 'We used to have a beautiful Citroën DS23. Daddy was driving Sappho, Nico and a carpenter who was doing some work for us in Wales. A lorry carrying railway tracks without the markers at the back to show how far they were sticking out, stoved the roof of the car in down to the steering wheel. Daddy had quite a charmed life in that respect.' Nobody was hurt and Alexis went straight round to see Pam Wynne (formerly Pam Mayall). He hadn't seen the railway tracks, probably because 'he hadn't slept for about four days'. He borrowed her car to make the journey to Wales. 'Bobbie was at the Chapel and he said, "If I don't get into a car and drive right now, I might never drive again." '

History of Rock was the most ambitious of the planned projects. Alexis came up with the notion of a multi-part series for which he would script, narrate and conduct the interviews following the history of the music from the forties onwards. The respect that Alexis commanded on both sides of the Atlantic meant that all interview requests, including Paul McCartney, B B King and Tina Turner, were granted.

Everything was set up, the interviewing process began and, according to the magazine *Television Weekly*, the £800,000 series was pre-sold to America. Problems with the production company caused delays, but this was simply the prelude to a complete cessation of activities for entirely different reasons.

In October 1983 Del, having secured a deal with Tony Stratton-Smith's Charisma Records, persuaded Alexis to try a studio album, his first one since the nightmare of *Just Easy*. Alexis had some songs he wanted to record, including two autobiographical tracks, 'Juvenile Delinquent' and 'Mean Fool', and a tribute number called 'King B.B.'. But in truth, the album was ill-starred. Some of the other material was less well chosen – for example, a dire song written by Peter Sarstedt called 'Beirut', which was also released as a single, and another, which mercifully didn't make it to vinyl, Prince's 'Jack You Off'. There was a dispute over the production. Alexis said he wouldn't do it without Damian as producer, while Damian wasn't keen on being written into a contract without being asked first. Meanwhile Del brought in Thin Lizzy and Commander Cody producer John Alcock, who had previously produced Liar and Bandit, both managed by Del. John had worked with Alexis before, in 1976 down at the R. G. Jones studio, in an abortive attempt to work with drum machines. 'It was lunacy to try and tie Alexis down with synthesizers and drum machines to build the recording process like most normal people do. I never should have thought of trying this with Alexis – he was a total free spirit.'

But here they were at Konk Studios trying to record again with members of a new band called HRH, with Colin Hodgkinson, who took over much of what went on musically. 'I said to Alexis that I would take care of everything. You come in and when you get fed up, just go out and do something else.' Damian came in as co-producer and the recording process picked up momentum. The cartoonist Ralph Steadman was commissioned to do the cover. Alexis did go out, but he never came back. Every engagement listed on the office calendar for 12 October 1983 and weeks ahead is scratched through 'cancelled'. The last entry in his personal diary reads: 'Fell over in the street 3pm. Was taken to hospital. Getting very bad headaches.'

Alexis had been concerned about his health for some time. He told a reporter in 1983 that he would play until he died, like so many of the famous bluesmen. Privately he felt he had to cut down on playing because he feared he was suffering from 'white finger', an occupational hazard of guitarists, some of whom lose the feeling in their fingers. According to his friend Ellie Buchanan, Alexis stopped smoking cigarettes in 1981 (although Bobbie says he didn't) and as early as the summer of 1982, Ellie says, he told her he felt he was going to die. Ellie's sister had died of cancer and Alexis pumped Ellie for information. Not that this scare stopped him from smoking cannabis. He was still an ardent campaigner for legalization. In 1980 he gave a speech at the First International Cannabis Conference in Amsterdam, where he spoke of his enjoyment of both dope and cocaine. But for all the dope, coke and speed Alexis had consumed over the years, he never had what could remotely be called a psychological 'drug problem'. The potential physical damage inflicted by years of smoking tobacco and cannabis was another matter.

He had been losing weight through 1982 and 1983 and friends began to remark on his appearance. In the autumn of 1983 he went to Texas, where he was made an honorary Admiral in the Texan Navy, which raised a few eyebrows back home among those who hadn't realized Texas had a coastline. But he was unwell and suffering badly from as yet undiagnosed headaches.

Initially it was thought that the headaches might have been caused by dental work. Then sinus trouble was proposed and he was sent for X-rays. The doctor said that he did have bad sinuses, but when the nurse told Alexis: 'I'd rather have that than the operation to cure it,' he was gone.

He needed a medical for the *History of Rock* series and it was then discovered that he had scars on his lungs caused by the childhood TB of which he had been completely ignorant all his adult life. But the head pains just got worse; one October night when Bobbie and Alexis were at the Chapel, 'Alexi was just weeping with the pain it was so bad. I phoned the doctor and he said, "Drive him straight into Hereford." The only thing they could do to stop the pain was to give him steroids because the painkillers no longer worked. They didn't know what was wrong. He felt quite a lot better. But they said he needed a scan and he got recommended to somebody at the Westminster Hospital.'

Alexis went into that hospital, at which time, Bobbie says, there was no pain, no sign of brain tumour. She says the doctors performed two biopsies, which were both negative. He was sent home but collapsed the next day from a massive infection. Bobbie says that the huge dose of steroids Alexis was taking for pain was not reduced before the biopsy operations and this, Bobbie maintains, left Alexis vulnerable to infection. The hospital was still convinced that there was something wrong with the lung and wanted to remove part of it. Bobbie said no, but the doctors told Alexis he would be home for Christmas.

However, at some point there must have been a diagnosis of terminal cancer either in the form of a brain tumour or lung cancer with secondaries because Damian says it fell to him to break the news to his father. 'The consultants called us in and said it was terminal and that he probably wouldn't come out. I told him . . . it was one of the things that you remember for the rest of your life.' Bobbie had been under enormous strain. Her mother had recently died and her father was too elderly to take care of himself. Jenny Marriott was with her when they found out that Alexis was not coming home for the holidays, and she recalls: 'Up to that point she had been so calm and patient and for Alexis' sake, not making waves. But I saw her outside in the corridor and she just shouted out, "It's true what they say. If the illness doesn't kill you, the hospital will." '

Meanwhile nobody outside the family and a few close friends had any idea that Alexis was so ill. Those who visited him found him in good spirits. Charlie Watts remembers that 'he had all these tubes coming out of him. He was going, "I'm fine, cock. I've got my stuff here," and he brought out this tiny little screw of hash. "They don't know what the hell this is." He had a little tape recorder and he'd go out and play his guitar on the balcony so the smoke would blow away. I thought, what an amazing attitude. Not a bloody word about how ill he was.' Alexis was actually composing in hospital. He recorded a set of 'Westminster Songs', including 'Cat Scan', 'Westminster Rock', 'Lung Leak' and 'Hanging Fire In The Air', which Damian is determined will never see the light of day 'because they are far too personal'. Alexis had demonstrably good days. When Anthea Joseph came calling, he wasn't even in the hospital. ' "Where's Mr Korner?" "Oh, he's gone round to the pub." I found him surrounded by pretty nurses and glasses of brandy. "Have a drink." We finally persuaded him to go back to the hospital and back into bed and then he said, "Can you find my stash – it's under the bed somewhere." And I just sat there and rolled a couple of joints.'

More than anything, Alexis wanted to be home for Christmas at the Chapel, but the doctors changed their minds and said no. Just before Christmas, Alexis wrote his last letter to Norman Beaker, saying he now hoped to be out for New Year and enclosing a cheque for Alexis Beaker, Norman's son. Alexis, the boy's godfather, had got quietly stoned at the christening, but still left the impression of 'what a nice man' with all the unsuspecting guests.

Alexis underwent more surgery, but he was fading fast. The situation was not helped by what Bobbie maintains was the reduction of care over the holiday period. 'I went in on Christmas Day, he could hardly breathe and his oxygen mask was rolled up in the cupboard.' She says there were few staff on and the intensive care unit was shut. As soon as the ICU opened up again, he was transferred. Damian feels that if there was really nothing to be done, they should have let out to be with his family.

Jeff Griffin was one of the last of Alexis' close friends to see him alive. He visited on New Year's Eve. 'He was on a drip feed and I don't think we exchanged more than about half a dozen words. He was in a very bad way – but even so hope springs eternal. I should have been ready for it, but I wasn't.'

On 1 January 1984 Alexis, aged only fifty-five, quietly slipped away. The causes of death were listed as brain tumour, lung cancer and infection.

There was a very private funeral for the immediate family. Alexis was cremated and his ashes scattered on the grounds of his beloved Chapel. And right to the end, the stars turned out for him. Guests were invited to a 'wake' at Dingwalls on Friday 13 January. It was a filthy night, with the rain hammering down, but still they came from all walks of Alexis' rich and varied life: musicians, producers, record-company executives and music journalists, radio bosses and DJs, and the advertising world all gathered together to pay their last respects.

There was no live music; instead John Mayall's son Gaz played records and there were speeches by Guido Toffoletti, writers Ian Carr and Peter Clayton and the host for the evening, Jeff Griffin, who recalls: 'I tried to be quite light-hearted about it, which a couple of people thought was a bit funny. But I felt that, knowing Alexis as I did, he wouldn't have minded me trying to lighten the situation up with a few jokes about it. Fortunately my wife was standing on the right-hand side of the stage. As I came off she grabbed me and I just cried for about ten minutes.'

The obituaries were a predictable career résumé, highlighting in particular his role in the formation of the Rolling Stones. What was more impressive was the number and size of them. Many of the nationals, major regionals and rock press carried substantial appreciations: one issue of *Music Week* devoted five pages to Alexis, with a full-page advertisement from the Stones. The best of the obituaries came from those who had known him; worthy of special mention was the obituary by the late Peter Clayton for the *Sunday Telegraph*.

'Death cannot have succeeded in snatching my old friend Alexis Korner last weekend without descending to some kind of trick. Alexis was too fast on his feet, too full of the human spark, too defiant to have succumbed at the age of 55 to a fate that was playing the game according to the rules.

'Apart from anything else, there was his invincible charm. Only a stone-deaf emissary could have failed to have his purpose deflected, his resolve demolished, by the sweet eloquence of that oaken voice, the blandishments of that unruffled courtesy (his blues voice was different – throaty and deliberately harsh).'

Peter described how their lives touched even before they had met.

'When I worked in the cataloguing department of a record company in 1956, I found that Alexis had been the previous incumbent in the same job. The impression he'd made on the catalogue editor, a man in a state of permanent exasperation with printers, proofreaders and people in general, was lasting if unfavourable.

'It pained him to remember when he had to sit and look at Alexis in what he described as "outlandish" clothes – the bootlace ties and narrow black trousers were particular sources of irritation I recall – and he was distressed by the villainous little black cigarettes. The more I heard about Alexis Korner, the more I warmed to him by proxy. Clearly he was someone who should go far.'

Peter co-presented a long series of Forces Radio shows with him, but never failed to be 'in awe of Alexis. And I shall always be in his debt, for he freely gave away that most precious of all possessions – knowledge. You only had to ask him something about the blues and if he knew he would tell you. What's more, he usually knew.'

The 'feel-good' factor around Alexis has continued long after his death. In February 1984 Bill Wyman presented Bobbie with a posthumous award for Alexis as Best Radio 1 DJ for 1983 – an award which Ellie Buchanan described in a long, cogent appreciation for *The Times Educational Supplement*, as 'Too Little Too Late'. That the *TES*, not noted for its music coverage, should devote several column inches to a blues musician was indicative of his stature throughout the media. The following June the Nottingham Festival played host to a cancer charity benefit concert in Alexis' name starring Charlie Watts, Ian Stewart, Jack Bruce, Jimmy Page, Paul Jones and many others. In the words of the organizer: 'One day when this night is talked about you can say you were there.'

And so ten years on to May 1994 and the start of what has been, at the time of writing in 1996, an annual Alexis Korner Memorial concert in aid of the Beechwood Cancer Care Centre, held at Buxton Opera House, Derbyshire. From that first concert in 1994 came one image which somehow typified what Alexis was all about.

Musicians were milling about the stage area during the afternoon, running through some numbers, sound checking and generally chewing the fat. Robert Plant was there, surrounded by a gaggle of admirers. To one side Chris Barber stood chatting with Dick Heckstall-Smith. Robert and Chris just happened to look up at the same moment, caught each other's eye, reached over and decades of British jazz, blues and rock respectfully shook hands. It was that sort of day.

TESTAMENT

'We were playing Lillehammer in Norway – it was jokingly called "The Lillehammer Blues Festival". It was a tragedy really – they were nice, well-meaning people, but honestly . . .
' "Have a beer."
' "What about the gear?"
' "Have a beer."
'And it got to the stage where we realized the gear we needed was just not there. The stage was really poky, people milling about. We kept our cool, but . . . Dave, our keyboard player suddenly had these keyboards put in front of him. "Thank God it's a DX7." He started playing. "Hey, Mick, I think we'll just about get away with this." Halfway through the sound check this guy strolls up on stage – "So I must have my DX7 now, thank you" – and walks off with it under his arm.

'Eventually we went on stage to do the gig with anything we could lay our hands on. I thought, this is going to be a total disaster. What am I going to do?

'And right behind me there was this big smiling face, a big poster of Alexis on the wall. And I could hear his voice saying, "Don't worry, Mick, it's going to be all right, just do it, it'll be fine.' So I thought, right, fuck 'em. And we tore the arse out of the place. Nothing went wrong and the crowd loved it.

'The man had so much soul in everything he did – even when he played bad it was good. He was one of the very few musicians on the scene that actually meant what he did.'

Mick Abrahams

TESTAMENT

'My most endearing recollection of Alexis is that when my career such as it has been was faltering and I was just at the point when I was thinking, Jesus, is this really worth doing?, there'd be a phone call and Alexis would say, "Hey Bob, do you fancy coming and doing a bit of radio?" And it happened to me so many times.'

Bob Hall

'He kept on doing it; when the times were fat for the music he was there and when times were thin for the music he was there. I've seen him in some of the worst clubs filled with drunks and he'd be sitting in the corner, rag tied around his head, playing. He was one of the very few musicians that I not only admired but mixed with socially.'

Eric Burdon

'I can honestly say that I still miss him, even now – as a mate as much as anything else.'

Colin Hodgkinson

'He was a friend, a father figure, a brilliant raconteur, enjoyed everything, very exciting musician, great presence. All in all one of the most wonderful people I have ever met. When he died it was just an enormous part of my life gone.'

Jeff Griffin

'The most articulate man I have ever talked to – no question.'

Zoot Money

'He was one of the most genuine human beings I've ever met – knowledgeable, articulate and absolutely true to his principles.'

Del Taylor

'The warmth and charisma that he had on that first performance [at Finchden] for that bunch of boys who had been where he had been – a lot of fellow feeling, humanity and real connection with us which I'll never forget and always value.'

Tom Robinson

'Alexi still dominates. If Bobbie and I are talking for a few minutes and suddenly one of us recounts something, immediately Alexi becomes part of it. It's really very strange, he's still controlling from beyond the grave.'

Steve Clyne

'He was probably my closest ever friend and it was disgusting that he died at fifty-five. He had so much more to give. But he lived his life to the full. He enjoyed life and he IS my father – not WAS, because his body may have died, but his spirit certainly hasn't.

'There was something about him that made you feel that if there was reincarnation, then he was on his last one. He was very advanced spiritually – his capacity to listen, to give, to communicate yet at the same time his frailty, made you feel that his spirit was very nearly complete.'

Damian Korner

'He gave me my love of music . . . every time I hear something brilliant, I want to say, "Hey, Dad, listen to this." '

Sappho Korner

'I once woke up in the middle of the night and he was on the radio and I heard his voice in a kind of detached way and I realized then that it was a special voice he had. When I think of him, I don't think how he looked or anything like that, but I think of when he phoned and his opening words, "Hello, darl' . . ." '

Bobbie Korner

DISCOGRAPHY by Mark Troster

This discography covers all of Alexis' offical recordings, with the exception of those tracks which have over the years appeared on endless repackagings of British R & B. There is possibly only one Alexis Korner bootleg – *Alexis Korner Meets Jack Daniels* (Flash Records) – an indifferent recording of the first New Church gig in June 1969.

Various Alexis compilations and reissues (like the Cavern album) are in the pipeline and may have appeared by the time this book is published. Meanwhile, if you have £28.99 lying around you could impress your friends with a 24 carat gold US CD audiophile of *R & B From The Marquee*, recently spotted in *Mojo* magazine!

Entries are listed chronologically by the date of recordings. Except for where otherwise stated, line-up list is for all tracks on individual recordings.

KEN COLYER'S SKIFFLE GROUP
Back To The Delta (Decca 10" LP, LF 1196)
Rec: Decca West Hampstead Studios, London, June 25 1954
Prod: Ken Colyer/Arthur Lilley
Rel: November 1954
'Midnight Special', 'Casey Jones', 'K. C. Moan'
Ken Colyer: vocals/acoustic guitar; Alexis Korner: acoustic guitar, mandolin ('Midnight Special'); Mickey Ashman: string bass; Bill Colyer: washboard

KEN COLYER'S SKIFFLE GROUP
Ken Colyer's Skiffle Group (Decca EP, DFE 6286)
Rec: Decca West Hampstead Studios, London, July 28 1955
Prod: Ken Colyer/Arthur Lilley
Rel: October 1955
'Take This Hammer', 'Down By The Riverside', 'Go Down Old Hannah', 'Streamline Train'
Ken Colyer: vocals/acoustic guitar; Alexis Korner: acoustic guitar (except for 'Go Down Old Hannah'), mandolin ('Go Down Old Hannah'); John Bastable: banjo, acoustic guitar ('Go Down Old Hannah'); Dick Smith: string bass; Bill Colyer: washboard

KEN COLYER'S SKIFFLE GROUP
Take This Hammer (Decca 45 and 78, F 10631)
Rec: Decca West Hampstead Studios, London, July 28 1955
Prod: Ken Colyer/Arthur Lilley
Rel: October 1955
'Take This Hammer', 'Down By The Riverside'
Ken Colyer: vocals/acoustic guitar; Alexis Korner: acoustic guitar; John Bastable: banjo; Dick Smith: string bass; Bill Colyer: washboard

KEN COLYER'S SKIFFLE GROUP
Go Down Old Hannah (Decca 45 and 78, F 10711)
Rec: Decca West Hampstead Studios, London, July 28 1955
Prod: Ken Colyer/Arthur Lilley
Rel: March 1956
'Go Down Old Hannah', 'Streamline Train'
Ken Colyer: vocals/acoustic guitar; Alexis Korner: mandolin ('Go Down Old Hannah'), acoustic guitar ('Streamline Train'); John Bastable: acoustic guitar ('Go Down Old Hannah'), banjo (Streamline Train'); Dick Smith: string bass; Bill Colyer: washboard

BERYL BRYDEN'S BACK-ROOM SKIFFLE
Kansas City Blues (Decca 45 and 78, F-J 10823)
Rec: Decca West Hampstead Studios, London, November 9 1956
Prod: unknown
Rel: December 1956
'Kansas City Blues', 'Casey Jones'
Beryl Bryden: vocals/washboard; Alexis Korner: acoustic guitar, backing vocals ('Casey Jones'); Cyril Davies: acoustic guitar, harmonica ('Kansas City Blues'), backing vocals ('Casey Jones'); Frank Clarke: string bass; Dave Stevens: piano

Note: Two further titles, 'Rock Me' (matrix DRF 23020) and 'This Train' (matrix DRF 23021), were recorded by this line-up on January 25 1957. Decca planned to release them on another 45/78, but this did not happen and it is believed that only internal 'demonstration' discs were released.

ALEXIS KORNER'S BREAKDOWN GROUP FEATURING CYRIL DAVIES
Blues From The Roundhouse (77 10" LP, 77 LP/2)
Rec: The Roundhouse, London, February 13 1957
Prod: Brian Harvey
Rel: November 1957
'Leaving Blues', 'Rotten Break', 'Alberta', 'Roundhouse Stomp', 'Skip To My Lou', 'Good Morning', 'Boll Weevil', 'Ella Speed'
Cyril Davies: vocals (except for 'Roundhouse Stomp', 'Rotten Break')/acoustic guitar, harmonica ('Roundhouse Stomp'); Alexis Korner: vocals ('Rotten Break'), acoustic guitar ('Rotten Break', 'Good Morning', 'Boll Weevil'), mandolin ('Roundhouse Stomp', 'Skip To My Lou', 'Ella Speed'), backing vocals ('Skip To My Lou'); Terry Plant: string bass ('Roundhouse Stomp', 'Skip To My Lou', 'Good Morning', 'Boll Weevil', 'Ella Speed'); Mike Collins: washboard ('Roundhouse Stomp', 'Good Morning', 'Boll Weevil', 'Ella Speed')

Note: Only 100 copies were pressed – 99 for sale and one for test purposes. All titles were re-issued in April 1970, along with titles by The Roundhouse Jug Four, on the Folklore LP *The Legendary Cyril Davies With Alexis Korner's Breakdown Group And The Roundhouse Jug Four* (F LEUT/9).

ALEXIS KORNER'S BREAKDOWN GROUP
Alexis 1957 (Krazy Kat LP, KK 789)
Rec: The Roundhouse, London, February 13 1957
Prod: Brian Harvey
Rel: November 1984
'Streamline Train'
Alexis Korner: vocals/acoustic guitar; Cyril Davies: acoustic guitar/ harmonica; Terry Plant: string bass; Mike Collins: washboard

ALEXIS KORNER
Alexis 1957 (Krazy Kat LP, KK 789)
Rec: Walnut Tree Cottage, Burnham, Buckinghamshire, March 29 1957
Prod: John R. T. Davies
Rel: November 1984
'County Jail', 'Doggone My Good Luck Soul', 'Badly Mistreated Man'
Alexis Korner: vocals/acoustic guitar

ALEXIS KORNER SKIFFLE GROUP
County Jail (Tempo 45 and 78, A 166)
Rec: Decca West Hampstead Studios, London, July 22 1957
Prod: Geoff Milne
Rel: May 1958
'County Jail', 'I Ain't Gonna Worry No More'
Alexis Korner: vocals/acoustic guitar; Cyril Davies: harmonica, acoustic guitar ('I Ain't Gonna Worry No More'); Dave Stevens: piano ('County Jail'); Chris Capon: string bass; Mike Collins: washboard

ALEXIS KORNER SKIFFLE GROUP
Blues From The Roundhouse Volume 1 (Tempo EP, EXA 76)
Rec: Decca West Hampstead Studios, London, July 22 1957
Prod: Geoff Milne
Rel: July 1958
'I Ain't Gonna Worry No More', 'County Jail', 'Easy Rider', 'Kid Man'

DISCOGRAPHY

Alexis Korner: vocals (except for 'Easy Rider')/acoustic guitar; Cyril Davies: acoustic guitar ('I Ain't Gonna Worry No More', 'Easy Rider'), harmonica ('I Ain't Gonna Worry No More', 'County Jail', 'Kid Man'), vocals ('Easy Rider'); Chris Capon: string bass; Dave Stevens: piano ('County Jail', 'Kid Man'); Mike Collins: washboard

ALAN LOMAX
Alan Lomax Sings Great American Ballads (HMV LP, CLP 1192)
Rec: Abbey Road Studios, London, February 4 1958
Prod: Peter Kennedy
Rel: July 1958
'Long John', 'John Crossed The Water', 'Boll Weevil', 'The Grey Goose', 'Po' Lazarus', 'Frankie'
Alan Lomax: vocals/acoustic guitar; 'Nick Wheatstraw' (Alexis Korner): acoustic guitar

Note: Alexis presumably used the pseudonym 'Nick Wheatstraw' because he was actually under contract with Tempo Records at the time of this recording.

ALEXIS KORNER'S BLUES INCORPORATED
Blues From The Roundhouse Volume 2 (Tempo EP, EXA 102)
Rec: Decca West Hampstead Studios, London, April 29 1958
Prod: Geoff Milne
Rel: December 1958
'Sail On', 'National Defence Blues', 'Go Down Sunshine', 'Death Letter'
Alexis Korner: acoustic guitar, vocals ('Go Down Sunshine'); Cyril Davies: vocals/acoustic guitar (except for 'Go Down Sunshine'), harmonica ('Go Down Sunshine'); Jim Bray: string bass; Mike Collins: washboard; Dave Stevens: piano ('National Defence Blues')

RAMBLING JACK ELLIOTT
Kid Stuff (Columbia EP, SEG 8046)
Rec: Lansdowne Studios, London, October 29 1959
Prod: Denis Preston
Rel: November 1960
'Howdido', 'My Daddy', 'Why, Oh Why?', 'Riding In My Car', 'Hey, Rattler'

Rambling Jack Elliott: vocals/acoustic guitar; Alexis Korner: mandolin; Jack Fullon: string bass

CHAMPION JACK DUPREE
Natural And Soulful Blues (London Atlantic LP, SA11-K 6151)
Rec: Lansdowne Studios, London, November 9 1959
Prod: Denis Preston
Rel: May 1961
'Death Of Big Bill Broonzy', 'Don't Leave Me, Mary', 'Bad Life', 'Bad Luck Round To Change'
Champion Jack Dupree: vocals/piano; Alexis Korner: acoustic guitar; Jack Fallon: string bass

RAMBLING JACK ELLIOTT
Rambling Jack Elliott Sings Songs By Woody Guthrie And Jimmie Rodgers (Columbia LP, 33SX 1291)
Rec: Lansdowne Studios, London, November 24 1959
Prod: Denis Preston
Rel: January 1961
'Dead or Alive', 'Grand Coulee Dam'
Rambling Jack Elliott: vocals/acoustic guitar; Alexis Korner: mandolin; Danny Levan: violin; Jack Fallon: string bass

MEMPHIS SLIM
Memphis Slim USA (Collector LP, JGN 1004)
Rec: City of London Studios, London, July 14 1960
Prod: Colin Pomroy
Rel: February 1961
'Memphis Slim USA', 'Caught The Old Coon At Last', 'Whiskey And Gin', 'Two Of A Kind', 'I Love You More And More', 'Me Myself And I'
Memphis Slim: vocals/piano; Alexis Korner: acoustic guitar; Stan Greig: drums

MEMPHIS SLIM
Memphis Slim (Collector LP, JGN 1005)
Rec: City of London Studios, London, July 14 1960
Prod: Colin Pomroy
Rel: February 1960
'Ain't Nobody's Business If I Do', 'Sun

Gonna Shine In My Backdoor Someday',
'In The Evening', 'I Believe I'll Settle
Down', 'Darlin' I Miss You', 'Roll 'n'
Tumble'
Memphis Slim: vocals/piano; Alexis Korner:
acoustic guitar; Stan Greig: drums ('Ain't Nobody's
Business If I Do')

MEMPHIS SLIM
Goes To Kansas City (Collector EP, JEN 5)
Rec: City of London Studios, London, July
14 1960
Prod: Colin Pomroy
Rel: February 1961
'Kansas City'
Memphis Slim: vocals/piano; Alexis Korner:
acoustic guitar; Stan Greig: drums

MEMPHIS SLIM
Pinetops Blues (Collector 45, JDN 102)
Rec: City of London Studios, London, July
14 1960
Prod: Colin Pomroy
Rel: February 1961
'How Long'
Memphis Slim: vocals/piano; Alexis Korner:
acoustic guitar; Stan Greig: drums

LITTLE BROTHER MONTGOMERY
Little Brother (Columbia LP, 33SX 1289)
Rec: Lansdowne Studios, London, August
18 1960
Prod: Denis Preston
Rel: January 1961
'I Keep Drinkin'', 'Old Maid Blues'
Little Brother Montgomery: vocals/piano; Alexis
Korner: acoustic guitar; Jack Fallon: string bass; Bob
Guthrie: drums

ROOSEVELT SKYES
The Honeydupper (Columbia LP, 33SX
1422)
Rec: Lansdowne Studios, London, January
21 1961
Prod: Denis Preston
Rel: May 1962
'Sweet Old Chicago', 'Hot Nuts', 'Little
And Low', 'How Long, How Long Blues'
Roosevelt Skyes: vocals/piano; Alexis Korner:
acoustic guitar; Phil Seamen: drums

ALEXIS KORNER AND DAVY GRAHAM
3/4 A. D. (Topic EP, TOP 70)
Rec: North Villas, London, April 1961
Prod: Alexis Korner
Rel: April 1962
'3/4 A. D.'
Alexis Korner: acoustic guitar; Davy Graham:
acoustic guitar

Note: The recording was made by Bill Leader at his
home, 'North Villas'.

JIMMY COTTON
Chris Barber Presents Jimmy Cotton
(Columbia EP, SEG 8141)
Rec: Lansdowne Studios, London, August
10 1961
Prod: Denis Preston
Rel: February 1962
'Dealing With The Devil', 'Standing
Around Crying', 'Slow And Easy', 'Rock
Me Mama'
Jimmy Cotton: vocals (except for 'Slow And
Easy')/harmonica; Alexis Korner: electric guitar;
Chris Barber: string bass ('Dealing With The
Devil'), acoustic guitar ('Standing Around Crying',
'Slow And Easy'), trombone ('Rock Me Mama');
Keith Scott: piano ('Dealing With The Devil',
'Rock Me Mama')

JIMMY COTTON
Chris Barber Presents Jimmy Cotton Volume 2
(Columbia EP, SEG 8189)
Rec: Lansdowne Studios, London, August
10 1961
Prod: Denis Preston
Rel: October 1962
'Jimmy's Jump', 'Decoration Day Blues',
'Polly Put The Kettle On', 'Goin'
Down Slow'
Jimmy Cotton: vocals (except for 'Jimmy's
Jump')/harmonica; Alexis Korner: electric guitar;
Chris Barber: string bass ('Jimmy's Jump', 'Polly Put
The Kettle On'), acoustic guitar ('Decoration Day
Blues', 'Goin' Down Slow'); Keith Scott: piano
('Jimmy's Jump', 'Polly Put The Kettle On')

DISCOGRAPHY

OTTILLE PATTERSON
Ottille Patterson Back In The Old Days
(Timeless Historical LP, CBC 4001)
Rec: Lansdowne Studios, London,
September 22 1961
Prod: Denis Preston
Rel: 1988
'Lawdy, Lawd (It Hurts So Bad)', 'Only
The Blues'
Ottille Patterson: vocals; Alexis Korner: electric
guitar; Keith Scott: piano; Dick Smith: string bass;
Graham Burbridge: drums; Eddie Smith: banjo
('Only The Blues')

**ALEXIS KORNER'S BLUES
INCORPORATED**
Bootleg Him – Alexis Korner (RAK D/LP,
SRAK 511-2)
Rec: Olympic Studios, London, January
17 1962
Prod: unknown
Rel: July 1972
'She Fooled Me'
Alexis Korner: vocals/electric guitar; Cyril Davies:
harmonica; Keith Scott: piano; Graham Beazley:
string bass; Colin Bowden: drums

**ALEXIS KORNER'S BLUES
INCORPORATED**
R & B From The Marquee (Decca Ace of
Clubs LP, ACL 1130)
Rec: Decca West Hampstead Studios,
London, June 8 1962
Prod: Jack Good
Rel: November 1962
'Gotta Move', 'Rain Is Such A Lonesome
Sound', 'I Got My Brand On You',
'Spooky But Nice', 'Keep Your Hands
Off', 'I Wanna Put A Tiger In Your Tank',
'I Got My Mojo Working', 'Finkle's Cafe',
'Hoochie Coochie', 'Down Town', 'How
Long, How Long Blues', 'I Thought I
Heard That Train Whistle Blow'
Alexis Korner: acoustic guitar; Cyril Davies:
vocal ('I Got My Brand On You', 'Keep Your
Hands Off', 'I Wanna Put A Tiger In Your
Tank', 'I Got My Mojo Working', 'Hoochie
Coochie')/harmonica (except for 'I Wanna Put A
Tiger In Your Tank'); Dick Heckstall-Smith: tenor
saxophone (except for 'I Got My Brand On You'),

vocal chorus ('I Got My Mojo Working'); Keith
Scott: piano; Spike Heatley: string bass (except for
'I Got My Mojo Working'); Graham Burbridge:
drums; Long John Baldry: vocals ('Rain Is Such A
Lonesome Sound', 'How Long, How Long Blues',
'I Thought I Heard That Train Whistle Blow'),
vocal chorus ('I Got My Mojo Working'); Teddy
Wadmore: bass guitar ('I Got My Mojo Working');
Big Jim Sullivan: vocal chorus ('I Got My Mojo
Working')

Note: These recordings were re-released by
Decca in February 1984 with the same sleeve and
catalogue number, and later by Deram (Decca
Group) on CD only.

**ALEXIS KORNER'S BLUES
INCORPORATED**
Alexis Korner's Blues Incorporated (Decca
Teldec LP, 6.24475 – Germany only)
Rec: Decca West Hampstead Studios,
London, June 8 1962
Prod: Jack Good
Rel: May 1981
'I'm Built For Comfort' (a.k.a. 'Everything
She Needs')
Alexis Korner: acoustic guitar; Cyril Davies:
harmonica; Long John Baldry: vocals; Dick
Heckstall-Smith: tenor saxophone; Keith Scott:
piano; Spike Heatley: string bass; Graham
Burbridge: drums

**ALEXIS KORNER'S BLUES
INCORPORATED**
Bootleg Him – Alexis Korner (RAK D/LP,
SRAK 511-2)
Rec: BBC *Jazz Club*, Paris Theatre,
London, July 12 1962
Prod: Terry Henebery
Rel: July 1972
'Hoochie Coochie Man'
Alexis Korner: electric guitar; Cyril Davies:
vocals/harmonica; Dick Heckstall-Smith: tenor
saxophone; Dave Stevens: piano; Jack Bruce: string
bass; Charlie Watts: drums

**NANCY SPAIN WITH ALEXIS
KORNER AND HIS BAND**
Blaydon Races (Lyntone 45, LYN298)
Rec: unknown studio, London, October
1962

Prod: John Mordler
Rel: December 1962
'Blaydon Races'
Nancy Spain: vocals; Alexis Korner: electric guitar;
Cyril Davies: harmonica; Dick Heckstall-Smith:
tenor saxophone; Jack Bruce: string bass; Ginger
Baker: drums

BLUES INCORPORATED
Up Town (Lyntone 45, LYN299)
Rec: unknown studio, London, October
1962
Prod: John Mordler
Rel: December 1962
'Up Town'
Alexis Korner: electric guitar; Cyril Davies:
harmonica; Dick Heckstall-Smith: tenor saxophone;
Johnny Parker: piano; Jack Bruce: string bass;
Ginger Baker: drums

Note: LYN298 and LYN299 are the 'A' and 'B'
sides of a flexidisc given away free to promote *Trio*
magazine.

ALEXIS KORNER'S BLUES
INCORPORATED
Rhythm And Blues – Various Artists (Decca
LP, LK 4616)
Rec: Decca West Hampstead Studios,
London, January 3 1963
Prod: Roy Lister
Rel: October 1964
'Night Time Is The Right Time', 'Early In
The Morning'
Alexis Korner: electric guitar; Ronnie Jones:
vocals ('Night Time Is The Right Time'); Graham
Bond: alto saxophone; Dick Heckstall-Smith: tenor
saxophone; Johnny Parker: piano; Jack Bruce: string
bass; Ginger Baker: drums

ALEXIS KORNER'S BLUES
INCORPORATED
Bootleg Him – Alexis Korner (RAK D/LP,
SRAK 511-2)
Rec: BBC *Jazz Club*, Paris Theatre,
London, January 24 1963
Prod: Terry Henebery
Rel: July 1972
'Rockin''
Alexis Korner: electric guitar; Graham Bond: alto

saxophone; Dick Heckstall-Smith: tenor saxophone;
Johnny Parker: piano; Jack Bruce: string bass;
Ginger Baker: drums

ALEXIS KORNER'S BLUES
INCORPORATED
Alexis Korner's Blues Incorporated (Decca Ace
of Clubs LP, ACL 1187)
Rec: Lansdowne Studios, London, May
10–12 1963
Prod: Vic Keary
Rel: June 1965
'Blue Mink', 'Rainy Tuesday', 'Yogi',
'Sappho', 'Navy Blue', 'Royal Dooji' (a.k.a.
'Dooji Wooji'), 'Preachin' The Blues', 'The
Captain's Tiger', 'A Little Bit Groovy',
'Anything For Now', 'Chris Trundle's
Habit', 'Trundlin'' (a.k.a. 'Skippin'')
Alexis Korner: electric guitar (except for 'Preachin'
The Blues', 'A Little Bit Groovy', Chris Trundle's
Habit'), bouzouki ('Preachin' The Blues'); Dick
Heckstall-Smith: tenor saxophone (except for
'A Little Bit Groovy'); Art Themen: tenor
saxophone (except for 'Rainy Tuesday', 'A Little
Bit Groovy', 'Anything for Now'), alto saxophone
('Rainy Tuesday'); Johnny Parker: piano (except
for 'Preachin' The Blues'); Mike Scott: string
bass (except for 'Preachin' The Blues'); Phil
Seamen: drums

Note: The above tracks were originally recorded
for the Seeburg Jukebox Corporation for possible
distribution to US jukeboxes. However, this plan
did not proceed beyond the pressing of a test
acetate, and the titles were later licensed by Decca.

ALEXIS KORNER ALL STARS
See See Rider (King 45, KG 1017)
Rec: Lansdowne Studios, London, May
10–12 1963
Prod: Vic Keary
Rel: 1965
'Blues a la King' (a.k.a. 'Navy Blue')
Alexis Korner: vocals/electric guitar; Dick
Heckstall-Smith: tenor saxophone; Art Themen:
tenor saxophone; Johnny Parker: piano; Mike Scott:
string bass; Phil Seamen: drums

Note: This alternative take of 'Navy Blue' was
re-named 'Blues a la King' and used for the 'B' side
of the King 45.

DISCOGRAPHY

ALEXIS KORNER
See See Rider (King 45, KG 1017)
Rec: Lansdowne Studios, London,
June 1 1963
Prod: Vic Keary
Rel: 1965
'See See Rider'
Alexis Korner: vocals/electric guitar; Dick
Heckstall-Smith: tenor saxophone; Art Themen:
tenor saxophone; Johnny Parker: piano; Vernon
Bown: string bass; Phil Seamen: drums

CURTIS JONES
Curtis Jones In London (Decca LP, LK 4587)
Rec: Decca West Hampstead Studios,
London, November 27–28 1963
Prod: Mike Vernon
Rel: May 1964
'Shake It Baby', 'Lonesome Bedroom
Blues', 'Dust My Broom', 'Good
Woman Blues'
Curtis Jones: vocals/piano; Alexis Korner: electric
guitar; Jack Fallon: string bass; Eddie Taylor: drums

CURTIS JONES
Raw Blues – Various Artists (Decca Ace of
Clubs LP, ACL 1220)
Rec: Decca West Hampstead Studios,
London, November 27–28 1963
Prod: Mike Vernon
Rel: January 1967
'Roll Me Over', 'You Got Good Business'
Curtis Jones: vocals/piano; Alexis Korner: acoustic
guitar; Neil Slaven: acoustic guitar ('You Got Good
Business'); Mike Vernon: foot-tapping ('You Got
Good Business')

**ALEXIS KORNER'S BLUES
INCORPORATED**
At The Cavern (Oriole LP, PS40058)
Rec: concert at The Cavern, Liverpool,
February 23 1964
Prod: Geoff Frost
Rel: October 1964
'Overdrive', 'Whoa Babe', 'Everyday I
Have The Blues', 'Hoochie Coochie Man',
'Herbie's Tune' (a.k.a. 'Dooji Wooji'),
'Little Bitty Gal Blues', 'Well All Right,
OK, You Win', 'Kansas City'
Alexis Korner: vocals ('Overdrive', 'Whoa

Babe', 'Hoochie Coochie Man', 'Little Bitty Gal
Blues')/electric guitar, backing vocals ('Kansas
City'); Dave Castle: alto saxophone; Malcom Saul:
organ; Vernon Bown: string bass; Mike Scott:
drums; Herbie Goins: vocals ('Everyday I Have
The Blues', 'Well All Right, OK, You Win',
'Kansas City')

**ALEXIS KORNER'S BLUES
INCORPORATED**
Red Hot From Alex (Transatlantic LP,
TRA 117)
Rec: Olympic Studios, London, March
16–19 1964
Prod: Nathan Joseph
Rel: June 1964
'Woke Up This Morning', 'Skippin''
(a.k.a. 'Trundlin''), 'Herbie's Tune' (a.k.a.
'Dooji Wooji'), 'Stormy Monday', 'It's
Happening', 'Roberta', 'Jones', 'Cabbage
Greens', 'Chicken Shack', 'Haitian
Fight Song'
Alexis Korner: electric guitar; Herbie Goins: vocals
('Woke Up This Morning', 'Stormy Monday',
'Roberta'), tumbas ('Woke Up This Morning',
'Roberta'); Dave Castle: alto saxophone (except
for 'Stormy Monday', 'Cabbage Greens'), flute
('Stormy Monday'); Art Themen: tenor saxophone
(except for 'Cabbage Greens'); Ron Edgeworth:
piano (except for 'Skippin'', 'Herbie's Tune',
'Chicken Shack'), organ ('Skippin'', 'Herbie's Tune',
'Chicken Shack'); Dick Heckstall-Smith: tenor
saxophone ('Skippin'', 'Herbie's Tune', 'Chicken
Shack'); Danny Thompson: string bass; Barry
Howten: drums

Note: The *Red Hot From Alex* recordings were
re-issued in July 1969 under the title *Alexis
Korner's All Stars Blues Incorporated* (Transatlantic
LP, TRASAM 7), and again under this later title
in 1974 (Just Sunshine LP, JSS 13 – US only) and
1989 (Line CD, TACD 9.00634 – Germany only).

**ALEXIS KORNER'S BLUES
INCORPORATED**
I Need Your Loving (Parlaphone 45, R 5206)
Rec: Olympic Studios, London, September
15 1964
Prod: Eric Easton
Rel: November 1964

'I Need Your Loving', 'Please, Please, Please, Please'
Alexis Korner: electric guitar, vocal chorus ('I Need Your Loving'); Herbie Goins: vocals; Ray Warleigh: alto saxophone; Mick Pyne: tenor saxophone; Danny Thompson: string bass, vocal chorus ('I Need Your Loving'); Ronnie Dunn: drums, vocal chorus ('I Need Your Loving')

ALEXIS KORNER'S BLUES INCORPORATED
I Got Money (Sonet 45, T8223 – Scandinavia only)
Rec: Olympic Studios, London, September 15 1964
Prod: Eric Easton
Rel: January 1965
'I Got Money'
Alexis Korner: electric guitar; Herbie Goins: vocals; Ray Warleigh: alto saxophone; Mick Pyne: tenor saxophone; Danny Thompson: string bass; Ronnie Dunn: drums

Note: 'B' side was the same version of 'I Need Your Loving' released in the UK as Parlaphone R 5206.

ALEXIS KORNER'S BLUES INCORPORATED
The BBC Radio Sessions – Alexis Korner (Music Collections International CD, MCCD 179)
Rec: BBC *Top Gear*, Playhouse Theatre, London, November 27 1964
Prod: Bernie Andrews
Rel: October 1994
'Overdrive', 'Please, Please, Please, Please'
Alexis Korner: vocals ('Overdrive')/electric guitar; Ray Warleigh: alto saxophone; Mick Pyne: tenor saxophone; Danny Thompson: string bass; Ronnie Dunn: drums; Herbie Goins: vocals ('Please, Please, Please, Please')

ALEXIS KORNER'S BLUES INCORPORATED
Little Baby (Parlaphone 45, R 5247)
Rec: Olympic Studios, London, December 17 1964
Prod: Eric Easton
Rel: February 1965

'Little Baby', 'Roberta'
Alexis Korner: electric guitar; Herbie Goins: vocals; Ray Warleigh: alto saxophone; Dave Castle: baritone saxophone, piano ('Little Baby'); Danny Thompson: string bass; Ronnie Dunn: drums, tambourine ('Little Baby')

ALEXIS KORNER'S BLUES INCORPORATED
Bootleg Him – Alexis Korner (RAK D/LP SRAK 511-2)
Rec: BBC *Rhythm & Blues*, Maida Vale Studio 5, London, April 21 1965
Prod: Jeff Griffin
Rel: July 1972
'I Got A Woman' (excerpt)
Alexis Korner: electric guitar; Herbie Goins: vocals; Ray Warleigh: alto saxophone; Nigel Stanger: tenor saxophone; Brian Smith: tenor saxophone; Danny Thompson: string bass; Terry Cox: drums

ALEXIS KORNER'S BLUES INCORPORATED
Sky High (Spot LP, JW551)
Rec: Ryemuse Studios, London, April–June 1965
Prod: Jack Winsley
Rel: April 1966
'Long Black Train', 'Rock Me', 'I'm So Glad (You're Mine)', 'Wednesday Night Prayer Meeting', 'Honesty', 'Yellow Dog Blues', 'Let The Good Times Roll', 'Ooo Wee Baby', 'Rivers Invitation', 'Money Honey', 'Big Road Blues', 'Louise', 'Floating', 'Anchor 5 Miles', 'Daph's Dance'
Alexis Korner: vocals ('Rock Me', 'Let The Good Times Roll', 'Rivers Invitation', 'Money Honey', 'Big Road Blues')/electric guitar (except for 'Louise', 'Floating', 'Anchor 5 Miles', 'Daph's Dance'), acoustic guitar ('Louise', solo on 'Floating', 'Anchor 5 Miles', 'Daph's Dance'); Duffy Power: vocals ('Long Black Train', 'I'm So Glad (You're Mine)', 'Ooo Wee Baby', 'Louise')/harmonica ('Long Black Train', 'Rock Me', 'I'm So Glad (You're Mine)', 'Let The Good Times Roll', 'Ooo Wee Baby', 'Money, Honey', 'Big Road Blues', 'Louise'; Danny Thompson: string bass (except for 'Louise', 'Floating', 'Anchor 5 Miles', 'Daph's Dance'); Alan Skidmore: tenor saxophone

DISCOGRAPHY

('Wednesday Night Prayer Meeting', 'Honesty',
'Yellow Dog Blues', 'Rivers Invitation'); Chris
Pyne: trombone ('Wednesday Night Prayer
Meeting', 'Honesty', 'Yellow Dog Blues', 'Rivers
Invitation'); Terry Cox: drums (except for 'Louise',
'Floating', 'Anchor 5 Miles', 'Daph's Dance')

Note: Some of these recordings were re-released
in 1967 as *Alexis Korner's Blues Incorporated* (Polydor
Special LP, 236 206). *Sky High* was re-issued in
November 1994 (Indigo CD, IGO 2012), though
sound quality is extremely variable.

ALEXIS KORNER'S BLUES INCORPORATED
Bootleg Him – Alexis Korner (RAK D/LP,
SRAK 511-2)
Rec: BBC *Jazz Club*, Paris Theatre,
London, May 31 1965
Prod: Bill Bebb
Rel: July 1972
'Oh Lord, Don't Let Them Drop That
Atomic Bomb On Me'
Alexis Korner: vocals/electric guitar; Alan
Skidmore: tenor saxophone; Chris Pyne: trombone;
Danny Thompson: string bass; Terry Cox: drums

ALEXIS KORNER'S BLUES INCORPORATED
The BBC Radio Sessions – Alexis Korner
(Music Collection International CD,
MCCD 179)
Rec: BBC *Band Beat*, Maida Vale Studio 4,
London, December 10 1965
Prod: Jeff Griffin
Rel: October 1994
'Back At The Chicken Shack', 'Trouble
In Mind'
Alexis Korner: vocals ('Trouble In Mind')/electric
guitar; Brian Auger: organ ('Back At The Chicken
Shack'); Vic Briggs: electric guitar ('Back At The
Chicken Shack'); Ray Warleigh: alto saxophone;
Bernie George: baritone saxophone; Chris Pyne:
trombone; Danny Thompson: string bass; Terry
Cox: drums

ALEXIS KORNER'S BLUES INCORPORATED
Bootleg Him – Alexis Korner (RAK D/LP,
SRAK 511-2)

Rec: BBC *Jazz Club*, Paris Theatre,
London, December 13 1965
Prod: Bryant Marriott
Rel: July 1972
'Honesty'
Alexis Korner: electric guitar; Ray Warleigh:
alto saxophone; Chris Pyne: trombone; Danny
Thompson: string bass; Terry Cox: drums

ALEXIS KORNER'S BLUES INCORPORATED
The BBC Radio Sessions – Alexis Korner
(Music Collection International CD,
MCCD 179)
Rec: BBC *Jazz Beat*, Playhouse Theatre,
London, January 19 1966
Prod: Bryant Marriott
Rel: October 1994
'Going Down Slow', 'Blue Mink'
Alexis Korner: vocals ('Going Down Slow')/electric
guitar; Ray Warleigh: alto saxophone; Chris Pyne:
trombone; Danny Thompson: string bass; Terry
Cox: drums

ALEXIS KORNER
Rivers Invitation (Fontana 45, TF 706)
Rec: Philips Studios, London, April 7 1966
Prod: Terry Brown
Rel: May 1966
'Rivers Invitation', 'Everday (I Have
The Blues)'
Alexis Korner: vocals, tipple guitar ('Rivers
Invitation'), electric guitar ('Everyday (I Have
The Blues)'); Danny Thompson: string bass; Terry
Cox: drums

ALEXIS KORNER
I Wonder Who? (Fontana LP, STL 5381)
Rec: Philips Studios, London, April 7 1966
Prod: Terry Brown
Rel: April 1967
'Rock Me', 'Going Down Slow', 'Rivers
Invitation', 'I Wonder Who?', 'Chicken
Shack Back Home', 'See See Rider'
Alexis Korner: vocals (except for 'Chicken Shack
Back Home')/electric guitar (except for 'Rivers
Invitation'), tipple guitar ('Rivers Invitation');
Danny Thompson: string bass; Terry Cox: drums

Note: Recordings re-released on CD by BGO

in March 1992 under the title *I Wonder Who?* (BGOCD 136).

ALEXIS KORNER
I Wonder Who? (Fontana LP, STL 5381)
Rec: Philips Studios, London, April
27 1966
Prod: Terry Brown
Rel: April 1967
'Watermelon Man', 'Streamline Train',
'Come Back', '2.19 Blues', 'County Jail
Blues', 'Roll 'Em Pete', 'Betty & Dupree'
Alexis Korner: vocals/electric guitar; Danny
Thompson: string bass; Terry Cox: drums

ALEXIS KORNER'S BLUES
INCORPORATED
Bootleg Him – Alexis Korner (RAK D/LP,
SRAK 511-2)
Rec: BBC *Jazz Beat*, Picadilly Studio 1,
London, April 28 1966
Prod: Bryant Marriott
Rel: July 1972
'Yellow Dog Blues'
Alexis Korner: electric guitar; Ray Warleigh:
alto saxophone; Chris Pyne: trombone; Mick
Pyne: piano; Danny Thompson: string bass; Terry
Cox: drums

ALEXIS KORNER'S BLUES
INCORPORATED
The BBC Radio Sessions – Alexis Korner
(Music Collection International CD,
MCCD 179)
Rec: BBC *Jazz Beat*, Picadilly Studio 1,
London, April 28 1966
Prod: Bryant Marriott
Rel: October 1994
'When Will I Be Called A Man',
'Wednesday Night Prayer Meeting'
Alexis Korner: electric guitar; Jimmy Witherspoon:
vocals ('When Will I Be Called A Man'); Ray
Warleigh: alto saxophone; Chris Pyne: trombone;
Mick Pyne: piano; Danny Thompson: string bass;
Terry Cox: drums

ALEXIS KORNER'S BLUES
INCORPORATED
The BBC Radio Sessions – Alexis Korner
(Music Collection International CD,
MCCD 179)
Rec: BBC *Band Beat*, Studio S2,
Broadcasting House, London, July 22 1966
Prod: Jeff Griffin
Rel: October 1994
'Rock Me'
Alexis Korner: vocals/electric guitar; Ray Warleigh:
alto saxophone; Chris Pyne: trombone; Ian Fenby:
trumpet; Danny Thompson: string bass; Terry
Cox: drums

ALEXIS KORNER
Rosie (Fontana 45, TF 817)
Rec: Philips Studios, London, January
31 1967
Prod: Terry Brown
Rel: April 1967
'Rosie'
Alexis Korner: vocals/electric guitar; Binkie
McKenzie: bass guitar; Hughie Flint: drums

Note: Although released under Alexis' name, this
recording was actually by Free at Last. The 'B' side
was 'Rock Me', which was recorded on April 7
1966 (with a different line-up) and released on the *I
Wonder Who* LP.

JIMI HENDRIX EXPERIENCE
Radio One (Rykodisc CD, RCD 20078 –
US only)
Rec: BBC *Rhythm & Blues*, Aolian Studio
2, London, October 17 1967
Prod: Jeff Griffin
Rel: 1988
'Hoochie Coochie Man'
Jimi Hendrix: vocals/electric guitar; Alexis Korner:
electric guitar; Noel Redding: bass guitar; Mitch
Mitchell: drums

ALEXIS KORNER AND VICTOR
BROX
Bootleg Him – Alexis Korner (RAK D/LP,
SRAK 511-2)
Rec: Pinna Studios, London, November
13 1967

Prod: Mark Edwards
Rel: July 1972
'Corina Corina', 'The Love You Save'
Alexis Korner: vocals/acoustic guitar; Victor Brox: vocals/trumpet ('Corina Corina'), piano ('The Love You Save')

ALEXIS KORNER AND VICTOR BROX

Alexis Korner And ... 1961–1972 (Castle Communications D/LP, CCSLP 150)
Rec: Pinna Studios, London, November 13 1967
Prod: Mark Edwards
Rel: September 1986
'Louisiana Blues'
Alexis Korner: vocals/acoustic guitar; Victor Brox: violin

ALEXIS KORNER

Alexis Korner And ... 1961–1972 (Castle Communications D/LP, CCSLP 150)
Rec: concert at the Frankfurt Jazz Festival, Germany, March 24 1968
Prod: Sigi Schmidt-Joos
Rel: September 1986
'Everyday (I Have The Blues)'
Alexis Korner: vocals/electric guitar; 'Clarence': piano; Gunter Lenz: string bass; Rafel Luderitz: drums

ALEXIS KORNER

A New Generation Of Blues (Liberty LP, LBS 83147B)
Rec: Sound Techniques Studios, London, March–April 1968
Prod: Ian Samwell
Rel: May 1968
'Mary Open The Door', 'Little Bitty Gal', 'Baby Don't You Love Me', 'Go Down Sunshine', 'The Same For You', 'I'm Tore Down', 'In The Evening', 'Somethin' You Got', 'New Worried Blues', 'What's That Sound I Hear?', 'A Flower'
Alexis Korner: vocals, electric guitar (except for 'Go Down Sunshine', 'In The Evening', 'New Worried Blues', 'A Flower'), acoustic guitar ('Go Down Sunshine', 'In The Evening', 'Somethin' You Got', 'New Worried Blues', 'A Flower'); Ray Warleigh: flute ('Mary Open The Door', 'Little Bitty Gal',

'The Same for You'), alto saxophone ('Baby Don't You Love Me', 'I'm Tore Down'); Danny Thompson: string bass ('Mary Open The Door', 'Little Bitty Gal', 'Baby Don't You Love Me', 'The Same For You', 'I'm Tore Down'); Steve Miller: piano ('I'm Tore Down', 'What's That Sound I Hear?'); Terry Cox: drums ('Mary Open The Door', 'Little Bitty Gal', 'Baby Don't You Love Me', 'The Same For You', 'I'm Tore Down')

Note: These recordings were re-released in July 1991 under this original title (BGO LP, 102/BGO CD, 102). An earlier planned re-release in 1971, under the title *What's That Sound I Hear?* (Sunset LP, SLS50245), did not take place.

ALEXIS KORNER

Internationales Hot Jazz Meeting, Hamburg '68 – Various Artists (WAM LP, JL 0368 – Germany only)
Rec: concert at Auditorium Maximum, Hamburg, Germany, May 9 1968
Prod: unknown
Rel: 1968
'Go Down Sunshine'
Alexis Korner: vocals/acoustic guitar

ALEXIS KORNER

Bootleg Him – Alexis Korner (RAK D/LP, SRAK 511-2)
Rec: BBC *Jazz Club*, Maida Vale Studio 5, London, August 8 1968
Prod: Roger Eames
Rel: July 1972
'I Wonder Who', 'Dee' (correct title is 'Eadie')
Alexis Korner: vocals/electric guitar ('I Wonder Who'), acoustic guitar ('Dee'); John Surman: baritone saxophone; Chris Pyne: trombone; Dave Holland: string bass

ALEXIS KORNER WITH ROBERT PLANT AND STEVE MILLER

Bootleg Him – Alexis Korner (RAK D/LP, SRAK 511-2)
Rec: De Lane Lea Studios, London, September 1968
Prod: Ian Samwell
Rel: July 1972
'Operator'

ALEXIS KORNER

Alexis Korner: vocals/acoustic guitar; Robert Plant: vocals/harmonica; Steve Miller: piano

CUBY AND THE BLIZZARDS
Live (Philips LP, PY 844 087 – Holland only)
Rec: concert at the Rheinhalle, Düsseldorf, Germany, October 26 1968
Prod: Tony Vos
Rel: 1969
'No Way Out', 'Don't Love You Twice'
Harry Muskee: vocals/harmonica; Alexis Korner: vocals/electric guitar; Eelco Gelling: electric guitar; Herman Brood: piano; Jaap van Eik: bass guitar; Dick Breekman: drums

THE BEEFEATERS
Meet You There (Sonet LP, SLPS 1509 – Scandinavia only)
Rec: Ivar Rosenberg Lydteknik, Copenhagen, Denmark, November 1968
Prod: H. H. Koltze
Rel: 1970
'Night Train', 'Stormy Monday'
Peter Thorup: electric guitar; Alexis Korner: vocals ('Stormy Monday')/electric guitar; Morten Kjrumgaard: organ; Keith Volkersen: bass guitar; Max Nhuthzht: drums

NEW CHURCH AND FRIENDS
Both Sides (Metronome LP, MLP 15364 – Germany only)
Rec: Olympic Studios, London, September 23–October 1 1969
Prod: Jeff Griffin
Rel May 1970
'Mighty Mighty Spade And Whitey', 'Funky' (a.k.a. 'Soul Twist'), 'Wild Injun Woman', ' I See It', 'You Don't Miss Your Water (Till Your Well Runs Dry)'
Alexis Korner: vocals (except for 'Funky')/electric guitar; Peter Thorup: vocals ('Mighty Mighty Spade And Whitey')/electric guitar, backing vocals ('Wild Injun Woman', 'I See It', 'You Don't Miss Your Water'); Paul Rodgers: vocals ('Mighty Mighty Spade And Whitey'), backing vocals ('Wild Injun Woman', 'I See It'); Annette Brox: vocals ('Mighty Mighty Spade And Whitey')/tambourine ('Mighty Mighty Spade And Whitey', 'I See It'), backing vocals ('Wild Injun Woman', 'I See It');

Ray Warleigh: alto saxophone ('Mighty Mighty Spade And Whitey', 'Funky', 'You Don't Miss Your Water'); Lol Coxhill: tenor saxophone ('Mighty Mighty Spade And Whitey', 'Wild Injun Woman', 'You Don't Miss Your Water')/soprano saxophone ('Wild Injun Woman'); John Surman: baritone saxophone ('Mighty Mighty Spade And Whitey'), piano ('You Don't Miss Your Water'); Malcom Griffiths: trombone ('Mighty Mighty Spade And Whitey'); Chris Pyne: trombone ('Mighty Mighty Spade And Whitey', 'You Don't Miss Your Water'); Henry Lowther: trumpet ('Mighty Mighty Spade And Whitey', 'You Don't Miss Your Water'); Harry Beckett: trumpet ('Mighty Mighty Spade And Whitey', 'You Don't Miss Your Water'); Andy Fraser: bass guitar; John Marshall: drums ('Mighty Mighty Spade And Whitey', 'You Don't Miss Your Water')

NEW CHURCH AND FRIENDS
Both Sides (Metronome LP, MLP 15364 – Germany only)
Rec: concert at the Auditorium Maximum, Hamburg, Germany, December 9 1969
Prod: Alexis Korner
Rel: May 1970
'Polly Put The Kettle On', 'Worried Blues', 'The Duo Thing', 'Rosie'
Alexis Korner: vocals ('Polly Put The Kettle On', 'Rosie'), mando guitar ('Worried Blues', 'Rosie'), backing vocals ('Worried Blues'); Peter Thorup: vocals (except for 'The Duo Thing'), harmonica ('Polly Put The Kettle On'), acoustic guitar ('Worried Blues'), electric guitar ('Rosie'); Ray Warleigh: alto saxophone ('The Duo Thing', 'Rosie'); Colin Hodgkinson: bass guitar ('The Duo Thing', 'Rosie')

JACK GRUNSKY
Toronto (Amadeo LP, AVRS 9260 – Austria only)
Rec: De Lane Lea Studios, London, January 5–9 1970
Prod: Alexis Korner
Rel: January 1972
'Travels', 'Moon Child Song'
Jack Grunsky: vocals/electric guitar ('Moon Child Song'); Alexis Korner: electric guitar; Mick Taylor: acoustic guitar; Annette Brox: vocals ('Moon Child Song')

242

DISCOGRAPHY

NEW CHURCH
Bootleg Him – Alexis Korner (RAK D/LP, SRAK 511-2)
Rec: BBC *Rythm & Blues*, Maida Vale Studio 4, London, April 1 1970
Prod: Jeff Griffin
Rel: July 1972
'Jesus Is Just Alright With Me'
Alexis Korner: vocals/mando guitar; Peter Thorup: vocals/electric guitar; Annette Brox: vocals/tambourine; Peter Fensome: vocals; Roy Babbington: bass guitar

CCS
Whole Lotta Love/Boom Boom (RAK 45, RAK 104)
Rec: Abbey Road Studios, London, May 1970
Prod: Mickie Most
Rel: September 1970
'Whole Lotta Love', 'Boom Boom'
Alexis Korner: vocals/acoustic guitar; Peter Thorup: vocals/acoustic guitar; John Cameron: conductor/electric piano; Alan Parker: electric guitar; Herbie Flowers: bass guitar; Spike Heatley: string bass; Barry Morgan: drums; Tony Carr: drums; Jim Lawless: percussion; Bill le Sage: percussion; Neil Sanders: French horn; Harold McNair, Tony Coe, Pete King, Danny Moss, Bob Efford, Ron Ross: woodwind; Harold Beckett, Henry Lowther, Greg Bowen, Tony Fisher, Les Condon, Kenny Wheeler: trumpets; Don Lusher, John Marshall, Brian Perrin, Bill Geldard: trombones

Note: This was issued as a double 'A'-side.

CCS
CCS (RAK LP, SRAK 6751)
Rec: Abbey Road Studios, London, May–July 1970
Prod: Mickie Most
Rel: October 1970
'Boom Boom', '(I Can't Get No) Satisfaction', 'Waiting Song', 'Lookin' For Fun', 'Whole Lotta Love', 'Living In The Past', 'Sunrise', 'Dos Cantos', 'Wade In The Water'
Alexis Korner: vocals/acoustic; Peter Thorup: vocals/acoustic guitar; John Cameron:

conductor/electric piano; Alan Parker: electric guitar; Herbie Flowers: bass guitar; Spike Heatley: string bass; Barry Morgan: drums; Tony Carr: drums; Jim Lawless: percussion; Bill le Sage: percussion; Neil Sanders: French horn; Harold McNair, Tony Coe, Pete King, Danny Moss, Bob Efford, Ron Moss: woodwind; Harold Beckett, Henry Lowther, Greg Bowen, Tony Fisher, Les Condon, Kenny Wheeler: trumpets; Don Lusher, John Marshall, Brian Perrin, Bill Geldard: trombones

ALEXIS KORNER
Alexis Korner (Metronome LP, 15 802 – Germany only)
Rec: ZBM Studios, Bermuda, August 1970
Prod: Jean Paul Salvatori
Rel: June 1971
'Black Woman (The Wild Ox Moan)', 'Frankie Diamond', 'Clay House Inn', 'Stump Blues', 'You Can Make It Like You Want It To Be', 'Gold', 'Saturday Sun', 'I Don't Know', 'Am I My Brother's Keeper', 'Stop Playing Games', 'That's All'
Alexis Korner: vocals/acoustic guitar ('Clay House Inn', 'Am I My Brother's Keeper'), backing vocals ('You Can Make It Like You Want It To Be'); Chris McGregor: electric piano ('Frankie Diamond', 'Gold', 'Saturday Sun', 'Stop Playing Games'), piano ('Clay House Inn', 'You Can Make It Like You Want It To Be', 'I Don't Know'), organ ('You Can Make It Like You Want It To Be'); Larry Power: electric guitar ('Frankie Diamond', 'Clay House Inn', 'You Can Make It Like You Want It To Be', 'I Don't Know'), acoustic guitar ('Gold', 'Saturday Sun'); Colin Hodgkinson: bass guitar (except for 'Black Woman', 'Stump Blues'), backing vocals ('You Can Make It Like You Want It To Be'); Joe Walsh: backing vocals ('You Can Make It Like You Want It To Be'); Jack Brooks: drums (except for 'Black Woman', 'Stump Blues', 'That's All')

Note: Released in the UK in July 1971 with a different sleeve (RAK LP, SRAK 501).

ALEXIS KORNER
Bootleg Him – Alexis Korner (RAK LP, SRAK 511-2)
Rec: ZBM Studios, Bermuda, August 1970
Prod: Jean Paul Salvatori

ALEXIS KORNER

Rel: July 1972
'Love Is Gonna Go'
Alexis Korner: vocals/acoustic guitar; Colin
Hodgkinson: bass guitar

ALEXIS KORNER
The BBC Radio Sessions – Alexis Korner
(Music Collection International CD,
MCCD 179)
Rec: BBC *Mike Raven's R & B Show*,
Maida Vale Studio 4, London, October
14 1970
Prod: Jeff Griffin
Rel: October 1994
'Stump Blues'
Alexis Korner: vocals/acoustic guitar

CCS
Walking (RAK 45, RAK 109)
Rec: Abbey Road Studios, London,
December 17–21 1970
Prod: Mickie Most
Rel: January 1971
'Walking', 'Salome'
Alexis Korner: vocals/acoustic guitar; Peter Thorup:
vocals/acoustic guitar; plus various members of the
CCS band

CCS
CCS (RAK LP, SRAK 503)
Rec: Morgan Studios, London, May
1971–January 1972
Prod: Mickie Most
Rel: March 1972
'Brother', 'Black Dog', 'I Want You Back',
'Sky Diver', 'Whole Lotta Rock 'n' Roll',
'Chaos, Can't We Ever Get It Back', 'This
Is My Life', 'Misunderstood', 'Maggie's
Song', 'City'
Alexis Korner: vocals/acoustic guitar; Peter Thorup:
vocals/acoustic guitar; plus various members of the
CCS band

B. B. KING
In London (ABC LP, ABCX US only)
Rec: Olympic Studios, London, June
11 1971
Prod: Ed Michel/Jo Zagarino
Rel: November 1971
'Alexis' Boogie'

B. B. King: acoustic guitar; Alexis Korner: acoustic
guitar; Steve Marriot: harmonica; Greg Ridley: bass
guitar; Jerry Shirley: drums

Note: Released in the UK on Probe LP, SBP 0141.

CCS
Tap Turns On The Water (RAK 45,
RAK 119)
Rec: Abbey Road Studios, London,
July 1971
Prod: Mickie Most
Rel: August 1971
'Tap Turns On The Water'
Alexis Korner: vocals/acoustic guitar; Peter Thorup:
vocals/acoustic guitar; plus various members of the
CCS band

CCS
Sixteen Tons (RAK 45, RAK 141)
Rec: Abbey Road Studios, London,
July 1971
Prod: Mickie Most
Rel: October 1972
'This Is My Life'
Alexis Korner: vocals/acoustic guitar; Peter Thorup:
vocals/acoustic guitar; plus various members of the
CCS band

CCS
Brother (RAK 45, RAK 126)
Rec: Abbey Road Studios, London,
July 1971
Prod: Mickie Most
Rel: February 1972
'Mister, What You Want I Can Get'
Alexis Korner: vocals/acoustic guitar; Peter Thorup:
vocals/acoustic guitar; plus various members of the
CCS band

ALEXIS KORNER AND PETER THORUP
Bootleg Him – Alexis Korner (RAK D/LP,
SRAK 511-2)
Rec: Lansdowne Studios, London, August
24 1971
Prod: Jean Paul Salvatori
Rel: July 1972
'Evil Hearted Woman', 'Hellbound On
My Trail'

Alexis Korner: vocals ('Evil Hearted Woman)/tipple guitar, backing vocals ('Hellbound On My Trail'); Peter Thorup: vocals ('Hellbound On My Trail'/acoustic guitar; Colin Hodgkinson: bass guitar ('Evil Hearted Woman')

ALEXIS KORNER AND PETER THORUP

Alexis Korner And ... 1961–1972 (Castle Communications D/LP, CCSLP 150)
Rec: Lansdowne Studios, London, August 24 1971
Prod: Jean Paul Salvatori
Rel: September 1986
'Lo And Behold'
Alexis Korner: backing vocals/tambourine; Peter Thorup: vocals/acoustic guitar; Zoot Money: backing vocals

CCS

Brother (RAK 45, RAK 126)
Rec: Abbey Road Studios, London, January 1972
Prod: Mickie Most
Rel: February 1972
'Brother'
Alexis Korner:vocals/acoustic guitar; Peter Thorup: vocals/acoustic guitar; plus various members of the CCS band

ALEXIS KORNER AND PETER THORUP – SNAPE

Accidentally Born In New Orleans (Brain LP, 1022 – Germany only)
Rec: Wally Heider Studios, San Francisco/Island Studios, London, April–July 1972
Prod: Snape
Rel: December 1972
'Gospel Ship', 'One Scotch, One Bourbon, One Beer', 'Sweet Sympathy', 'Rock Me', 'Don't Change On Me', 'You Got The Power (To Turn Me On)', 'Lo And Behold', 'Country Shoes'
Alexis Korner: vocals (except for 'You Got The Power', 'Lo And Behold')/electric guitar (except for 'Lo And Behold', 'Country Shoes'), backing vocals ('You Got The Power', 'Lo And Behold'), acoustic guitar ('Lo and Behold'), tipple guitar ('Country Shoes'); Peter Thorup: vocals

(except for 'Rock Me')/electric guitar, backing vocals ('Rock Me'); Mel Collins: saxophones (except for 'Rock Me'), piano ('You Got The Power'), flute ('Lo And Behold'); Zoot Money: piano ('Gospel Ship'); Boz Burrell: bass guitar, backing vocals ('Sweet Sympathy', 'Rock Me', 'Don't Change On Me'); Tim Hinkley: piano ('Lo And Behold'), backing vocals; Steve Marriott: organ ('Country Shoes'), backing vocals; Ian Wallace: drums; Ollie Halsall, Sappho Korner, Mike Patto: backing vocals

Note: Released in the UK in June 1973 on Transatlantic LP, TRA 269 with the same sleeve.

ALEXIS KORNER AND SNAPE

The BBC Radio Sessions – Alexis Korner (Music Collection International CD, MCCD 179)
Rec: BBC *In Concert*, Paris Theatre, London, June 15 1972
Prod: Jeff Griffin
Rel: October 1994
'Looking For Fun'
Alexis Korner: vocals/electric guitar; Peter Thorup: vocals/electric guitar; Mel Collins: tenor saxophone; Boz Burrell: bass guitar; Ian Wallace: drums

DUFFY POWER

Duffy Power (GSF LP, GS 502)
Rec: Island/Nova Studios, London, June–July 1972
Prod: Adrian Millar/Andrew Oldham
Rel: February 1973
Duffy Power: vocals/guitar; Alexis Korner: backing vocals; plus various session musicians

CCS

Sixteen Tons (RAK 45, RAK 141)
Rec: Abbey Road Studios, London, September 1972
Prod: Mickie Most
Rel: October 1972
'Sixteen Tons'
Alexis Korner: vocals/acoustic guitar; Peter Thorup: vocals/acoustic guitar; plus various members of the CCS band

ALEXIS KORNER AND PETER
THORUP WITH SNAPE
Live On Tour In Germany (Brain LP, 2/1039
– Germany only)
Rec: various concerts, Germany,
November 18–December 19 1972
Prod: Peter Walmsley
Rel: November 1973
'Going Down', 'Early In The Morning',
'You Got The Power (To Turn Me
On)', 'Snape', 'Rock Me Baby', 'These
Kind Of Blues', 'The Night Time Is The
Right Time', 'Bottom Of The Sea', 'Oo
Wee Baby'
Alexis Korner: vocals ('Going Down', 'Early
In The Morning', 'Rock Me Baby', 'Oo Wee
Baby')/electric guitar (except for 'Early In The
Morning'), backing vocals ('You Got The Power');
Peter Thorup: vocals ('Going Down', 'Early In
The Morning', 'You Got The Power', 'Oo Wee
Baby')/electric guitar, backing vocals ('Rock Me
Baby'); Boz Burrell: bass guitar/backing vocals
('Going Down', 'Early In The Morning', 'You Got
The Power', 'Rock Me Baby'), vocals ('These
Kind Of Blues', 'The Night Time Is The Right
Time', 'Bottom Of The Sea', 'Oo Wee Baby');
Mel Collins: saxophones; Tim Hinkley: piano
('Going Down'), organ ('Early In The Morning',
'The Night Time Is The Right Time', 'Bottom Of
The Sea', 'Oo Wee Baby'), electric piano ('Snape',
'These Kind Of Blues'; Gasper Lawal: African
drums (except for 'Going Down') percussion; Ian
Wallace: drums

CCS
The Band Played The Boogie (RAK 45,
RAK 154)
Rec: Abbey Road Studios, London, January
29 1973
Prod: Mickie Most
Rel: June 1973
'The Band Played The Boogie', 'Hang It
On Me'
Alexis Korner: vocals/acoustic guitar; Peter Thorup:
vocals/acoustic guitar; plus various members of the
CCS band

CCS
The Best Band In The Land (RAK LP,
SRAK 504)
Rec: Abbey Road Studios, London,
January–May 1973
Prod: Mickie Most
Rel: September 1973
'The Band Played The Boogie', Wild
Witch Lady', 'Lola', 'Primitive Love',
'Hundred Highways', 'Shakin' All Over',
'Memphis', 'Sunshine Of Your Love', 'Our
Man In London', 'Cannibal Sheep'
Alexis Korner: vocals; Peter Thorup: vocals; John
Cameron: conductor/electric piano; Alan Parker:
electric guitar; Herbie Flowers: bass guitar; Spike
Heatley: string bass; Neil Sanders: French horn; Jim
Lawless: percussion; Bill le Sage: percussion; Harold
McNair, Tony Coe, Pete King, Danny Moss, Bob
Efford, Ron Ross: saxophones/woodwind; Harold
Beckett, Henry Lowther, Greg Bowen, Tony
Fisher, Les Condon, Kenny Wheeler: trumpets;
Don Lusher, John Marshall, Brian Perrin, Bill
Geldard: trombones; Barry Morgan: drums; Tony
Carr: drums

ALEXIS KORNER
Alexis Korner (Polydor LP, 2374 109 –
Germany only)
Rec: CBS Studios, London, June–July 1973
Prod: Peter Thorup
Rel: April 1974
'Machine Gun And Julie', 'Lies', 'Wild
Women & Desperate Men', 'Geneva',
'Hey! Good Lookin'', 'The Thief', 'Captain
America', 'Casey Jones', 'Goodnight Irene',
'Doggone My Good Luck Soul', 'Vicksburg
Blues', 'Ford Engine Movements In My
Hips, 10,000 Miles Guaranteed'
Alexis Korner: vocals, electric guitar ('Hey! Good
Lookin''), tipple guitar ('Vicksburg Blues'), acoustic
guitar ('The Thief', 'Casey Jones', 'Goodnight
Irene', 'Doggone My Good Luck Soul', 'Ford
Engine ... '); Peter Thorup: vocals ('Machine Gun
And Julie'), electric guitar ('Machine Gun And
Julie', 'Lies', 'Wild Women & Desperate Men',
'Hey! Good Lookin'', 'Casey Jones'), acoustic guitar
('Geneva'), backing vocals ('Lies', 'Wild Women
& Desperate Men', 'Hey! Good Lookin'', 'Captain
America', 'Casey Jones', 'Goodnight Irene'); Boz
Burrell: bass guitar ('Machine Gun And Julie', 'Lies',
'Wild Women & Desperate Men', 'Casey Jones');
Tim Hinkley: piano ('Machine Gun And Julie',
'Casey Jones'); Mel Collins: tenor saxophone

246

('Lies', 'Wild Women & Desperate Men', 'Captain America'); Zoot Money: electric piano ('Wild Women & Desperate Men', 'Geneva'), piano ('Captain America', 'Doggone My Good Luck Soul'); Colin Hodgkinson: bass guitar ('Hey! Good Lookin'', 'Captain America', 'Ford Engine ...'); Elton Dean: alto saxophone ('Lies', 'Wild Women & Desperate Men', 'Captain America'); Nick Evans: trombone ('Lies', 'Wild Women & Desperate Men', 'Captain America'); Harry Beckett: trumpet ('Lies', 'Wild Women & Desperate Men', 'Captain America'); Mike Patto: piano ('Lies'); Ron Aspery: soprano saxophone ('Wild Women & Desperate Men'); Duster Bennett: harmonica ('Vicksburg Blues'); Eddie Mordue: baritone saxophone ('Captain America'); John Honeyman: string bass ('The Thief'); John Cameron: strings conductor ('The Thief'); John Meek: viola ('The Thief'); John Sharpe, Laurie Lewis: violins ('The Thief'); Charles Ford: cello ('The Thief'); Carol Morgan: backing vocals ('Lies'); Rick Mishlen: backing vocals; Ian Wallace: drums ('Machine Gun And Julie', 'Lies', 'Wild Women & Desperate Men', 'Casey Jones', 'Ford Engine ... '), percussion ('Machine Gun And Julie'); Tony Carr: drums ('Hey! Good Lookin'', 'Captain America')

ALEXIS KORNER
Wild Women & Desperate Men (Polydor 45, 2040 115 – Germany only)
Rec: CBS Studios, London, June–July 1973
Prod: Peter Thorup
Rel: 1974
'Wild Women & Desperate Men', 'Machine Gun And Julie'
Alexis Korner: vocals; Peter Thorup: electric guitar, backing vocals ('Wild Women & Desperate Men'),vocals ('Machine Gun And Julie'); Boz Burrell: bass guitar; Zoot Money: electric piano ('Wild Women & Desperate Men'); Mel Collins: tenor saxophone ('Wild Women & Desperate Men'); Elton Dean: tenor saxophone ('Wild Women & Desperate Men'); Ron Aspery: soprano saxophone ('Wild Women & Desperate Men'); Nick Evans: trombone ('Wild Women & Desperate Men'); Harry Beckett: trumpet ('Wild Women & Desperate Men'); Tim Hinkley: piano ('Machine Gun And Julie'); Ian Wallace: drums

ALEXIS KORNER
Captain America (Polydor 45, 2040 125 – Germany only)
Rec: CBS Studios, London, June–July 1973
Prod: Peter Thorup
Rel: 1974
'Captain America', 'The Thief'
Alexis Korner: vocals, acoustic guitar ('The Thief'); Colin Hodgkinson: bass guitar ('Captain America'); Zoot Money: piano ('Captain America'); Mel Collins: tenor saxophone ('Captain America'); Elton Dean: alto saxophone ('Captain America'); Eddie Mordue: baritone saxophone ('Captain America'); Nick Evans: trombone ('Captain America'); Harry Beckett: trumpet ('Captain America'); Peter Thorup: backing vocals ('Captain America'); John Honeyman: string bass ('The Thief'); John Meek: viola ('The Thief'); John Sharpe, Laurie Lewis: violin ('The Thief'); Charles Ford: cello ('The Thief'); John Cameron: string conductor ('The Thief'); Tony Carr: drums ('Captain America')

ALEXIS KORNER
The BBC Radio Sessions – Alexis Korner (Music Collection International CD, MCCD 179)
Rec: BBC *In Concert*, Paris Theatre, London, July 5 1973
Prod: Jeff Griffin
Rel: October 1994
'Vicksburg Blues', 'Love Is Gonna Go'
Alexis Korner: vocals, tipple guitar ('Vicksburg Blues'), acoustic guitar ('Love Is Gonna Go')

CCS
Hurricane Coming (RAK 45, RAK 172)
Rec: Abbey Road Studios, London, September 1973
Prod: Mickie Most
Rel: April 1974
'Dragster'
Alexis Korner: vocals/acoustic guitar; Peter Thorup: vocals/acoustic guitar; plus various members of the CCS band

KLAUS DOLDINGER
Doldinger Jubilee Concert (Atlantic LP, ATL 50070 – Germany only)
Rec: concert at the Reinhalle, Düsseldorf, Germany, October 16 1973

ALEXIS KORNER

Prod: Dieter Dierks
Rel: September 1974
'Rockport', 'Rock Me Baby', 'Lemuria's Dance'
Klaus Doldinger: tenor saxophone (except for 'Rock Me Baby'), soprano saxophone ('Rock Me Baby'); Alexis Korner: electric guitar, vocals ('Rock Me Baby'); Johnny Griffin: tenor saxophone (except for 'Rock Me baby'); Volker Kriegel: electric guitar; Brian Auger: organ (except for 'Rock Me baby'), piano ('Rock Me Baby'); Wolfgang Schmidt: bass guitar; Kristian Schultze: electric piano/mellotron ('Rockport'), piano ('Lemuria's Dance'); Curt Cress: percussion ('Rock Me Baby'), drums ('Lemuria's Dance'); Pete York: drums (except for 'Lemuria's Dance'), percussion ('Lemuria's Dance')

CCS
Hurricane Coming (RAK 45, RAK 172)
Rec: Abbey Road Studios, London, January 1974
Prod: Mickie Most
Rel: April 1974
'Hurricane Coming'
Alexis Korner: vocals/acoustic guitar; Peter Thorup: vocals/acoustic guitar; plus various members of the CCS band

ALEXIS KORNER
Get Off My Cloud (Polydor LP, 2374 117 – Germany only)
Rec: CBS Studios, London, September–December 1974
Prod: George Caldwell
Rel: March 1975
'I Got Cha Number', 'The Wasp (Texas Radio)', 'Robert Johnson', 'Tree Top Fever', 'You Are My Sunshine', 'Strange 'n' Deranged', 'Slow Down', 'Song For Jimi', 'Ain't That Peculiar', 'Get Off My Cloud'
Alexis Korner: vocals, acoustic guitar ('Robert Johnson', 'You Are My Sunshine', 'Song For Jimi'), tipple guitar ('Robert Johnson'), piano ('Song For Jimi'); Peter Frampton: electric guitar (except for 'Robert Johnson', 'Tree Top Fever', 'Strange 'n' Deranged', 'Song For Jimi'); Neil Hubbard: electric guitar ('I Got Cha Number', 'Robert Johnson', 'Tree Top Fever', 'Song For Jimi'); Nicky Hopkins: piano ('I Got Cha Number', 'The Wasp (Texas Radio)', 'You Are My Sunshine', 'Slow Down', 'Ain't That Peculiar', 'Get Off My Cloud'); Colin Hodgkinson: bass guitar ('I Got Cha Number', 'The Wasp (Texas Radio)', 'Robert Johnson', 'Song For Jimi'); Steve Marriott: electric guitar ('Tree Top Fever', 'Strange 'n' Deranged', 'Get Off My Cloud'); Tony O'Malley: piano ('Strange 'n' Deranged'); Keith Richard: vocals/electric guitar ('Get Off My Cloud'); Alan Spenner: bass guitar ('Tree Top Fever', 'Strange 'n' Deranged'); Rick Wills: bass guitar ('You Are My Sunshine', 'Slow Down', 'Ain't That Peculiar', 'Get Off My Cloud'); Morris Pert: percussion ('Tree Top Fever'); Jason Caine: percussion ('Song For Jimi'); Terry Stannard: drums; plus various backing vocalists

Note: Released in the UK on CBS Records LP, 69155 with a different sleeve, then re-released in the UK on Sequel Records LP, NEXLP 134 with a different sleeve.

ALEXIS KORNER
Get Off My Cloud (Polydor 45, 3040 136 – Germany only)
Rec: CBS Studios, London, September–December 1974
Prod: George Caldwell
Rel: February 1975
'Get Off My Cloud', 'Strange 'n' Deranged'
Alexis Korner: vocals; Peter Frampton: electric guitar; Steve Marriott: electric guitar; Keith Richard: vocals/electric guitar ('Get Off My Cloud'); Rick Wills: bass guitar ('Get Off My Cloud'); Alan Spenner: bass guitar ('Strange 'n' Deranged'); Nicky Hopkins: piano ('Get Off My Cloud'); Tony O'Malley: piano ('Strange 'n' Deranged'); Terry Stannard: drums; plus various backing vocalists

Note: Released in the UK on CBS 45, 3520 in August 1975.

ALEXIS KORNER
Ain't That Peculiar (CBS 45, S CBS 3877)
Rec: CBS Studios, London, September–December 1974
Prod: George Caldwell
Rel: January 1976
'Ain't That Peculiar', 'Tree Top Fever'
Alexis Korner: vocals; Peter Frampton: electric guitar ('Ain't That Peculiar'); Steve Marriott:

electric guitar ('Tree Top Fever'); Nicky Hopkins: piano ('Ain't That Peculiar'); Neil Hubbard: electric guitar ('Tree Top Fever'); Rick Wills: bass guitar; Morris Pert: percussion ('Tree Top Fever'); Terry Stannard: drums; plus various backing vocalists

ALEXIS KORNER
Alexis Korner And ... 1972–1983 (Castle Communications D/LP, CCSLP 192)
Rec: concert in Mainz, Germany, April 24 1975
Prod: unknown
Rel: September 1988
'Honky Tonk Woman', 'Spoonful'
Alexis Korner: vocals/acoustic guitar

ALEXIS KORNER
Live In Paris Bonus Tracks (CD Label CD, CDTL001)
Rec: Pebble Beach Studio, Worthing, October 1976
Prod: John Alcock
Rel: February 1988
'Working In A Coalmine', 'Flocking With You'
Alexis Korner: vocals/electric guitar; Adam Sieff: guitar/bass guitar; Derek Austin: synthesiser

ERIC BURDON
Survivor (Polydor LP, 230 2078)
Rec: Advision Studios, London, February–March 1977
Prod: Chas Chandler
Rel: March 1978
'Rocky', 'Woman Of The Rings', 'The Kid', 'Tomb Of The Unknown Singer', 'Famous Flames', 'Hollywood Woman', 'Hook Of Holland', 'I Was Born To Live The Blues', 'Highway Dealer', 'P. O. Box 500'
Eric Burdon: vocals; Alexis Korner: electric guitar; plus various session musicians

ALEXIS KORNER
The King Of Elfland's Daughter – Various Artists (Chrysalis LP, CHR 1137)
Rec: Wessex Studios, London, February 1977
Prod: Bob Johnson/Pete Knight
Rel: May 1977
'The Coming Of The Troll'

Alexis Korner: vocals; Bob Johnson: electric guitar; Herbie Flowers: bass guitar; Pete Knight: violin; Mike Batt: clarinet; Nigel Pegrum: drums

Note: Soundtrack LP which also features Chris Farlowe, Mary Hopkin, Frankie Miller and P. P. Arnold.

ALEXIS KORNER
Tell –Various Artists (Telefunken LP, 6.23075 AS – Germany only)
Rec: Dierks Studios, Stommeln, Germany, May–June 1977
Prod: Dieter Dierks
Rel: August 1977
'Schüsse', 'Gesslerlied', 'Willhelm Tell'
Alexis Korner: vocals

Note: Alexis played the part of Gessler on this soundtrack LP from the German production of the William Tell rock musical.

ALEXIS KORNER
Just Easy (Intercord LP, INT 160.099 – Germany only)
Rec: Foel Studio, Wales/Advision Studios, London/Pebble Beach Studios, Worthing/Basing Street Studios, London/Island Studios, London, October 1976–April 1977
Prod: Jean Paul Salvatori
Rel: 1978
'Roll Me', 'If I Never Sing Another Song', 'Lend Me Some Time', 'Everyday Since You've Been Gone', 'Daytime Song', 'The Gambler', 'Angel Band', 'The Love You Save'
Alexis Korner: vocals, electric guitar ('If I Never Sing Another Song', 'The Gambler'), electric piano ('Lend Me Some Time'), acoustic guitar ('Angel Band', 'The Love You Save'); Jim Diamond: vocals ('I'll Never Sing Another Song', 'Daytime Song', 'The Gambler'), backing vocals ('Roll Me', 'Lend Me Some Time', 'Everyday Since You've Been Gone'); Richie Zito: electric guitar ('Roll Me'); Peter Ward: electric guitar ('If I Never Sing Another Song'); Danny Mackintosh Jr: electric guitar ('Lend Me Some Time', 'Daytime Song', 'The Gambler'); Mick Weaver: piano/organ ('Roll Me'); Dick Morrisey: tenor saxophone ('Daytime Song'); Dave Winter: bass guitar ('Roll Me');

Colin Hodgkinson: bass guitar (except for 'Roll Me', 'Angel Band'); Sappho Korner: backing vocals ('Lend Me Some Time'); Henry Spinetti: drums ('Roll Me'); Graham Bond: drums (except for 'Roll Me', 'Angel Band')

ALEXIS KORNER AND FRIENDS
The Party Album (Intercord D/LP, INT 155.055 – Germany only)
Rec: concert at the Gatsby Room, Pinewood Studios, London, April 19 1978
Prod: Damien Korner
Rel: 1979
'Things Ain't What They Used To Be', 'The Captain's Tiger', 'Skippin'', 'Spoonful', 'Finkle's Cafe', 'Dooji Wooji', 'Mess Of Blues', 'Lining Track', 'Robert Johnson', 'Hey Pretty Mama', 'High-Heel Sneakers', 'Stormy Monday Blues'
Alexis Korner: vocals ('Spoonful', 'Robert Johnson'), electric guitar (except for 'Lining Track', 'Robert Johnson'), acoustic guitar ('Robert Johnson'), cowbell/backing vocals ('Lining Track'); Zoot Money: electric piano (except for 'Lining Track'), vocals ('Mess Of Blues', 'High-Heel Sneakers'), backing vocals ('Spoonful', 'Lining Track'), tambourine ('Lining Track'); Mel Collins: tenor saxophone ('Things Ain't What They Used To Be', 'The Captain's Tiger', 'Skippin'', 'Spoonful', 'Finkle's Cafe'), soprano saxophone ('Dooji Wooji'); Dick Heckstall-Smith: tenor saxophone (except for 'Mess Of Blues', 'Lining Track', 'Robert Johnson', 'Hey Pretty Mama', 'High-Heel Sneakers'); John Surman: baritone saxophone (except for 'Dooji Wooji', 'Mess Of Blues', 'Lining Track', 'Robert Johnson', 'Stormy Monday Blues'), soprano saxophone ('Spoonful', 'Dooji Wooji'); Dick Morrisey, Art Themen: tenor saxophones (except for 'Mess Of Blues', 'Lining Track', 'Robert Johnson', 'Hey Pretty Mama', 'High-Heel Sneakers'); Mike Zwerin: trombone (except for 'Mess Of Blues', 'Lining Track', 'Robert Johnson', 'Stormy Monday Blues'); Sappho Gillet: tambourine/backing vocals ('Robert Johnson'); Chris Farlowe: vocals ('Hey Pretty Mama', 'High-Heel Sneakers', 'Stormy Monday Blues'), tambourine ('High-Heel Sneakers'); Eric Clapton: electric guitar ('Hey Pretty Mama', 'High-Heel Sneakers', 'Stormy Monday Blues'); Colin Hodgkinson: bass guitar; Stu Speer: drums

ALEXIS KORNER
Eat A Little Rhythm And Blues (BBC Video, BBCV 3011)
Rec: concert at the Gatsby Room, Pinewood Studios, London, April 19 1978
Prod: Damien Korner
Rel: April 1984
'Louisiana Blues', 'Mess Of Blues', 'Lining Track', 'Blue Monday', 'Skippin'', 'Spoonful', 'Finkle's Cafe', 'Dooji Wooji', 'Got To Get You Off My Mind', 'Stormy Monday Blues', 'High-Heel Sneakers'
Alexis Korner: vocals ('Louisiana Blues', 'Spoonful'), electric guitar (except for 'Louisiana Blues', 'Lining Track'), acoustic guitar ('Louisiana Blues'), cowbell ('Lining Track'), backing vocals ('Lining Track', 'Blue Monday'); Zoot Money: vocals ('Mess Of Blues', 'High-Heel Sneakers'), electric piano (except for 'Louisiana Blues', 'Lining Track'), backing vocals ('Lining Track', 'Blue Monday', 'Spoonful', 'Got To Get You Off My Mind'), tambourine ('Lining Track'); Dick Morrissey, Art Themen, Dick Heckstall-Smith: tenor saxophones (except for 'Louisiana Blues', 'Lining Track', 'Blue Monday', 'High-Heel Sneakers'); Mel Collins: tenor saxophone ('Skippin'', 'Spoonful', 'Finkle's Cafe'), soprano saxophone ('Dooji Wooji', 'Got To Get You Off My Mind'); John Surman: baritone saxophone ('Skippin'', 'Spoonful', 'Finkle's Cafe', 'Got To Get You Off My Mind', 'High-Heel Sneakers'), soprano saxophone ('Spoonful', 'Dooji Wooji'); Mike Zwerin: trombone (except for 'Louisiana Blues', 'Mess Of Blues', 'Lining Track', 'Stormy Monday Blues'); Chris Farlowe: vocals ('Got To Get You Off My Mind', 'Stormy Monday Blues', 'High-Heel Sneakers'), tambourine ('High-Heel Sneakers'); Eric Clapton: electric guitar ('Got To Get You Off My Mind', 'Stormy Monday Blues', 'High-Heel Sneakers'); Duffy Power: harmonica ('Stormy Monday Blues', 'High-Heel Sneakers'); Neil Ford: electric guitar ('High-Heel Sneakers'); Paul Jones: harmonica ('High-Heel Sneakers'); Colin Hodgkinson: bass guitar (except for 'Louisiana Blues'); Stu Speer: drums (except for 'Louisiana Blues')

ROB HALL WITH ALEXIS KORNER
Pinetops Boogie Woogie (Logo 45, GO 331)
Rec: Morgan Studios, London, September 1978

Prod: Neil Slaven
Rel: December 1978
'Pinetops Boogie Woogie', 'All I
Got Is You'
Alexis Korner: vocals; Bob Hall: piano; Colin
Hodgkinson: bass guitar; Stu Speer: drums

ALEXIS KORNER
Me (Jeton LP, 100–3305 – Germany only)
Rec: Tonstudio Bauer, Ludwigsburg,
Germany, July 12 1979
Prod: Alexis Korner
Rel: 1980
'Honky Tonk Woman', 'Louise', 'Hammer
And Nails', 'Santa Fé Blues', 'How Long
Blues', 'Roberta', 'Precious Lord', 'Honour
The Young Man', 'And Again', 'East St
Louis Blues'
Alexis Korner plays all tracks solo

Note: Recordings released in the UK in
January 1987 under the title *Hammer And Nails*
(Thunderbolt LP, THBL 037).

ROCKET 88
Rocket 88 (Atlantic LP, K50776)
Rec: concert at the Rotation Club,
Hanover, Germany, November 1979
Prod: Ian Stewart
Rel: March 1981
'Rocket 88', 'Waiting For The Call', 'St
Louis Blues', 'Roll 'Em Pete', 'Swindon
Swing', 'Roadhouse Boogie', 'Talking
About Louise' (a.k.a. 'Little Bitty
Gal Blues')
Alexis Korner: vocals ('Roll 'Em Pete', 'Talking
About Louise')/electric guitar; Jack Bruce: vocals
('Waiting For The Call')/string bass; Bob Hall:
piano; George Green: piano; Hal Singer, Don
Weller: tenor saxophones; Ian Stewart: piano
('Swindon Swing'); Colin Smith: trumpet; John
Pickard: trombone; Charlie Watts: drums

ALEXIS KORNER WITH COLIN
HODGKINSON
Testament (Thunderbolt LP, THBL 2.026)
Rec: concert at La Chapelle des Lombards,
Paris, March 1980
Prod: Serge Loupien
Rel: June 1985

'One Scotch, One Bourbon, One Beer',
'Stump Blues', 'Streamline Train/My
Babe', '3220 Blues', 'Will The Circle Be
Unbroken', 'Mary Open The Door'
Alexis Korner: vocals (except for '3220 Blues'),
acoustic guitar ('One Scotch, One Bourbon, One
Beer', 'Stump Blues', 'Streamline Train/My Babe'),
electric guitar ('High-Heel Sneakers', 'Will The
Circle Be Unbroken', 'Mary Open The Door');
Colin Hodgkinson: vocals ('3220 Blues', 'High-Heel
Sneakers', 'Will The Circle Be Unbroken')/bass
guitar (except for 'One Scotch, One Bourbon, One
Beer', 'Stump Blues', 'Streamline Train/My Babe')

Note: Recordings were first issued in 1984 on a
bootleg LP titled *White & Blue* (Blue Silver LP,
C3328 – France only).

ALEXIS KORNER
Live In Paris (CD Label CD, CDTL001)
Rec: concert at La Chapelle des Lombards,
Paris, March 1980
Prod: Serge Loupien
Rel: February 1988
'Blue Monday', 'Key To The Highway',
'Catcote Bag', 'Phonograph Blues', 'Little
Bitty Gal Blues', 'Sweet Home Chicago',
'Cherry Red', 'I Got My Mojo Working',
'Gospel Ship', 'Geneva'
Alexis Korner: electric guitar ('Blue Monday', 'Key
To The Highway', 'Sweet Home Chicago', 'I Got
My Mojo Working', 'Gospel Ship'), vocals ('Little
Bitty Gal Blues', 'Cherry Red', 'I Got My Mojo
Working', 'Gospel Ship'), piano ('Phonograph
Blues', 'Little Bittly Gal Blues', ' Cherry Red', 'I
Got My Mojo Working', 'Gospel Ship'), backing
vocals ('Sweet Home Chicago'); Colin Hodgkinson:
vocals ('Blue Monday', 'Key To The Highway',
'Phonograph Blues', 'Sweet Home Chicago',
'Gospel Ship'), backing vocals ('I Got My Mojo
Working', 'Geneva'), bass guitar

SCHTICK AND FUTZ
Alexis Korner And … 1972–1983 (Castle
Communications D/LP, CCSLP 192)
Rec: Satril Studios, London, May 6 1981
and June 8–9 1981
Prod: Damien Korner
Rel: September 1988
'Wreck Of The Old '97', 'Casey Jones'

Alexis Korner: vocals, acoustic guitar ('Casey Jones');
Colin Hodgkinson: bass guitar/backing vocals; Pete
Sayers: dobro, banjo ('Wreck Of The Old '97')

ALEXIS KORNER AND COLIN HODGKINSON
Open-Air Arbon – Various Artists (Delta LP,
8355 001 – Switzerland only)
Rec: concert in Arbon, Switzerland, June
20 1982
Prod: Victor Waldeburger
Rel: December 1983
'High-Heel Sneakers', 'Juvenile Delinquent'
Alexis Korner: vocals/electric guitar; Colin
Hodgkinson: vocals/bass guitar

ALEXIS KORNER AND FRIENDS
The BBC Radio Sessions – Alexis Korner
(Music Collections International CD,
MCCD 179)
Rec: BBC *In Concert*, Marquee Club,
London, April 28 1983
Prod: Jeff Griffin
Rel: October 1994
'Bring It On Home To Me', 'Money
Honey'
Alexis Korner: vocals/electric guitar; Georgie Fame:
organ/backing vocals; Ruby Turner: vocals ('Bring
It On Home To Me'), backing vocals ('Money
Honey'); Jacki Graham: backing vocals; Nico
Korner: electric guitar; Bill Wyman: bass guitar;
John Pickard: trombone; Dick Heckstall-Smith;
Willy Carnet: tenor saxophones; Charlie
Watts: drums

FRANKFURT CITY BLUES BAND
*Live – Frankfurt City Blues Band Meets Alexis
Korner, Louisiana Red* (Joke LP, JLP 218 –
Germany only)
Rec: concert at Lauterbach, Germany, May
15 1983
Prod: Wolfgang Neumann
Rel: unknown
'Mississippi River Blues', 'High-Heel
Sneakers'
Alexis Korner: vocals/acoustic guitar (solo
on 'Mississippi Blues'); Luiz Sommer: electric
guitar; Andreas August: organ; Achim Farr: tenor
saxophone/harmonica; Thomas Schilling: bass guitar;
Werner Fromm: drums

ALEXIS KORNER
The BBC Radio Sessions – Alexis Korner
(Music Collection International CD,
MCCD 179)
Rec: BBC *Alexis Korner's Rhythm &
Blues Show*, Bush House, London, August
22 1983
Prod: Jeff Griffin
Rel: October 1994
'How Can A Poor Man Stand Such Times
And Live'
Alexis Korner: vocals/acoustic guitar

ALEXIS KORNER
Beirut (Charisma 45, CB 412)
Rec: Konk Studios, London,
September–October 1983
Prod: John Alcock/Damien Korner
Rel: April 1984
'Beirut', 'Mean Fool'
Alexis Korner: vocals/electric guitar; Colin
Hodgkinson: bass guitar; Alan Ross: vocals/electric
guitar; Robin Lumley: synthisisers; Morris Pert:
percussion; Tony Hicks: drums

ALEXIS KORNER
Juvenile Delinquent (Charisma LP,
CAS 1165)
Rec: Konk Studios, London,
September–October 1983
Prod: John Alcock/Damien Korner
Rel: June 1984
'Beirut', 'Mean Fool', 'The Sphinx', 'Get
Off My Cloud', 'King B. B.', ' Juvenile
Delinquent'
Alexis Korner: vocals/acoustic guitar (except
for 'Juvenile Delinquent'); Alan Ross: electric
guitar/backing vocals; Colin Hodgkinson: bass
guitar; Adam Sieff: slide guitar; Robin Lumley:
synthisisers; Morris Pert: percussion; Tony
Hicks: drums

Note: Recordings were re-released in August 1988
under the same title (Charisma LP, CHC 64).

INDEX

INDEX

Harris, Bob 40, 201, 205
Harris, Jet 115–16
Harris, Rex 57
Harry, Bill 5
Hasted, Professor John 85
Hawdon, Dicky 44
Hayes, Tubby 44, 133
Heartsong 136
Heatley, Spike 108–9
Heckstall-Smith, Dick 106–7,
    109–11, 113, 115, 117,
    119–22, 124–5, 128–9, 134,
    187, 212
Hendricks, Jon 162
Hendrix, Jimi 158–9, 180, 196
Herbidge, Alex 135
'Herbie's Tune' 134
Hill, Trevor 36
Hinkley, Tim 192
Hiseman, Jon 165
History of British Jazz (Godbolt)
    39
History of Rock 222, 224
Hobbstweedle 160
Hodgkinson, Colin 175–6, 179,
    186, 190, 194, 198, 208,
    211–12, 217–18, 223, 229
Holland Park Comprehensive
    150, 152–3
Holly, Buddy 68
Home and School 18
Hope Hall, Liverpool 131
'Hoochie Coochie Man' 97,
    133, 159
Hoogenboom, Andy 99,
    103, 108
Hooker, John Lee 57
Hopkins, Nicky 117
Hopkins, Syd 21
Horovitz, Michael 78
Hot Club de France 59
How It Is 163
'How You Want It Done' 59
Howard, Brian 7–8
Howton, Barry 134
HRH 223
Humble Pie 188–90
100 Club 39, 44, 58, 163
Hunt, Marsha 145–6
Hutchinson, Denny 98
Hyde Park 171–2, 181

'I Ain't Gonna Worry No
    More' 79
'I Can't Hold Out Much
    Longer' 170
'I Gotcha Number' 196

'I Need Your Loving' 134–5
I Play As I Please (Lyttleton) 42
I Used To Be An Animal
    (Burdon) 104
I Wonder Who 141
'I'm So Glad' 139
Individual Voices 218–19
Intercord Label 179, 208, 216
International Artists
    Representation 165
International Essen Song
    Days 168
International Hot Jazz Meeting
    168
Island Records 161, 189
It's All Happening 136
ITV 139
'I've Got My Mojo Working'
    109

'Jack You Off' 222
Jackson, Mahalia 64
Jagger, Mick 100, 102, 104,
    108–9, 111–12, 119, 155, 157,
    166, 170, 172, 196
Jahnke, Karsten 177, 199–200,
    214
James, Elmore 91, 101
James, Jim 178–9
James, Skip 74, 91
Jansch, Bert 143, 164
Jazz Appreciation Society 85
Jazz at Night 163
Jazz Centre 163
Jazz Club 44, 112, 135
Jazz Jamboree, Warsaw 168
Jazz Journal 46, 119
Jazz News 90, 92–7, 109,
    112, 119
Jazz News & Review 92, 118–19
Jazz on Record 1960 65
Jazz Review 71
Jazz Session 88, 135
Jazz Sociological Society 85
Jefferson, Blind Lemon 42, 57,
    93, 143
Jethro Tull 162, 183, 216
Jody Grinder 221
Johnny Burch Octet 113
Johnson, Bob 208
Johnson, Bunk 47
Johnson, Lonnie 58–9
Johnson, Pete 15
Johnson, Robert 37, 40, 57, 59,
    71–3, 117, 143, 196
Johnson, Tommy 74
Jones, Brian 101–5, 112, 155,
    170–2, 216
Jones, Curtis 163

Jones, Max 46, 57, 60, 64, 70,
    71, 75, 85
Jones, Paul 102, 104, 111,
    213–14, 227
Jones, Ronnie 111, 113–15, 121,
    125, 127, 129
Jones, Tom 135
Joseph, Anthea 85–6, 105,
    157–8, 161, 225
Joseph, Nathan 133
Just Easy 208, 222
'Juvenile Delinquent' 219–20,
    222

'Kansas City' 122
Kelly, Bob 84
Kelly, Jo-Ann 162, 178
Ken Colyer Club 119
Kensington Register Office 6,
    43
'Kid Man' 79
King, B.B. 188, 222
King, Pete 53, 183
King Alfred School 10, 39
'King B.B.' 222
King Crimson 189
King label 128
The King of Elfland's Daughter
    208
Kingsway Hall 59
Kinorra, Phil 138
Kirk, Roland 143
Kirke, Simon 160
Knight, Brian 117–18
Knight, Peter 208
Konk Studios 223
Korner, Alexis
    agents 165
    attitude to drugs 154–5, 223
    awards 227
    band leader 94–6, 106, 108,
        110–13, 115–16, 119–21,
        124–6, 129–30, 132,
        145, 169, 175–6, 182–3,
        189–91, 220
    and blues 55–6, 62–4, 72–4,
        76, 90, 93–4, 121, 129,
        134, 141–3, 162, 167
    broadcasting 11, 35–7, 88–91,
        112, 135–6, 139–41, 157–9,
        161, 163, 178, 186, 196,
        203–7, 220–2
    character 149
    childhood 7–12
    commercials 161
    death 226
    driving 221–2
    early musical experiences
        14–15, 30

INDEX

INDEX

Powley, Captain Neville 36
'Preachin' The Blues' 117, 128
Preston, Dennis 128
Pretty Things 134
Priestley, Brian 89
Pula 209
Put Out More Flags (Waugh) 8
Pye 59, 117
Pyne, Chris 139, 175

Quarrymen 80

R&B from the Marquee 108,
  118–19, 122, 133
Radio Oxford 40
Rainey, Ma 57, 93
'Rainy Tuesday' 128
RAK label 181, 185–6
Rambling Jack's Blues Club 170
Raven, Mike 178
Record Mirror 184
Red Barn, Bexleyheath 39
Red Hot From Alex 133
Rediffusion 136, 140
Refectory, Golder's Green 134
Reid, Terry 160
Renbourn, John 143, 164
Rendell, Don 44, 68, 117
Rhodes, John 140
Rhythm & Blues 122
*Rhythm & Blues with Alexis
  Korner* 136
Richard, Cliff 89
Richard, Keith 14, 100, 102–3,
  108, 111–12, 155, 170, 195–6
Richardson, Clive 204
Richmond Jazz Club 119
Ridley, Greg 189
'Rivers Invitation' 141
Roberge, Phil 165–7, 171–2,
  175, 178–9, 182, 184, 186–7,
  190, 193–5, 201, 205
'Roberta' 122
Robertson, Phil 94
Robinson, Tom 28–9, 150–1,
  164, 229
'Rock Island Line' 49,
  55, 62, 82
'Rock Me' 170, 189
Rock On 188
Rocket 88 47, 213–15, 217
Rodgers, Paul 160–1, 175
Rolling Stone 186, 188, 196
Rolling Stones 112, 118–19,
  134–6, 139, 170–1, 196,
  213, 226
Rome 126–7, 129
Ronnie Scott's 134, 182, 184
Roosters 104

Rose, Tim 159
'Rosie' 145
Ross, Annie 162
Ross, Ronnie 182–3
Rostov 3, 5
Rothschild, Baron 114
Roundabout 90
Roundhouse 63, 74, 76, 81,
  84–6, 91, 95, 98, 101, 106
Royal Albert Hall 158, 184, 187
Royal Festival Hall 58; 64
Russell, Dora 21, 41
Russia 2–5, 8
Ryemuse Studios 137–8

The Safest Place In The World
  (Heckstall-Smith) 106
St John's Convent School 41
St Pancras Town Hall 70
St Paul's School 13–14, 25, 39
Salvatori, Jean-Paul 186, 208
'The Same For You' 164
Sandford, Chris 103
Sandy Brown's Quartet 163
Sarstedt, Peter 222
'Satisfaction' 183
Saturday Club 115
Saul, Malcolm 133
Savages 117
Savoy Brown Blues Band 162
Sayers, Pete 218
Schlosser, Willi 195
Scotsville Jazz Band 110
Scott, Keith 92, 95–8, 103, 109,
  113, 116, 119, 126
Scott, Mike 125, 145
Scott, Ronnie 42
Seamen, Phil 60, 110, 124–5,
  127–30, 136
Second World War 12–13, 17
See My Music Talking 159
Seeburg Corporation 128
Sellers, Brother John 64
77 label 79
Shade, Will 96
Shadows 80
Shalit, Emile 45–6
'She Fooled Me' 98
Sheffield Morning Telegraph 221
Shelton, Bob 157
Shepherd's Bush Empire 58
Shepp, Archie 143
Sheridan, Tony 168
Shirley, Jerry 189
Six Bells, Chelsea 134
Skidmore, Alan 139
Skiffle Cellar 80, 85, 101
'Skiffle is Piffle' (Korner) 83
'Skip To My Lou' 79

Sky High 138–9
Slim, Memphis 64, 75, 95
'Slow Down' 199
Smith, Bessie 57, 93
Smith, Colin 213
Smith, Jimmy 120, 141
Smokin' 188
Snape 189–94, 200, 202, 209
Snell, Gordon 55
Somers, Andy 130
South, Nick 163–4, 166, 169,
  172, 174–5, 199
Southcombe & West 165–6
Spann, Otis 70
Speer, Stu 211–12
Spock, Dr 179
Spooky Tooth 176, 190
'Spoonful' 212
'Sportin' Life' 44
Spot Records 137–8
Stanger, Nigel 167
Stannard, Martin 8
Stannard, Terry 197
Star and Garter Hotel, Windsor
  134
Stars Campaign for Interracial
  Friendship 85
Steadman, Ralph 223
'Steal Away' 160
Steve Lane's Southern Stompers
  56
Stevens, Dave 40, 44, 64, 67–9,
  79, 109, 113–14, 163
Stevens, Trixie 43, 44, 63, 78
Stewart, Al 144
Stewart, Ian 104, 112, 188,
  213–15, 227
Stewart, Rod 111
Stickells, Gerry 180
Stigwood, Robert 165
Stone House 147–8, 152, 167
'Stormy Monday' 122
'Stump Blues' 186
*The Submerged Seven-Eighths Of
  The
Blues* 162
Suez War 54–5
'Sugar Man' 122
Sullivan, Jim 109, 137
Sullivan, Red 85, 86
Sunday Telegraph 226
Sunderland 28
Sunshine 208
Sunshine, Monty 49, 115, 123
Surman, John 175, 212
Sutch, Screaming Lord 117
Swing Club 39
Switzerland 10, 37, 207–8,
  215

259